MEDIEVAL CATHEDRALS

Titles in the Series
Greenwood Guides to Historic Events of the Medieval World

The Black Death

The Crusades

Eleanor of Aquitaine, Courtly Love, and the Troubadours

Genghis Khan and Mongol Rule

Joan of Arc and the Hundred Years War

Magna Carta

Medieval Castles

Medieval Cathedrals

The Medieval City

Medieval Science and Technology

The Puebloan Society of Chaco Canyon

The Rise of Islam

MEDIEVAL CATHEDRALS

William W. Clark

Greenwood Guides to Historic Events of the Medieval World
Jane Chance, Series Editor

GREENWOOD PRESS
Westport, Connecticut • London

Library of Congress Cataloging-in-Publication Data

Clark, William W., 1940–
  Medieval cathedrals / William W. Clark
      p.   cm. — (Greenwood guides to historic events of the medieval world)
  Includes bibliographical references and index.
  ISBN 0–313–32693–2 (alk. paper)
  1. Cathedrals—Europe. 2. Architecture, Medieval 3. Architecture and society—
Europe. I. Title. II. Series.
NA4830.C57 2006
726.6'094'0902—dc22   2005022204

British Library Cataloguing in Publication Data is available.

Library of Congress Catalog Card Number: 2005022204
ISBN: 0–313–32693–2

First published in 2006

Greenwood Press, 88 Post Road West, Westport, CT 06881
An imprint of Greenwood Publishing Group, Inc.
www.greenwood.com

Printed in the United States of America

The paper used in this book complies with the
Permanent Paper Standard issued by the National
Information Standards Organization (Z39.48–1984).

10 9 8 7 6 5 4 3 2 1

Copyright Acknowledgment

Every reasonable effort has been made to trace the owners of copyright materials in this
book, but in some instances this has proven impossible. The author and publisher will
be glad to receive information leading to more complete acknowledgments in subsequent
printings of the book, and in the meantime extend their apologies for any omissions.

CONTENTS

Primary Documents

ILLUSTRATIONS

SERIES FOREWORD

The Middle Ages are no longer considered the "Dark Ages" (as Petrarch termed them), sandwiched between the two enlightened periods of classical antiquity and the Renaissance. Often defined as a historical period lasting, roughly, from 500 to 1500 c.e., the Middle Ages span an enormous amount of time (if we consider the way other time periods have been constructed by historians) as well as an astonishing range of countries and regions very different from one another. That is, we call the "Middle" Ages the period beginning with the fall of the Roman Empire as a result of raids by northern European tribes of "barbarians" in the late antiquity of the fifth and sixth centuries and continuing until the advent of the so-called Italian and English renaissances, or rebirths of classical learning, in the fifteenth and sixteenth centuries. How this age could be termed either "Middle" or "Dark" is a mystery to those who study it. Certainly it is no longer understood as embracing merely the classical inheritance in the west or excluding eastern Europe, the Middle East, Asia, or even, as I would argue, North and Central America.

Whatever the arbitrary, archaic, and hegemonic limitations of these temporal parameters—the old-fashioned approach to them was that they were mainly not classical antiquity, and therefore not important—the Middle Ages represent a time when certain events occurred that have continued to affect modern cultures and that also, inevitably, catalyzed other medieval events. Among other important events, the Middle Ages saw the birth of Muhammad (c. 570–632) and his foundation of Islam in the seventh century as a rejection of Christianity, which led to the imperial conflict between East and West in the eleventh and twelfth centuries. In western Europe in the Middle Ages the foundations for modern nationalism and modern law were laid and the concept of romantic love arose in the Middle Ages, this latter event partly one of the indirect consequences of the Crusades. With the shaping of national identity came the need to defend boundaries against invasion; so the castle emerged as a military outpost—whether in northern Africa, during the Crusades, or in Wales, in the eleventh century, to defend William of Normandy's newly acquired provinces—to satisfy that need. From Asia the invasions of Genghis Khan changed the literal and cultural shape of eastern and southern Europe.

In addition to triggering the development of the concept of chivalry and the knight, the Crusades influenced the European concepts of the lyric, music, and musical instruments; introduced to Europe an appetite for spices like cinnamon, coriander, and saffron and for dried fruits like prunes and figs as well as a desire for fabrics such as silk; and brought Aristotle to the European university through Arabic and then Latin translations. As a result of study of the "new" Aristotle, science and philosophy dramatically changed direction—and their emphasis on this material world helped to undermine the power of the Catholic Church as a monolithic institution in the thirteenth century.

By the twelfth century, with the centralization of the one (Catholic) Church, came a new architecture for the cathedral—the Gothic—to replace the older Romanesque architecture and thereby to manifest the Church's role in the community in a material way as well as in spiritual and political ways. Also from the cathedral as an institution and its need to dramatize the symbolic events of the liturgy came medieval drama— the mystery and the morality play, from which modern drama derives in large part. Out of the cathedral and its schools to train new priests (formerly handled by monasteries) emerged the medieval institution of the university. Around the same time, the community known as a town rose up in eastern and western Europe as a consequence of trade and the necessity for a new economic center to accompany the development of a bourgeoisie, or middle class. Because of the town's existence, the need for an itinerant mendicancy that could preach the teachings of the Church and beg for alms in urban centers sprang up.

Elsewhere in the world, in North America the eleventh-century settlement of Chaco Canyon by the Pueblo peoples created a social model like no other, one centered on ritual and ceremony in which the "priests" were key, but one that lasted barely two hundred years before it collapsed and its central structures were abandoned.

In addition to their influence on the development of central features of modern culture, the Middle Ages have long fascinated the modern age because of parallels that exist between the two periods. In both, terrible wars devastated whole nations and peoples; in both, incurable diseases plagued cities and killed large percentages of the world's population. In both periods, dramatic social and cultural changes took place as a result of these events: marginalized and overtaxed groups in societies rebelled against imperious governments; trade and a burgeoning middle class came to the fore; outside the privacy of the family, women began to have a greater role in Western societies and their cultures.

How different cultures of that age grappled with such historical change is the subject of the Greenwood Guides to Historic Events of the Medieval World. This series features individual volumes that illuminate key events in medieval world history. In some cases, an "event" occurred during a relatively limited time period. The troubadour lyric as a phenomenon, for example, flowered and died in the courts of Aquitaine in the twelfth century, as did the courtly romance in northern Europe a few decades later. The Hundred Years War between France and England generally took place during a precise time period, from the fourteenth to mid-fifteenth centuries.

In other cases, the event may have lasted for centuries before it played itself out: the medieval Gothic cathedral, for example, may have been first built in the twelfth century at Saint-Denis in Paris (c. 1140), but cathedrals, often of a slightly different style of Gothic architecture, were still being built in the fifteenth century all over Europe and, again, as the symbolic representation of a bishop's seat, or chair, are still being built today. And the medieval city, whatever its incarnation in the early Middle Ages, basically blossomed between the eleventh and thirteenth centuries as a result of social, economic, and cultural changes. Events—beyond a single dramatic historically limited happening—took longer to affect societies in the Middle Ages because of the lack of political and social centralization, the primarily agricultural and rural nature of most countries, difficulties in communication, and the distances between important cultural centers.

Each volume includes necessary tools for understanding such key events in the Middle Ages. Because of the postmodern critique of authority that modern societies underwent at the end of the twentieth century, students and scholars as well as general readers have come to mistrust the commentary and expertise of any one individual scholar or commentator and to identify the text as an arbiter of "history." For this reason, each book in the series can be described as a "library in a book." The intent of the series is to provide a quick, in-depth examination and current perspectives on the event to stimulate critical thinking as well as ready-reference materials, including primary documents and biographies of key individuals, for additional research.

Specifically, in addition to a narrative historical overview that places the specific event within the larger context of a contemporary perspective, five to seven developmental chapters explore related focused aspects of the event. In addition, each volume begins with a brief chronology and ends with a conclusion that discusses the consequences and impact of the event. There are also brief biographies of twelve to twenty key individuals (or places or buildings, in the book on the cathedral); primary documents from the period (for example, letters, chronicles, memoirs, diaries, and other writings) that illustrate states of mind or the turn of events at the time, whether historical, literary, scientific, or philosophical; illustrations (maps, diagrams, manuscript illuminations, portraits); a glossary of terms; and an annotated bibliography of important books, articles, films, and CD-ROMs available for additional research. An index concludes each volume.

No particular theoretical approach or historical perspective characterizes the series; authors developed their topics as they chose, generally taking into account the latest thinking on any particular event. The editors selected final topics from a list provided by an advisory board of high school teachers and public and school librarians. On the basis of nominations of scholars made by distinguished writers, the series editor also tapped internationally known scholars, both those with lifelong expertise and others with fresh new perspectives on a topic, to author the twelve books in the series. Finally, the series editor selected distinguished medievalists, art historians, and archaeologists to complete an advisory board: Gwinn Vivian, retired professor of archaeology at the University of Arizona Museum; Sharon Kinoshita, associate professor of French literature, world literature, and cultural studies at the University of California–Santa Cruz; Nancy Wu, associate museum educator at the Metropolitan Museum of Art, The Cloisters, New York City; and Christopher A. Snyder, chair of the Department of History and Politics at Marymount University.

In addition to examining the event and its effects on the specific cultures involved through an array of documents and an overview, each volume provides a new approach to understanding these twelve events. Treated in the series are: the Black Death; the Crusades; Eleanor of Aquitaine, courtly love, and the troubadours; Genghis Khan and Mongol rule; Joan of Arc and the Hundred Years War; Magna Carta; the medieval castle, from the eleventh to the sixteenth centuries; the medieval cathedral; the medieval city, especially in the thirteenth century; medieval science and technology; Muhammad and the rise of Islam; and the Puebloan society of Chaco Canyon.

The Black Death, by Joseph Byrne, isolates the event of the epidemic of bubonic plague in 1347–52 as having had a signal impact on medieval Europe. It was, however, only the first of many related such episodes involving variations of pneumonic and septicemic plague that recurred over 350 years. Taking a twofold approach to the Black Death, Byrne investigates both the modern research on bubonic plague, its origins and spread, and also medieval documentation and illustration in diaries, artistic works, and scientific and religious accounts. The demographic, economic, and political effects of the Black Death are traced in one chapter, the social and psychological patterns of life in another, and cultural expressions in art and ritual in a third. Finally, Byrne investigates why bubonic plague disappeared and why we continue to be fascinated by it. Documents included provide a variety of medieval accounts—Byzantine, Arabic, French, German, English, and Italian—several of which are translated for the first time.

The Crusades, by Helen Nicholson, presents a balanced account of various crusades, or military campaigns, invented by Catholic or "Latin" Christians during the Middle Ages against those they perceived as threats to their faith. Such expeditions included the Crusades to the Holy Land between 1095 and 1291, expeditions to the Iberian Peninsula, the "crusade" to northeastern Europe, the Albigensian Crusades and the Hussite crusades—both against the heretics—and the crusades against the Ottoman Turks (in the Balkans). Although Muslim rulers included the concept of jihâd (a conflict fought for God against evil or his enemies) in their wars in the early centuries of Islam, it had become less important in the late tenth century. It was not until the middle decades of the twelfth century that jihâd was revived in the wars with the Latin Christian Crusaders. Most of the Crusades did not result in victory for the Latin Christians, although Nicholson concedes they slowed the advance of Islam. After Jerusalem was destroyed in 1291, Muslim rulers did permit Christian pilgrims to travel to holy sites. In the Iberian Peninsula, Christian rulers replaced Muslim rulers, but Muslims, Jews, and dissident Christians were compelled to convert to Catholicism. In northeastern Europe, the Teutonic Order's campaigns allowed German colonization that later encouraged twentieth-century German claims to land and led to two world wars. The Albigensian Crusade wiped out thirteenth-century aristocratic families in southern France who held to the Cathar heresy, but the Hussite crusades in the 1420s failed to eliminate the Hussite heresy. As a result of the wars, however, many positive changes occurred: Arab learning founded on Greek scholarship entered western Europe through the acquisition of an extensive library in Toledo, Spain, in 1085; works of western European literature were inspired by the holy wars; trade was encouraged and with it the demand for certain products; and a more favorable image of Muslim men and women was fostered by the crusaders' contact with the Middle East. Nicholson also notes that America may have been discovered because Christopher Columbus avoided a route that had been closed by Muslim conquests and that the Reformation may have been advanced because Martin Luther protested against the crusader indulgence in his Ninety-five Theses (1517).

Eleanor of Aquitaine, Courtly Love, and the Troubadours, by ffiona Swabey, singles out the twelfth century as the age of the individual, in which a queen like Eleanor of Aquitaine could influence the development of a new social and artistic culture. The wife of King Louis VII of France and later the wife of his enemy Henry of Anjou, who became king of England, she patronized some of the troubadours, whose vernacular lyrics celebrated the personal expression of emotion and a passionate declaration of service to women. Love, marriage, and the pursuit of women were also the subject of the new romance literature, which flourished in northern Europe and was the inspiration behind concepts of courtly love. However, as Swabey points out, historians in the past have misjudged Eleanor, whose independent spirit fueled their misogynist attitudes. Similarly, Eleanor's divorce and subsequent stormy marriage have colored ideas about medieval "love courts" and courtly love, interpretations of which have now been challenged by scholars. The twelfth century is set in context, with commentaries on feudalism, the tenets of Christianity, and the position of women, as well as summaries of the cultural and philosophical background, the cathedral schools and universities, the influence of Islam, the revival of classical learning, vernacular literature, and Gothic architecture. Swabey provides two biographical chapters on Eleanor and two on the emergence of the troubadours and the origin of courtly love through verse romances. Within this latter subject Swabey also details the story of Abelard and Heloise, the treatise of Andreas Capellanus (André the Chaplain) on courtly love, and Arthurian legend as a subject of courtly love.

Genghis Khan and Mongol Rule, by George Lane, identifies the rise to power of Genghis Khan and his unification of the Mongol tribes in the thirteenth century as a kind of globalization with political, cultural, economic, mercantile, and spiritual effects akin to those of modern globalization. Normally viewed as synonymous with barbarian destruction, the rise to power of Genghis Khan and the Mongol hordes is here understood as a more positive event that initiated two centuries of regeneration and creativity. Lane discusses the nature of the society of the Eurasian steppes in the twelfth and thirteenth centuries into which Genghis Khan was born; his success at reshaping the relationship between the northern pastoral and nomadic society with the southern urban, agriculturalist society; and his unification of all the Turco-Mongol tribes in 1206 before his move to conquer Tanquit Xixia, the Chin of northern China, and the lands of Islam. Conquered thereafter were the Caucasus, the Ukraine, the Crimea, Russia, Siberia, Central Asia, Afghanistan, Pakistan, and Kashmir. After his death his sons and grandsons continued, conquering Korea, Persia, Armenia, Mesopotamia, Azerbaijan, and eastern Europe—chiefly Kiev, Poland, Moravia, Silesia, and Hungary—until 1259, the end of the Mongol Empire as a unified whole. Mongol rule created a golden age in the succeeding split of the Empire into two, the Yuan dynasty of greater China and the Il-Khanate dynasty of greater Iran. Lane adds biographies of important political figures, famous names such as Marco Polo, and artists and scientists. Documents derive from universal histories, chronicles, local histories and travel accounts, official government documents, and poetry, in French, Armenian, Georgian, Chinese, Persian, Arabic, Chaghatai Turkish, Russian, and Latin.

Joan of Arc and the Hundred Years War, by Deborah Fraioli, presents the Hundred Years War between France and England in the fourteenth and fifteenth centuries within contexts whose importance has sometimes been blurred or ignored in past studies. An episode of apparently only moderate significance, a feudal lord's seizure of his vassal's land for harboring his mortal enemy, sparked the Hundred Years War, yet on the face of it the event should not have led inevitably to war. But the lord was the king of France and the vassal the king of England, who resented losing his claim to the French throne to his Valois cousin. The land in dispute, extending roughly from Bordeaux to the Pyrenees mountains, was crucial coastline for the economic interests of both kingdoms. The series of skirmishes, pitched battles, truces, stalemates, and diplomatic wrangling that resulted from the confiscation of English Aquitaine by the French form the narrative of this Anglo-French conflict, which was in fact not given the name Hundred Years War until the nineteenth century.

Fraioli emphasizes how dismissing women's inheritance and succession rights came at the high price of unleashing discontent in their male heirs, including Edward III, Robert of Artois, and Charles of Navarre. Fraioli also demonstrates the centrality of side issues, such as Flemish involvement in the war, the peasants' revolts that resulted from the costs of the war, and Joan of Arc's unusually clear understanding of French "sacred kingship." Among the primary sources provided are letters from key players such as Edward III, Etienne Marcel, and Joan of Arc; a supply list for towns about to be besieged; and a contemporary poem by the celebrated scholar and court poet Christine de Pizan in praise of Joan of Arc.

Magna Carta, by Katherine Drew, is a detailed study of the importance of the Magna Carta in comprehending England's legal and constitutional history. Providing a model for the rights of citizens found in the United States Declaration of Independence and Constitution's first ten amendments, the Magna Carta has had a role in the legal and parliamentary history of all modern states bearing some colonial or government connection with the British Empire. Constructed at a time when modern nations began to appear, in the early thirteenth century, the Magna Carta (signed in 1215) presented a formula for balancing the liberties of the people with the power of modern governmental institutions. This unique English document influenced the growth of a form of law (the English common law) and provided a vehicle for the evolution of representative (parliamentary) government. Drew demonstrates how the Magna Carta came to be—the roles of the Church, the English towns, barons, common law, and the parliament in its making—as well as how myths concerning its provisions were established. Also provided are biographies of Thomas Becket, Charlemagne, Frederick II, Henry II and his sons, Innocent III, and many other key figures, and primary documents—among them, the Magna Cartas of 1215 and 1225, and the Coronation Oath of Henry I.

Medieval Castles, by Marilyn Stokstad, traces the historical, political, and social function of the castle from the late eleventh century to the sixteenth by means of a typology of castles. This typology ranges from the early "motte and bailey"—military fortification, and government and economic center—to the palace as an expression of the castle owners' needs and purposes. An introduction defines the various contexts—military, political, economic, and social—in which the castle appeared in the Middle Ages. A concluding interpretive essay suggests the impact of the castle and its symbolic role as an idealized construct lasting until the modern day.

Medieval Cathedrals, by William Clark, examines one of the chief contributions of the Middle Ages, at least from an elitist perspective—that is, the religious architecture found in the cathedral ("chair" of the bishop) or great church, studied in terms of its architecture, sculpture, and stained glass. Clark begins with a brief contextual history of the concept of the bishop and his role within the church hierarchy, the growth of the church in the early Christian era and its affiliation with the bishop (deriving from that of the bishop of Rome), and the social history of cathedrals. Because of economic and political conflicts among the three authorities who held power in medieval towns—the king, the bishop, and the cathedral clergy—cathedral construction and maintenance always remained a vexed issue, even though the owners—the cathedral clergy—usually held the civic responsibility for the cathedral. In an interpretive essay, Clark then focuses on Reims Cathedral in France, because both it and the bishop's palace survive, as well as on contemporary information about surrounding buildings. Clark also supplies a historical overview on the social, political, and religious history of the cathedral in the Middle Ages: an essay on patrons, builders, and artists; aspects of cathedral construction (which was not always successful); and then a chapter on Romanesque and Gothic cathedrals and a "gazetteer" of twenty-five important examples.

The Medieval City, by Norman J. G. Pounds, documents the origin of the medieval city in the flight from the dangers or difficulties found in the country, whether economic, physically threatening, or cultural. Identifying the attraction of the city in its *urbanitas*, its "urbanity," or the way of living in a city, Pounds discusses first its origins in prehistoric and classical Greek urban revolutions. During the Middle Ages, the city grew primarily between the eleventh and thirteenth centuries, remaining essentially the same until the Industrial Revolution. Pounds provides chapters on the medieval city's planning, in terms of streets and structures; life in the medieval city; the roles of the Church and the city government in its operation; the development of crafts and trade in the city; and the issues of urban health, wealth, and welfare. Concluding with the role of the city in history, Pounds suggests that the value of the city depended upon its balance of social classes, its need for trade and profit to satisfy personal desires through the accumulation of wealth and its consequent economic power, its political power as a representative body within the kingdom, and its social role in the rise of literacy and education and in nationalism. Indeed, the concept of a middle class, a bourgeoisie, derives from the city—from the *bourg*, or "borough." According to Pounds, the rise of modern civilization would not have taken place without the growth of the city in the Middle Ages and its concomitant artistic and cultural contribution.

Medieval Science and Technology, by Elspeth Whitney, examines science and technology from the early Middle Ages to 1500 within the context of the classical learning that so influenced it. She looks at institutional history, both early and late, and what was taught in the medieval schools and, later, the universities (both of which were overseen by the Catholic Church). Her discussion of Aristotelian natural philosophy illustrates its impact on the medieval scientific worldview. She presents chapters on the exact sciences, meaning mathematics, astronomy, cosmology, astrology, statics, kinematics, dynamics, and optics; the biological and earth sciences, meaning chemistry and alchemy, medicine, zoology, botany, geology and meteorology, and geography; and technology. In an interpretive conclusion, Whitney demonstrates the impact of medieval science on the preconditions and structure that permitted the emergence of the modern world. Most especially, technology transformed an agricultural society into a more commercial and engine-driven society: waterpower and inventions like the blast furnace and horizontal loom turned iron working and cloth making into manufacturing operations. The invention of the mechanical clock helped to organize human activities through timetables rather than through experiential perception and thus facilitated the advent of modern life. Also influential in the establishment of a middle class were the inventions of the musket and pistol and the printing press. Technology, according to Whitney, helped advance the habits of mechanization and precise methodology. Her biographies introduce major medieval Latin and Arabic and classical natural philosophers and scientists. Extracts from various kinds of scientific treatises allow a window into the medieval concept of knowledge.

The Puebloan Society of Chaco Canyon, by Paul Reed, is unlike other volumes in this series, whose historic events boast a long-established historical record. Reed's study offers instead an original reconstruction of the Puebloan Indian society of Chaco, in what is now New Mexico, but originally extending into Colorado, Utah, and Arizona. He is primarily interested in its leaders, ritual and craft specialists, and commoners during the time of its chief flourishing, in the eleventh and twelfth centuries, as understood from archaeological data alone. To this new material he adds biographies of key Euro-American archaeologists and other individuals from the nineteenth and twentieth centuries who have made important discoveries about Chaco Canyon. Also provided are documents of archaeological description and narrative from early explorers' journals and archaeological reports, narratives, and monographs. In his overview chapters, Reed discusses the cultural and environmental setting of Chaco Canyon; its history (in terms of exploration and research); the Puebloan society and how it emerged chronologically; the Chaco society and how it appeared in 1100 c.e.; the "Outliers," or outlying communities of Chaco; Chaco as a ritual center of the eleventh-century Pueblo world; and, finally, what is and is not known about Chaco society. Reed concludes that ritual and ceremony played an important role in Chacoan society and that ritual specialists, or priests, conducted ceremonies, maintained ritual artifacts, and charted the ritual calendar. Its social organization matches no known social pattern or type: it was complicated, multiethnic, centered around ritual and ceremony, and without any overtly hierarchical political system. The Chacoans were ancestors to the later Pueblo people, part of a society that rose, fell, and evolved within a very short time period.

The Rise of Islam, by Matthew Gordon, introduces the early history of the Islamic world, beginning in the late sixth century with the career of the Prophet Muhammad (c. 570–c. 632) on the Arabian Peninsula. From Muhammad's birth in an environment of religious plurality—Christianity, Judaism, and Zoroastrianism, along with paganism, were joined by Islam—to the collapse of the Islamic empire in the early tenth century, Gordon traces the history of the Islamic community. The book covers topics that include the life of the Prophet and divine revelation (the Qur'an) to the formation of the Islamic state, urbanization in the Islamic Near East, and the extraordinary culture of Islamic letters and scholarship. In addition to a historical overview, Gordon examines the Caliphate and early Islamic Empire, urban society and economy, and the emergence, under the Abbasid Caliphs, of a "world religious tradition" up to the year 925 C.E.

As editor of this series I am grateful to have had the help of Benjamin Burford, an undergraduate Century Scholar at Rice University assigned to me in 2002–2004 for this project; Gina Weaver, a third-year graduate student in English; and Cynthia Duffy, a second-year graduate student in English, who assisted me in target-reading select chapters from some of these books in an attempt to define an audience. For this purpose I would also like to thank Gale Stokes, former dean of humanities at Rice University, for the 2003 summer research grant and portions of the 2003–2004 annual research grant from Rice University that served that end.

This series, in its mixture of traditional and new approaches to medieval history and cultures, will ensure opportunities for dialogue in the classroom in its offerings of twelve different "libraries in books." It should also propel discussion among graduate students and scholars by means of the gentle insistence throughout on the text as primal. Most especially, it invites response and further study. Given its mixture of East and West, North and South, the series symbolizes the necessity for global understanding, both of the Middle Ages and in the postmodern age.

Jane Chance, Series Editor
Houston, Texas
February 19, 2004

CHRONOLOGY

313	Edict of Toleration: Christianity was given legal existence.
313	S. Giovanni Laterano (St. John Lateran), Cathedral of Rome, was begun.
313–17	Emperor Constantine's gifts to the Lateran basilica and Old St. Peter's (Document 1).
317–29	S. Pietro Vaticano (Old St. Peter's), Rome, was built.
325	Creed of Nicaea decreed equality of the Trinity.
380	Christianity became the official religion of the Empire.
381	Second Creed of Nicaea (Document 4).
c. 400	Prudentius described the Lateran basilica and Old St. Peter's (Document 2).
	The Marvels of Rome, twelfth-century descriptions of Roman churches (Document 3).
c. 500	Baptism of Clovis and the conversion of the Franks to orthodox Christianity.
591	Gregory of Tours recounted the Baptism of Clovis and described two basilicas of the fifth century (Documents 5 and 6).

597	The pope, Gregory I, sent Augustine to establish Christianity in Canterbury (Document 7).
601	Two letters of Pope Gregory the Great concerning Christianity in England (Document 8).
Early 7th century	Desiderius's lists of gifts to St.-Germain at Auxerre (Document 8).
7th century	Benedict Biscop explained the importation of builders and materials from Rome to Hexham, England (Document 10).
Late 7th and 12th centuries	Two descriptions of Hexham (Document 11).
711	The Moslem conquest of Iberian Peninsula (Spain).
732	The Battle of Tours halted the Moslem invasion north of the Pyrenees.
742/3	St. Boniface's letter to Carloman on bishops' synods and the rules of election (Document 12).
744	Bishop Chrodegang of Metz organized cathedral clergy (Document 13).
751–54	The coronation of Pepin and his sons, Carloman and Charlemagne (Document 14).
768–75	The joint rule of Carloman and Charlemagne.
775–814	Charlemagne became sole ruler as King of the Franks.
820	Einhard described Charlemagne's buildings (Document 15).
843	Treaty of Verdun divided the Frankish kingdom into three parts (Document 16).
845–911	Invasions and incursions of the Vikings ended when Rollo was made duke of Normandy and given lands around the mouth of the river Seine.

858	Hincmar of Reims explained why the French bishops rejected Louis the German (Document 17).
885	How the German bishops fought the Vikings (Document 18).
End 9th century	The rules for the election of bishops without royal interference in Germany (Document 19).
936	The election of Otto I (Document 20).
936–73	Otto I, the Great, was named Holy Roman Emperor in 962.
963	Pope Leo VIII gave Otto I the right to choose bishops (Document 21).
965	Otto I gave the Archbishop of Hamburg permission to establish a market (Document 22).
987	Hugh Capet elected King of the Franks; the dynasty continued until 1328.
1030–61, 1082–1106	Speyer Cathedral, Germany, was built.
1063–1118	The first phase of the construction of Pisa Cathedral, Italy.
1066	Duke William of Normandy conquered England, became king of England.
1067	Eadmer described the cathedral of Canterbury (Document 23).
1074	Two texts describe the expulsion of the Archbishop of Cologne (Document 24).
1075–1122	Investiture Conflict between the papacy and the kings of Germany over the right to name bishops.
1076	The bishop of Liège and the Count of Hainaut divided power over the county (Document 25).

1076	Five letters describe the investiture conflict between Henry IV and Pope Gregory VII (Document 26).
Bet. 1075–80	Cathedral of Santiago de Compostela, Spain, was begun.
1082	Cathedral of Ely, England, was begun.
1085	Christian kings conquer Toledo, Spain.
1088	Trial of William of St.-Calais, bishop of Durham (Document 27).
1093–1133	Durham Cathedral, England, was constructed.
1095	First Crusade to the Holy Land was undertaken.
1106	Archbishop of Hamburg chartered his merchants (Document 28).
1115	Guibert de Nogent recounted the evil doings of bishops and citizens of Laon (Document 29).
1120–25	St.-Lazare at Autun, France, was begun; made the cathedral in 1195.
1120s	Cathedral of Angoulême, France, was begun.
1122	Concordat of Worms, the compromise of Calixtus II to remain pope (Document 30).
1125	German bishops demanded the election of the emperor (Document 31).
1135	German bishops made peace with the emperor (Document 32).
1142–45 to c. 1155	The royal portals at Chartres Cathedral, France, were constructed.
Mid-12th century	A description of Santiago de Compostela (Document 33).
1145	Archbishop of Rouen described the people pulling the carts at Chartres (Document 34).

1147–49	The Second Crusade ended badly.
c. 1155	Notre-Dame, Cathedral of Paris, was begun.
c. 1155	Notre-Dame, Cathedral of Laon, was begun.
1159	John of Salisbury described the duties of knights to the church (Document 35).
1164	Henry II of England published the Constitutions of Clarendon (Document 36).
1166	The number of knights owed by Archbishop of York to Henry II was explained (Document 37).
1170	Thomas à Becket, archbishop of Canterbury, was murdered.
1173	Thomas à Becket was canonized (Document 38).
1174–84	Gervase described the rebuilding of Canterbury (Document 39).
by 1174	The church at Monreale, Sicily, was begun.
1177	The bishop of the Artois and the count of Flanders divided secular jurisdictions (Document 40).
1189–92	The Third Crusade was not successful.
1194	The nave of the cathedral of Chartres was rebuilt after a fire.
c. 1195	Cathedral of St. Stephen at Bourges, France, was begun.
1198	Pope Innocent III wrote the Archbishop of Rouen about absent canons (Document 41).
Bef. 1200	Universities were formed at Bologne, Oxford, and Paris.
1200	France was put under Papal Interdict because of the "illegal" marriage of Philip Augustus (Document 42).

1202–4	The Fourth Crusade ended with the Sack of Constantinople.
1206–10	The new Cathedral of Notre-Dame at Reims, France, was begun.
Bef. 1213	Cathedral of Naumburg, Germany, was begun.
1215–17	Cathedral of Auxerre, France, was rebuilt (Document 43).
1218	Emperor Frederick II denied municipal freedoms and communes in Germany (Document 44).
1218–20	Cathedral of Notre-Dame at Amiens, France, was begun.
1218–21	The Fifth Crusade was a failure.
c. 1220	Cathedrals at Salisbury, England, and Toledo, Spain, were begun.
1228–29	The Sixth Crusade achieved nothing.
1233–36, 1241	Municipal uprisings occurred in Reims (Document 45).
1237	Limits are put on the authority of the Archbishop of Cologne, Germany (Document 46).
1248	Cathedral of Cologne, Germany, was begun.
1248–54	The Seventh Crusade; the first for Louis IX, was undertaken.
1258	Etienne de Boileau drew up statutes concerning workers in Paris (Document 47).
1270	The Eighth Crusade was undertaken; Louis IX died at Tunis.
1279	Cathedral of Exeter, England, was rebuilt.
1280	Wimpfen-am-Tal, Germany, was to be built in the French Gothic style (Document 48).

1286	Durandus of Mende explained the symbolism and the meaning of churches (Document 49).
1287	Etienne de Bonneuil received a contract to work on the cathedral at Uppsala, Sweden (Document 50).
1296	Cathedral of Palma de Majorca, Spain, was begun.
1313	Builders advised on the condition of Chartres Cathedral (Document 51).
1315–22	The Great Famine spread through western Europe.
1323	Jean de Jandun described Notre-Dame in Paris (Document 52).
1337–1453	Hundred Years War was fought intermittently between France and England.
1342	Construction of Prague Cathedral, Czech Republic, was begun by Matthew of Arras.
1347–50	Black Death ravaged Europe.
1348	Henry Knighton described the effects of the Black Death in England (Document 53).
1352	Cathedral of Antwerp, Belgium, was begun.
1385	Cathedral of Milan, Italy, was begun.
1431	Joan of Arc was burned at the stake in Rouen.
1512	New Cathedral of Salamanca, Spain, was begun.

INTRODUCTION

Today when we think of cathedrals, we usually envision the great Gothic buildings of twelfth- and thirteenth-century Europe, but other than being a large church (usually the largest in the city), a cathedral is neither a specific building type nor just medieval. What makes a large church a cathedral—whether we think of Christopher Wren's St. Paul's in London (1675–1710), James Renwick's St. Patrick's in New York (begun 1858), or José Raphael Moneo's new Our Lady of the Angels in Los Angeles (1997–2002)—is the presence of a single item of furniture: the chair (in Latin: *cathedra*) or throne that is the symbol of the ecclesiastical and spiritual authority of a bishop (the Anglo-Saxon corruption of *episcopus*, from the Greek for "overseer").

This book is an introduction to the medieval cathedral, rather than to the broader and more inclusive topic, the medieval church. Thus, it focuses on a selected series of high points, those churches that are usually regarded as among the greatest achievements of medieval architecture. This selective perspective is necessary in a volume such as this because of the overwhelming numbers of surviving medieval churches, but by no means should it be understood that this selection endorses the view that *only* cathedrals should be studied or that cathedrals constitute a representative sample of medieval churches. Indeed, lots of other, equally important surviving medieval churches, mostly monastic, occasionally parish, are just as worthy of our attention today. However, it is generally true that cathedrals often embody the most advanced ideas in architecture, sculpture, and stained glass, although these great buildings are by no means the exclusive sites of experimentation. After all, the general consensus is that the Gothic style was first achieved in the remarkable synthesis of old and new found in the two additions made in the 1130s and 1140s to the abbey church of St.-Denis, just north of Paris. The new ideas explored there were shortly adopted in a number of monastic and cathedral projects, but within a couple of decades it was the cathedral workshops that produced the experimentation and achievements that became characteristic of the Gothic.

The cathedral, usually the largest and most important church in a town, had a big visual impact in that municipal complex. Even today, the cathedral is often the most prominent urban structure in many European cities. If we consider that the medieval population was but a fraction of the present population, then we can better understand the dominant physical presence of the cathedral in the town. Most older studies of medieval building tend to adopt the positivist, nineteenth-century viewpoint that the cathedral should be recognized as the symbol of civic pride. While such symbolization might dominate nineteenth-century attitudes, this belief glosses over the enormous burden that cathedral construction imposed on towns in the Middle Ages. Indeed, such older studies ignore the frequent hostilities between emerging town economies and ecclesiastical overlords. Until very late in the Middle Ages all the records and references to cathedral construction come from ecclesiastical sources, who were understandably reluctant to admit hostilities to their grand projects.

In most medieval cathedral towns there were three important landlords that held the majority of property and, through that ownership, controlled the local economy. The three were the local secular authority, the bishop, and the cathedral chapter. In Paris, for example, that tripartite division included the king, the bishop, and the cathedral clergy. In many cities and towns across western Europe, the bishop exercised local overlordship in addition to his ecclesiastical responsibilities, but in neither capacity was he required to pay for cathedral construction and upkeep, which was the responsibility of the clergy. Forceful episcopal personalities could obviously play a major role in inspiring cathedral construction, and there are numerous records of bishops helping to initiate cathedral construction by willingly donating a percentage of episcopal income (as much as 10 percent) for a period of years (ranging from three to ten years in the known examples). On the other hand, the relations between bishops and chapters were often contentious and hardly supportive. For example, as elaborated later, the archbishop of Reims was ut-

1. Map of Europe in the fifth and six centuries.

terly unsympathetic to the developing dispute between the cathedral chapter and the townsmen in the early thirteenth century. He was dragged into the conflict only when the townsmen openly attacked his officers and his fortress in Reims. Nor are there any indications that he contributed to the mounting cost of construction, even though he was memorialized by name in the stained glass.

Cathedral construction was never a civic responsibility but remained always the responsibility of the cathedral owners, namely, the clergy in charge of day-to-day activities and services. Beginning in the eighth century, that clergy was organized into chapters with their own officers and responsibilities. Their income was derived from the land that they held both inside the city and without. Until the twelfth century that income came largely in the form of agricultural commodities, which, in turn, were traded for other goods and services. As town economies grew and began to diversify into other areas—cloth production being an early example— the income of the canons was derived in the form of rents from their properties and taxes imposed on commerce. As the economies began to be based less on goods and more on money, diversity increased. A money economy was by its very nature less dependent, for example, on the whims of nature that might result in bad harvests. The process of transformation from an agricultural to a money economy was slow and by no means the same in every town. But as a general rule cathedral chapters were rarely disposed favorably toward the developing commercial enterprises, even though they produced greater income. Remarkably, hostilities between the clergy and the persons under their control is only rarely reflected in the great buildings themselves. The inability of chapters to complete their cathedrals within the norm of about seventy-five to eighty years in cities as diverse and separated as Cologne, Milan, and Prague is a direct reflection not just of economies but of a number of social factors unique to each place.

As for the bishop, he was both the spiritual leader and the administrative head of a group of churches that together formed a diocese, which was in turn part of a still larger administrative and spiritual unit, the archdiocese, presided over by an archbishop. The archbishop answered, as he still does, to the head of the Roman Catholic faith, the pope in Rome, and his council, the College of Cardinals. A number of other active Christian denominations, from the national branches of the Eastern Orthodox faith to Protestant denominations, among them the Church of

2. Map of Europe in the ninth century.

England (Anglicans), Episcopalians, Lutherans, Methodists, and others, use the title bishop for presiding officials and are organized along somewhat similar lines. The role of the bishop in Eastern Orthodox groups dates from the earliest centuries of Christianity, as in the case of the Roman Catholic bishops, whereas the other denominations retained the pattern of organization after the Protestant Reformation.

Although the concepts of the bishop and his role in church hierarchy are often thought to have developed in Apostolic times (the first century AD)—indeed, references to the heads of various Early Christian communities can be found in the writings of St. Paul—there is little evidence of an established church hierarchy before the late third or early fourth century AD. The charge of Christ to the Apostle Peter, "Thou art Peter, and upon this rock I will build my Church" (Matt. 16:18), is usually understood metaphorically as both a directive and an explanation in the Early Christian period. Peter is considered simultaneously the first bishop of Rome and, as the most senior of the founding fathers of Christianity, the first pope (or *Pontifex maximus*, "builder of big bridges," a Roman civic title that accrued to the pope). As church leaders gradually replaced secular authorities in the void created by the gradual withdrawal of Roman imperial authority, first to the north of Italy (Milan and Ravenna) and, ultimately, to the east in 285 (then in 324 to the Greek town named Byzantium, renamed Constantinople in honor of the emperor Constantine, and, finally, with the Turkish conquest in 1453, Istanbul), some of the secular, administrative roles in cities passed to bishops.

The spiritual and ecclesiastical authority of the bishop of Rome (the pope) was, in fact, confirmed first by the Edict of Toleration (313 AD), which gave Christianity the legal right to exist, and then by the emperor Constantine's gift to the bishop of Rome of the imperial palace on the Lateran hill as a residence worthy of his authority. This official recognition, combined with the gradual revelation that even members of the imperial family were Christian adherents, brought increasing numbers of converts and the need for more and larger churches, especially in the quarter-century between the Edict of Toleration and the death of Constantine in 337 AD. The small Christian communities that had been led by a single priest with one or two assistants and had converted private houses into places of worship might have functioned well in small towns, but other solutions had to be found in the great cities of the ancient world as increasing numbers of Christians occupied important social and

3. Map of Europe in the eleventh century.

government offices. The most common model in the Western Empire (Europe) is that adopted in Rome itself, where a new, large church was built on the site of the stables of the Lateran palace. Because the palace was the residence of the bishop of Rome and itself still carried associations with imperial power, the new church became the cathedral of

Rome. Most people incorrectly assume that St. Peter's, the church most often associated with the pope and with his now-official residence in the Vatican, is the cathedral of Rome, but that distinction still belongs to San Giovanni Laterano, or St. John Lateran.

The present church of St. John Lateran is a largely seventeenth-century rebuilding of the fourth-century one, the plan and details of which we have recovered through archeological excavations. Everything we know about the early building indicates that the intent was to produce a big church that could hold numbers of people—Richard Krautheimer (1986) estimated it could have easily held 3,000 worshipers and 200 clergy—rather than to create an architectural type. In fact, St. John was loosely based on large Roman public buildings, such as the big halls called basilicas or the large rectangular rooms in public baths. Its major requirement was the creation of a suitable place where the Mass, the most important Christian rite, could be solemnly celebrated. Thus, the altar where this took place was the principal focus in the building, but this relatively simple requirement could, in fact, fit into any of several other common building types in the Roman Empire.

More important than any standardized architectural type was the development of a permanent and unchangeable liturgy, which was largely established during the early fourth century. The basic components remained the same: the Mass, divided into the Mass of the Catechumens (those being taught the tenets of Christianity but not yet baptized into the community), which comprised the first sections of the service, and the Mass of the Faithful, celebrated after the departure of the Catechumens. This second part begins with the Eucharist, the central sacrifice of the Mass, and continues to the end. In addition to this fixed liturgy, the clear separation of the clergy (those performing the Mass) from the congregation (those witnessing the Mass and celebrating it through the clergy) was now established, as was the presiding position of the bishop. Bishops were then viewed as shepherds leading the flocks of worshipers, and Christ, under imperial sponsorship, was seen as the King of Heaven. We need to remember, however, that Christianity itself was still changing and was by no means either universal or the only religion.

The relatively simple requirements of a place of focus, where the services took place, and a place to house the throne of the bishop meant that there was considerable architectural variety among fourth- and fifth-century cathedrals, variety that expressed regional variations of archi-

4. Map of Europe in the thirteenth century.

tectural traditions and variety among those that fulfilled additional roles
as burial or pilgrimage sites. Most early cathedrals, even those as late as
the ninth century, are known only through modern archeological investigations and/or early texts. In the period covered by this book, primarily from the ninth to the early fifteenth century, there are no specific
architectural features that distinguish cathedrals from other large
churches constructed at the same time. Only the presence of the bishop's
throne marks a cathedral. The cathedral always had a central place reserved for the bishop and the clergy that was clearly separated from the
congregational space, even though most of these architectural barriers
have now been dismantled. Over time and reflecting major changes in
the liturgy, as well as changes in the attitudes of the clergy, most of the
interior divisions have disappeared so completely that today it is often
difficult to know where they existed.

   Most European cathedrals have lost some if not all of the buildings
that originally surrounded them and made up the cathedral complex. In
the early centuries, for example, every cathedral had a separate baptistry
adjacent to the main church; but outside Italy and southern France, almost none of these remain. Examples of bishops' palaces survive, but
many of them were rebuilt at later periods than the cathedrals beside
them. And what about buildings for the clergy? We must remember that
the cathedral was the property of the clergy, who, after the eighth or
ninth century, were usually organized into a chapter of canons. They had
the responsibility for building, owning, running, and maintaining the
cathedral, just as they had daily, regular communal obligations. Except
for those rare exceptions in England where the cathedral was established
in a monastic community, the canons did not live together but had individual houses, which, like their assigned incomes, came with the posi-
tions. Bishops and canons, though they often shared common interests,
rarely lived near one another. The bishop lived on one side and the
canons on the other. There is no hard and fast rule as to who lived where,
but it is usually true that the bishops had the better side, depending on
the physical situation of the church. A few traces of the canons' communal buildings still survive, but our knowledge of them largely depends
on old plans and views made prior to their destructions. In short, it is
difficult for the modern visitor to get a sense of the original complex because most European cathedrals now survive as isolated structures separated from the urban environments that surrounded them and that

reflected the collective enterprises responsible for their many and varied functions in their communities.

In the chapter that follows, we begin with a historic overview, a social history of cathedrals, which is succeeded by chapters examining such topics as patrons, builders, and artists, as well as planning and construction, with sections discussing the major technological components in Romanesque and Gothic cathedrals. The final chapter is an in-depth examination of the French cathedral of Reims, a seminal building with significant technological advances, important sculptural programs, as well as a surviving bishop's palace and substantial information about the other buildings that made up the cathedral precinct. The volume concludes with a series of illustrations, a selection of original texts, and a selected bibliography for further study. Before venturing to these topics, however, let us examine the layout and organization of churches and cathedrals and discuss the general characteristics of their plans.

ARCHITECTURAL ORGANIZATION, PLANS AND DRAWINGS

The pages that follow illustrate four church plans (Figure 1) reproduced at the same scale so they can be compared to one another in size. Three of the four, top to bottom, the cathedrals of Durham, Speyer, and Reims, are shown with north to the top, south to the bottom, east to the right, and west to the left. The other plan, representing Old St. Peter's in Rome and over which that of Durham has been drawn, has been inverted because its main apse is to the west, not the east, owing to the topography of the Vatican hill on which it was constructed in the fourth century. This occidentation ("occident" meaning western) was also followed in the present church of St. Peter's, as well as in St. John Lateran, the cathedral of Rome. Christian churches have always been laid out along an east-west axis, a reflection of burial practices taken over from Jewish practice, itself influenced by the revival of the cult of the sun in the first century BC. The dead were buried with their feet to the east, facing the rising sun. Christians continued the practice but gave it new meaning by likening the rising sun to the Resurrection of Christ, which is still reenacted on Easter Sunday. Since the Resurrection of Christ represents the fulfillment of the promise of Christianity, churches are still laid out with the altar to the east and the main entrance, or facade, to the west. These four plans also demonstrate the continuity of church planning from the fourth to the thirteenth centuries.

A building plan is not a complex guide to construction; it is merely a chart of the arrangement of the major spaces. These four plans of Durham, Speyer, Reims, and old St. Peter's, Rome, are easily recognizable in their similarities. They contain the three most basic requirements, namely, the place of the main or high altar, space for the clergy, and space for the congregation. The space for the congregation is the nave, a long, hall-like room flanked by corridor-like aisles. The aisles are lower in height than the central nave space and are separated from it by long rows of arches resting on columns. Since the main nave is taller than the aisles, it usually contains windows in the wall that rises above the aisles, hence "clerestory" is the name given that window wall. Prior to the later eleventh and twelfth centuries the nave was almost exclusively covered by a timber ceiling and timber roof. Later Romanesque examples, like Durham and Speyer, were given stone vaulted ceilings, partly to emphasize their importance and partly in an effort to prevent fire from destroying the whole building.

Because the nave is the main congregational space, it is usually fronted at the west by a decorated facade that proclaimed "entrance." The facade of Old St. Peter's was nothing more than the end wall of the nave, but we know from texts that it was richly decorated. Durham and Speyer both had paired towers rising over their facades that emphasized their entrances, and the facade of Reims is one of the most dazzling creations of the Gothic period, as we will see.

All four of these churches had a cross volume, called a transept, between the nave and the main liturgical space to the east. At Old St. Peter's, the singers might have occupied the transept, which was a continuous space lower in height than the nave. The transepts at Durham and Speyer are the same height as their naves. They are not continuous, however, but are divided by tall lantern (or windowed) towers built over the crossing, the intersection of the nave and the transept. At Durham the floor level of the transept is the same as in the nave, whereas at Speyer the eastern end of the nave and the entire transept and east end are stepped up to a much higher level. Under them is one of the largest crypts in all of medieval architecture. Rather than being completely underground, as was the case with most crypts, that at Speyer is only partly below ground level and originally contained a number of episcopal and royal burials. The transept at Reims is more complex than the others because it has been given aisles on the east and west sides. Furthermore, on the north side are three elaborately decorated portals (doorways) into the church. The central portal in the north transept marked the ceremonial entrance of the canons at Reims, whose houses and other buildings were on that side of the church. The south side had one small doorway that led directly into the archepiscopal palace. Gothic Reims may have been intended to have a crossing tower, like the ninth-century cathedral, but it was never constructed, in part because of the cost, in part because each transept arm has a pair of towers over the outer bays. These towers were only built up to the level of the transept roof and never completed to their full height. In the late fifteenth century the canons wanted to build a tall, thin spire over the crossing, but it too was never constructed.

The space behind the altar at Old St. Peter's, which is called the apse, was defined by a semicircular wall and covered by a half dome. It was less tall than the transept and served as a kind of visual frame for the altar, as well as providing seating for the clergy on tiers of semicircular benches against the wall. The altar itself, where the services took place, was aligned on the opening of the apse in the transept wall and set directly over what was believed to be the burial spot of the Apostle Peter.

By the ninth century the liturgical space, called the choir, included everything east of the transept and had become both larger and more complex. The liturgical space at Speyer, for example, extended through the transept into the second bay of the nave because it included all of the raised area over the crypt. There was one altar in the apse, which was made deeper to hold the clergy, and a second directly under the crossing tower. One of these two would have been the main or high altar, but a third, which served as the principal altar for the congregation, stood at the top of the stairs in the east end of the nave.

At Durham, because it was a monastic cathedral, the choir is very long, almost as long as the nave. To accommodate the number of monks, the choir space actually extended through the crossing and into the nave. The high altar was placed deep in the eastern end of this space, in front of the tomb of St. Cuthbert, founder of the diocese. In addition to the main apse that held the saint's tomb, the two choir aisles ended in separate little apses that each housed an altar. This triapsidal plan first appeared in the fifth century, so its later use at Durham may be a specific reference to the antiquity of St. Cuthbert. An additional altar, called the matutinal altar, was located in the second choir bay to serve the daily needs of the monastic ritual. Because the entire area of the transept and choir at Durham was reserved for the Benedictine monks, there would have been a separate altar for the cathedral congregation, probably just west of the easternmost columns in the nave, where a screen was located to separate the congregation from the monks.

The choir of Reims Cathedral is especially elaborate, containing a deep apse surrounded and flanked by aisles and chapels. The U-shaped aisle around the apse is called an ambulatory because it allowed the visitor to walk around (ambulate) without disturbing the clergy inside. Opening out of the ambulatory are a series of five deep, nearly circular chapels that, in plan, look as though they are laid out in a radial pattern from the center of the apse; hence they are termed radiating chapels. The center chapel was made deeper because it was the most important. In addition, the aisles in the straight bays flanking the apse are doubled on each side, resulting in two more chapels. The scheme of the ambulatory and radiating chapels was created in the later ninth or early tenth century, probably in northern France, but popularized in central and southern France. This scheme became the standard solution in the Gothic period. The thirteenth-century high altar at Reims was located not in the choir but in the crossing, directly over the ruins of the ninth-century altar, itself built very close to the location of the high altar in the first church on the site. The high altar has been replaced several times, but it has never been moved far from the original spot because that site represents the continuity of Christianity at Reims. There was an additional, secondary altar in the apse, but it was far less important than the high altar. The center space of the choir at Reims east of the high altar was where the archbishop held councils with the eleven bishops of the archdiocese. The cathedral canons and other clergy occupied the four eastern bays of the central nave space and were separated from the congregation in the rest of the nave by a tall choir screen. In most Gothic cathedrals the liturgical space was confined to the area east of the transept; Reims was one of the few where it spilled over the crossing and into the nave, possibly owing to the seventy-two canons.

The four elevation drawings (Figure 2), again reproduced at the same scale, are of Reims Cathedral. The two at the ends show cross sections, vertical slices through half of the building, from the floor through the roof, perpendicular to the longitudinal axis. The lefthand section is of the nave; that on the right is of the choir. The middle pair of drawings are interior and exterior vertical elevations of the nave of Reims. Drawings such as these make possible comparisons between exterior and interior, but they also reveal the proportional relationship between the parts. These four drawings were made in the nineteenth century, before any major restorations took place and, of course, prior to the damage inflicted on Reims during World War I.

The interior elevation of the nave has three stories: the main arcade, a row of tall, pointed arches resting on vertical supports (piers) that fronts the aisles; the wall passage; and the clerestory. It is often described as an "ABA" elevation because the height of the main arcades (A) and the clerestory (A) are the same and are separated by the wall passage (B) between them. The enormous size of the clerestory windows is made possible by several factors, the first being the flying buttresses (visible in the cross sections) on the exterior that brace the upper wall and the roof. Another factor are the big arches that frame the window openings, arches that relieve the weight on the window opening, thus permitting the wall to be opened to the maximum. The tripartite division of the interior is repeated on the exterior; the aisle wall and window are the same height as the clerestory window. The whole scheme on the outside is made more elaborate by the addition of the statues of angels and the pinnacles to the flying buttresses. The drawing makes it appear that the angels and pinnacles are framing the windows. In reality the tall piers of the buttresses make it difficult to see the aisle windows, let alone the clerestory windows that are that much higher and set in from the perimeter (compare the cross section with the outside elevation). The cross section on the far right makes it possible to compare the system of flying buttresses of the nave with that of the choir. The choir buttresses are doubled in depth and have an intermediary pier because of the double aisles and the radiating chapels, but even so the upright buttress piers define the perimeter of the building and give it a contained, vertical sense.

In the final analysis, building plans and drawings are useful aides in understanding the layout and disposition of spaces in the buildings, as well as the proportional relationships between the parts, but they cannot substitute for the experience of actually visiting a major cathedral.

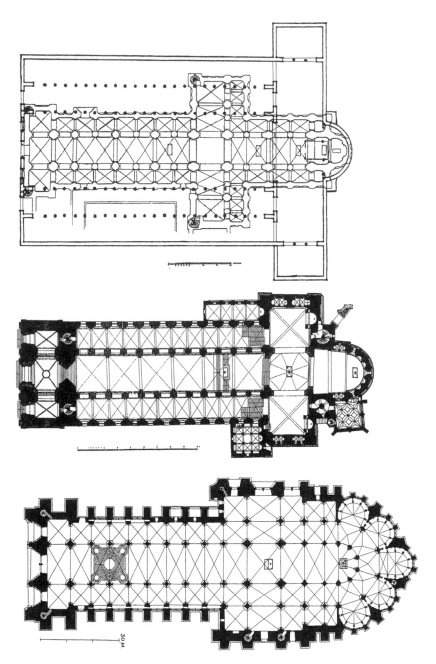

Figure 1. Plans of Four Churches at the Same Scale. Top: Rome, Old St. Peter's (east-west axis reversed) and Durham Cathedral superimposed. Middle: Speyer Cathedral. Bottom: Reims Cathedral. *Drawings: After William W. Clark.*

1

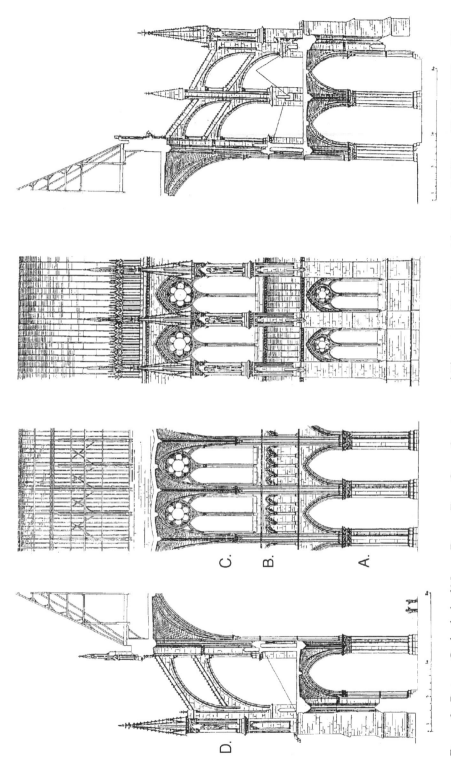

Figure 2. Reims, Cathedral of Notre-Dame. Four Cross Sections and Elevations. *Drawings: After King, 1858, modified by William W. Clark.* A. Main Arcade; B. Wall-Passage; C. Clerestory; D. Flying Buttress.

li

Figure 3. Excavations Showing Earlier Churches, Fourth to Eleventh Centuries, under and around the Cathedrals of Geneva and Rouen. *Drawings: Top, after Bonnet; bottom, after le Maho.*

CHAPTER 1

OVERVIEW: THE HISTORY OF CATHEDRALS AS SOCIAL HISTORY

A historical overview of the time of cathedrals would encompass a thousand-plus years of European history in the Middle Ages, which would either run into many volumes or be shrunk to little more than a timeline of major events and significant kings and queens, all of which can be found in current encyclopedias. Rather than string together a series of nearly meaningless facts and events, it is perhaps more useful to consider the cathedral as representative of a history of peoples and societies, of the growth of cities and social organization, and as an indicator of prosperity, if not always peace. After all, for the period we are considering, from the fourth to the fifteenth centuries, Christianity had no serious competition from within, except itself. The growth, expansion, enlargement, and even the empowerment of the church are all reflections of the society in which it operated in western Europe. The relationships between the church and the people can be seen as dependent on the personalities of religious and secular leaders. That is, strong popes in the eleventh, twelfth, and thirteenth centuries were often in contentious conflicts with strong secular rulers attempting to control the operations of the church in their lands, mainly in matters of income and of rights of justice (compare Documents 17, 19, 21, 22, 24–28, and 30–32). The same scenarios are played out over and over again with different casts of characters (Documents 35–37 and 40). With the exception of the Iberian Peninsula, the steady rise of Islam on the world scene had a far greater impact on the Byzantine east than in western Europe.

Throughout the period under consideration, as the dominant religion,

Christianity increasingly became the dominant social force in western and northern Europe. The emperor Theodosius made it the official state religion and forbad the celebration of other religions at the end of the fourth century. As Roman imperial power waned in the west outside the Italian peninsula, Christianity remained more or less intact, even as the great physical migrations of peoples across Europe began to increase. The English historian Edward Gibbon, in his classic nineteenth-century analysis of the fall of the Roman Empire, arbitrarily chose to mark the "fall" of Rome in the year 476 A.D., the year when a non-Roman-born citizen was elected emperor. Today we question even the concept of a fall and understand the more subtle nuances that accompanied the lengthy and complex transformation of the Roman Empire. What actually happened has been the subject of innumerable volumes since Gibbon and is still worthy of more, localized analyses. In one sense, perhaps the most accurate way to describe the multiple events is to see them as part of a gradual transformation from a Greco-Roman, Mediterranean worldview to a more abstract, northern European worldview.

The one constant was Christianity, although it was anything but a uniform or monolithic religion in the early centuries. As the westward-moving Indo-European tribal nations passed close to or even through the eastern Roman Empire over the course of the later fourth, fifth, and sixth centuries, many were Christianized by Byzantine missionaries, who themselves often reflected the different factions of Christianity vying for religious dominance in the eastern Empire. The result was that several tribal nations, among them the Burgundians, Ostrogoths, and Visigoths, were converted to Arian Christianity. Arians argued that the Trinity (Father, Son, and Holy Spirit) was not coequal, that God the Father was the only true God; Christ, being His Son, was lesser; Mary, therefore, was not "Theotokos" (Mother of God); and so forth. Faced with this problem in the fourth century, Constantine had insisted at the Council of Nicaea in 325 that the orthodox position on the coequality of the Trinity be promulgated (Document 4).

More important, Arian kings tended to disregard Rome and to appoint bishops themselves, as part of exercising control over religion. Arian beliefs were deemed heretical, which led to outright warfare between tribal nations and between some tribes and the empire. One well-known example concerns the Ostrogoths who settled in northern Italy and made the old imperial city of Ravenna their new capital. They soon held sway over most of the Italian peninsula, as far south as Rome. Cathedral construction was undertaken in several cities under Ostrogothic control, among them Ravenna and Florence, during the short period of peace in the later fifth and early sixth centuries.

Because the Ostrogoths followed the teaching of Arias and because the Byzantine emperor Justinian dreamt of reestablishing a new and larger empire in the name of orthodox Christianity, he sent an army against them in the early sixth century and conquered the Arians. His success in Italy was short-lived when the Lombards, another migrating people, arrived and seized Milan in 569. Pope Gregory the Great (590–604) organized the resistance to the Lombards in Rome and effectively took control of the city in the name of the papacy. On the whole, however, the popes had little authority to enforce their decrees before the eleventh and twelfth centuries.

In some instances, the new arrivals from the East found common ground with the extant Christian communities in western Europe; others, who arrived as pagans, like the Franks, were converted to orthodox (Roman) Christianity. Many of the tribal nations that pushed into the imploding Roman Empire in western Europe ahead of the advancing Huns were warrior societies with scant interest in or experience with agriculture, having been, only a few generations earlier, nomadic herdsmen. The defeat of the Huns near Troyes, in what is now eastern France, in 451, and the subsequent death of their great king Attila effectively removed the greatest threat to western Europe, although the social chaos occasioned by fighting between tribal overlords continued. Ultimately, many of these tribal nations are now remembered by having their names associated with modern European nations (the Franks and the Germans, for example), but many more of the names survive as geographic designations, from Bavaria to Burgundy to the Frisian Islands, Lombardy, Thuringia, and Swabia. Not surprisingly, the majority of such designations are on the edges or just beyond the limits of the Roman Empire.

The Visigoths, who were among the first peoples to cross into the Roman world, passed through western Europe and settled in the Iberian Peninsula, or what we know today as Spain. There they created what is usually considered the most advanced culture in the age of migrations and built, according to the surviving texts, magnificent churches whose walls were covered in gold and silver. This flourishing culture was absorbed and dismantled by the arrival of the Ummayid caliphs from Baghdad in the eighth century. Islam remained established in Iberia until 1492, when the last Moorish ruler of Granada withdrew across the straits of Gibralter. The first Islamic invaders continued unopposed across the Pyrenees until their advance was halted at the Battle of Tours, fought near Poitiers, in 732. The coalition army of Franks, Burgundians, and even Visigoths benefited from the social reorganization of the agricultural system just a generation before, when the large farms (patterned after the Roman manorial system) were required to provision horse soldiers, just as the cavalry itself benefited from a device unknown to the Islamic horsemen, the stirrup. Stirrups, which were apparently first known in the Indian subcontinent nearly two millennia before, effectively transferred the power of the horse to the rider and his weapons, which meant that his first concern was no longer whether or not he could stay on his mount.

It was the Franks in the eighth century who adopted stirrups, although scholars have not been able to learn exactly how the Franks learned about them. There is no evidence that they arrived in western Europe using them in the fifth century. The archeological evidence suggests a more northern route of migration for the Franks than for the Goths. The first Frankish center of power within the empire is found, through archeology, around Cologne. Within a generation their center of power has shifted to Tournai, a city in Belgium on the northern border with France. Their great king, Childeric, was buried in full pagan splendor at Tournai in 482. It was his son, Clovis, who moved the Franks into Gaul by conquest and by his selection of Paris as his capital, c. 500. Scholars are still arguing over the date of his conversion to Christianity, with the possibilities ranging from 495 to 508. More important than the date, however, is that he was baptized (so legend tells us, together with the entire Frankish army) an orthodox (Roman) Christian (Document 6), effectively driving a wedge between the Ostrogoths in northern Italy and the Visigoths in Iberia. Clovis married a Burgundian princess, Clotilde, who, unlike most Burgundians, was orthodox rather than Arian, and then proceeded to conquer the Burgundians and to extend his power base from the Pyrenees to the Rhineland. When he died in 511, he was buried in the church of the Holy Apostles that, together with Clotilde, he had founded in Paris. There was a cathedral in Paris at the time, since Christianity had arrived in the third century, but we know nothing about it.

Clovis's kingdom was, following Frankish custom, divided among his surviving sons and never again achieved the unity known under his rule.

After two centuries of nearly constant internal warfare, they had grown so weak and powerless that the kingdom was effectively run not by the king but by the descendent of Charles Martel (Charles the Hammer), the commander of the army that had defeated the Arab invaders in 732.

Charles's son, Pepin the Short, major domo of the last Merovingian king, contrived with the pope to replace that king with himself and his descendents and, in fact, Pepin, with his two sons, was crowned by Pope Stephen II at St.-Denis in 754 (Document 14). In return, Pepin intervened against the Lombards, on behalf of the pope, in 755 and 756. Pepin ruled until his death in 768, when he was succeeded, again according to Frankish law, by his two sons, Carolman and Charles, who ruled together until Carloman's death in 771, when Charles reigned alone until 814.

Charles, better known as Charlemagne (Charles the Great), set about consolidating and expanding his empire. The result of his expansion was the largest kingdom in northern Europe since the Roman Empire. It stretched from the Pyrennes to Hamburg, on the north sea, and included all the lands of the Germans as far east as the river Elbe and as far south as Rome and the Lombard kingdom of Beneventum.

The textual and, occasionally, archeological evidence indicates that most of the Christian communities in western Europe, established in many cities of the Roman Empire already in the third century, survived during the chaotic times of the fifth–eighth centuries. Most of the bishoprics in the cities date to the third or fourth century, and those in the border zones were established by the sixth century if not before. Even in the British Isles, where Christianity had to be reintroduced in the north from Ireland and in the south from Rome itself (Augustine was sent to be bishop of Canterbury by the pope in 597, Documents 7 and 8), the pattern of bishoprics was soon established (London in 604 and as far north as York by 627) in major population centers. A few were moved to other sites in Norman times, as was Old Sarum to Salisbury or Crediton to Exeter, as a result of population shifts. In the wake of the Anglo-Saxon invasions, England was divided into many small kingdoms that reflected the tribal divisions and the indigenous populations. Before the arrival of Alfred the Great (871–99), few kings were able to unite more than small areas, in part because of the waves of invaders from Denmark and other Viking lands. Alfred finally divided the kingdom, with the Danes taking the northeast and Alfred, London and the south. Alfred's descendants almost immediately began to recapture the Danelaw, but

English dominance in England was not secure until the mid-eleventh century. As a result, the English constructed few large Anglo-Saxon cathedrals, aside from Winchester, which was still only of moderate size.

If the Christian communities are known from historic records, the buildings that served them are known only from descriptions or, very occasionally, from archeology. But archeology rarely provides more than a plan and scattered fragments of the main church. Certain patterns can be discerned, however. Former imperial cities, from Rome and Milan to Cologne and Trier, generally retained their complexes centered around the large cathedrals, despite drastic decreases in the population. As newer Christian kingdoms emerged and populations began to stabilize, cathedral construction resumed, often following the same pattern. That is, we may be accustomed to thinking of the cathedral as a single monumental edifice, but in reality it was often several churches with differing functions grouped on a single site, as has been revealed at Geneva and Rouen (Figure 3), among others. For example, although the buildings have been several times rebuilt, the two parallel churches and several chapels at Trier, constructed on the site of a former imperial palace, still preserve an idea of the early complex, even though the surrounding buildings have disappeared. Elsewhere archeology and texts have revealed that the episcopal complex at Paris included four churches: the baptistry of St. John, the church of St. Denis du Pas, the basilica of St. Stephen, and the church of Notre-Dame, as well as other buildings that served as the residences of the bishop and clergy. In general, however, our knowledge of cathedrals constructed in the period between the early fourth century and the early eighth century, that is, between the Early Christian period and the beginning of the Carolingian era, is haphazard and piecemeal. Outside of major cities that existed in Roman times, the cathedrals were appropriately smaller and less indebted to the great churches of Rome, although the evidence suggests they were elaborately decorated with mosaic floors, had painted walls, and were furnished with gold and jeweled liturgical objects that would have been used on marble and gold-fronted altars (Documents 1–3, 5, and 9–11).

It is evident that Charlemagne and the scholars he gathered at his court saw the church as a key to power and as a tool to aid in the unification of his vast empire, almost on the model of the Byzantine emperors of the fifth and sixth centuries. Christianity was spread by conquest, and the new territories were frequently colonized and organized around new cathedral cities and Benedictine monasteries. The church in the north was reorganized into ecclesiastical provinces ruled by archbishops at Cologne (governing all the bishoprics to the north) and Mainz (the bishoprics to the east). In the year 800, Charlemagne was crowned emperor of the Romans by the pope in Rome. This proved mutually beneficial because on the one hand it made Charlemagne the protector of the church and especially the pope, while on the other it made official the Carolingian practice of using the church and its bishops as subordinates of the emperor and as tools of imperial policy. Perhaps the single most important change was the decision to impose the reformed liturgy of Pope Gregory the Great as the standard throughout the Carolingian Empire. Not only did this change necessitate new service books, especially sacramentaries, throughout the empire, but it also marked a step toward more elaborate liturgy.

Because of the relative peace created by Charlemagne and his successors, there was a great deal of major cathedral construction during the Carolingian period. Many of the buildings are deliberate attempts to revive the Early Christian architecture of Rome, Milan, and Ravenna, but others are interesting attempts to "copy" the past so loosely that the earlier sources are all but unidentifiable. Finally, we should recognize the originality of many Carolingian innovations in planning and in the organization of the space. For example, the area in which the liturgy was performed grew steadily in size and became more separated from the space of the congregation. Crypts that served as burial chambers for deceased bishops or, more important, provided safer, less exposed areas for the bodies of saints who were rapidly becoming the focus of veneration began to appear. Thus, the number of altars began to multiply: an altar in the liturgical choir reserved for the clergy necessitated another at which the rites could be performed for the congregation. Crypts were also outfitted with altars, especially an altar before the burial place of a local saint. Overall, the Carolingian period saw the widespread revival of large-scale stone architecture. As befitted the northern European climate, the buildings became more compact in plan and vertical in organization, often with emphasis on the east and west terminals by means of tall towers. Facade structures, termed westworks, became multistoried, multichambered complexes in themselves, often with an upper royal tribune from which visiting royalty could observe the liturgy, even in monasteries that were otherwise closed to them. From the evidence of plans and descriptions, it is apparent that the interior divisions between areas, some dictated by liturgy, others possibly by construction, became more pronounced. A few Carolingian buildings do, indeed, return to the Early Christian churches of Rome as sources (the monastery at Fulda, for example), but the majority present original solutions to planning and massing. Greater complexity in the liturgy led to greater variety in buildings, and as a result of advances in agriculture and population growth, greater riches were available to the churches, so their decoration and furnishing became more elaborate. Although no Carolingian cathedrals survive as standing structures, many have been discovered in excavations. Nevertheless, a great many liturgical objects and illuminated manuscripts have survived and testify to the richness of these buildings.

As the buildings and the liturgy grew more complex, so did the numbers and role of the clergy serving under the bishop (Document 12). Bishop Chrodegang of Metz, royal chancellor to Charlemagne's father, Pepin, reorganized the administration of his diocese and organized the clergy of Metz Cathedral into a chapter of canons (Document 13), all of whom were required to live by a common rule (not unlike the Rule of St. Benedict that governed the lives of monks). The clergy of the cathedral, however, were not isolated behind the walls of a monastery, but were active in the affairs of the diocese and took over the management and running of the cathedral itself. The system at Metz worked so effectively that Louis the Pious, Charlemagne's son, at a church council at Aachen in 817, made it universal throughout the empire. Such Carolingian reforms of the liturgy and of the clergy had far-reaching effects in western Europe and endured for several centuries. In like manner, the Carolingian policy of forced religious conversion following conquest not only ensured the spread of Christianity in the north but also formed the basis of Germanic royal policy right through the eleventh and twelfth centuries. The most significant political upheaval in the Carolingian world occurred when Louis the Pious began dividing the empire among his four sons just three years after he succeeded Charlemagne in 814 and long before his death in 840. After some years of squabbling among themselves, the three surviving sons came to a final decision regarding the partition with the Treaty of Verdun in 843 (Document 16), which had far-reaching consequences in European history. Louis, surnamed the German, as king of the East Franks received the northern and eastern part of the empire, which was by now largely Teutonic in blood, speech, and geography

(Document 17). Charles the Bald, as king of the West Franks, received the western part of the empire, an area that approximated later medieval France. Lothair, the eldest brother, kept the title of emperor and was king of a realm that included Italy and a middle or buffer zone bounded on the west by the Rhone, Saone, Meuse, and Scheldt rivers and on the east by the Rhine and Frisia on the coast. When Lothair died, following Frankish law, his kingdom was divided, first among his three sons and then between his two brothers. Once again Frankish law led to fragmentation and weakening of a once-powerful empire and dynasty. And, once again, cathedral construction became sporadic in the unsettled times. The architectural and liturgical innovations begun under Carolingian sponsorship, however, continued throughout the later ninth and tenth centuries.

Although warfare and political fragmentation continued throughout the tenth century, the great social upheaval caused by the massive migrations of peoples largely came to an end. A century of Viking raids and incursions along the coast and down the rivers of western Europe stopped when the Norsemen (hence "Normans") were given substantial land holdings on both sides of the mouth of the Seine by Charles III in 911 simply because he was unable to expel them (Document 18). On the eastern frontier of Christianity the Magyars settled in what would become modern Hungary and converted to Christianity in 996/7; the Christian kingdom of Bohemia was founded at the end of the tenth century; and Poland, settled 965–70, became Christian under King Boleslav. South of the Pyrenees, the Christian kingdom of Asturias emerged in the ninth century, while the tomb of the Apostle James was discovered further west in Galicia, c. 830, at Santiago de Compostela, prompting the first efforts to reconquer Iberia from Islam, which were celebrated in "The Song of Roland."

The two major political events that occurred in western Europe during the tenth century were the election of Otto I as king of the Germans in 936 (Document 20), followed by his elevation to Holy Roman Emperor in 962, and the election of Hugh Capet as king of the Franks in 987. The avowed aim of Otto and his successors was a return to Carolingian greatness by reuniting the north and the south, that is, Germany and Italy. Hugh's aims were less lofty in the beginning and basically centered on ensuring the succession of his son by having him crowned king at Reims before his own death, a practice that would continue his fam-

ily's rule until 1328. Hugh continued the Carolingian practice of supporting the pope in Rome in return for papal sanction of his right to approve the election of all bishops in his kingdom (Document 19), whereas
the Ottonians made the fatal mistake of trying to control the papacy.
Otto I, for example, proclaimed that all candidates for the papacy were
required to pledge an oath of support to the emperor at precisely the moment when popes were reforming the papacy and insisting on their independence: Pope Nicholas II decreed that only cardinals could elect the
pope; Gregory II declared papal supremacy, and so forth. Thus, the Ottonians and their successors through the eleventh and twelfth centuries
were almost continually involved in power struggles with an increasingly
stronger and independent papacy, a situation the Capetians exploited
many times to their own advantage in dealing with both.

Despite these international conflicts, the kingdoms of the Ottonians
and Capetians were sufficiently peaceful that major cathedral construction could be undertaken, especially in German lands. The architecture
of the Ottonian emperors and their successors was, like their avowed political goal, clearly based on the achievements of the Carolingians, but
larger and grander in every way. Unfortunately for historians, it is also a
period of unprecedented disasters, with the result that we know a number of important new cathedrals were undertaken but were all too soon
destroyed. The centerpiece of Otto I's new policy of conquest and conversion was the new cathedral at Magdeburg, begun in 955, in which he
was to be buried. The new building was damaged by fires in 1008 and
1049 and completely destroyed in a great conflagration in 1208. The
largest of all early Ottonian cathedrals, that built by Archbishop Willigis
at Mainz, burned to the ground on the day of its dedication. Willigis was
typical of the great Ottonian prelates in that he was close to the imperial family, as tutor to the Byzantine princess Theophanu, wife of Otto
II, and coregent with her during the minority of Otto III. That pattern
had begun with Archbishop Bruno of Cologne, the brother of Otto I.
The result of such close associations with the imperial families was a series of very large cathedrals that rivaled in size the great churches of
Rome and that culminated in the construction of the cathedral at Speyer,
intended as the dynastic burial church of Conrad II and his successors,
which for many years was the largest church in Europe outside of Rome
itself.

The dominant force in the tenth century was the Holy Roman Em-

pire, the Germanic Holy Roman Empire. Otto I dreamed of reestablishing the empire of Charlemagne and was crowned Holy Roman Emperor
on 9 February 962. He passed the crown to his son, Otto II, in 973. Otto
II ruled only ten years, with the result that Otto III was only three years
old when his father died. Otto III died young in 1002, and the throne
passed to his cousin, Henry II of Bavaria, who also died heirless. Conrad
II of Franconia was elected to succeed him in 1024. Thereafter, a number of dynasties of short duration ruled in German lands. Although they
frequently tried to assert their power in Italy, just as frequently German
ambitions were thwarted by increasingly powerful popes. In fact, this series of strong, reformist popes insisted on the primacy of the pope over
secular leaders and, under Nicholas II, in 1059 decreed that only cardinals of the church could elect the pope. On the whole the eleventh century was less favorable to the German emperors, who found themselves
in increasingly debilitating confrontations with the popes. Gregory VII
declared that the pope was the supreme spiritual authority over all Christians, clergy, and laity alike. Therefore, the pope insisted, secular and political authority had to give way to spiritual authority; hence the
confrontations collectively known as the Investiture Conflict (Document 26). That a later pope, Urban VIII, could instigate the First Crusade
in 1095 can be taken as a sign of the success of Gregory VII in establishing papal authority. The struggle between religious and secular authority continued into later centuries and was the basis of the struggle
between King Henry II of England and Thomas à Becket, Archbishop of
Canterbury (Documents 36 and 38).

While the German emperors were embroiled in these conflicts with
the pope and with their own attempts to reassert lost authority in Italy,
the Capetian kings of France were steadily accumulating the necessary
wealth and status to assert their authority over their wealthier and more
powerful dukes and counts. These actions began unassumingly enough
when Hugh Capet, elected in 987, had his son crowned king before his
own death to ensure continuity. The full fruits of this deed did not manifest themselves until the twelfth century, but the policy of having the
eldest son crowned king before the father's death continued to be the
cornerstone of Capetian success and meant an uninterrupted line of kings
from 987 to 1328. A second important key to the success of the Capetians
was the selling of town and city charters that began in the late eleventh
century and continued through most of the twelfth. For a sum of money

paid directly to the king, the merchants of a town or city were protected by him from interference by the local overlord, religious or secular. Taxes previously paid to that overlord now went to the king. The result was both an enrichment of the royal treasury and, in a more subtle way, the fostering of loyalty to a power greater than the local overlord. By the second quarter of the twelfth century, scholars and clerics in Paris were beginning to find a definition for that higher body that we now call a nation, but that they spoke of as the French People, with the king as its head. The success of this French royal policy was opposed by the Germans, who, in general, rejected city charters as late as 1218 (Document 44) but supported charters given in individual circumstances (Documents 22 and 28), and accepted the division of powers (Documents 25 and 40), as well as the obligations of bishops to kings (Documents 27, 35, and 37). Resistance to the power of bishops, specifically the archbishop of Cologne, is revealed by two documents (Documents 24 and 46). All these challenges to traditional social structure were accompanied by the clerical reforms emanating from Rome that were directed against such episcopal abuses as those described by Guibert de Nogent (Document 29) and that sought to limit the power of kings in social matters, such as Phillip Augustus's attempt to take a new wife without divorcing the previous one, an action that led to papal interdict (Document 42). But Phillip had become powerful enough to resist what he considered papal interference, even from a pope as powerful as Innocent III, so the stalemate was settled only by the death of Phillip's "disputed" wife, Agnes de Méran, in 1201.

The increasing size of the royal domain meant less internal warfare and fewer disruptions of commerce and agriculture. It also created a favorable climate for building. Agricultural surplus fed the growing towns, which in turn began to supply goods needed by both the residents and the farmers. Market economies, aided by the international trade fairs, such as the fairs of Champagne and the semiannual Lendit fairs of the abbey of St.-Denis, expanded the taste for luxury goods and products from as far away as Persia. The prized woolen fabrics of the north were traded for the luxury silks of Italy and, ultimately, Byzantium. The accumulation of wealth encouraged large-scale cathedral construction beginning in the middle of the twelfth century. By the thirteenth century, the Gothic style of France had become international, but, at the same time, even more closely identified with Paris. French architects were called to

Uppsala and Prague (Document 50), while German architects were hired for their ability to build in the French style (Document 48).

The most successful political development in the later eleventh century was the conquest of England by William, Duke of Normandy, who, after 1066, was known as the Conqueror. William introduced a new kind of administration in England that was ruthlessly imposed in the years immediately after the conquest, but that ultimately made England both remarkably well organized and efficiently run. That the system could survive the difficult years of the wars of succession between King Stephen and Empress Mathilda in the twelfth century is an indication of its success. The seemingly endless and endlessly inept battles of this civil war finally resulted in the succession of Mathilda's son, Henry, Duke of Anjou and of Normandy, as King Henry II in 1154. Freshly married to Eleanor of Aquitaine, who had only recently divorced Louis VII, king of France, Henry II controlled a vast empire that included not only all of England, Normandy, and Anjou but, thanks to Eleanor, most of the southern half of the modern state of France as well. Henry and Eleanor had four sons, two of whom, Richard I, the Lionhearted, and John, Lackland, ruled successively as kings of England into the thirteenth century. John had the misfortune to lose most of the continental empire to his Capetian overlord and rival, Phillip II, in 1204.

If the tenth century was marked by the ascendance of the Holy Roman Empire in Germany, and the eleventh by the conquest of England, then the twelfth and thirteenth centuries were the years of Capetian hegemony and dominance in western Europe. True, the rise of the Capetians began in 987, but their path to dominance was a slow but steady progression until c. 1130, the moment when Louis VI settled more or less permanently in Paris. The high point of early Capetian success was the Battle of Bouvines, on 27 July 1214, at which Phillip II decisively defeated the combined might of all his enemies at once, ruining John of England, assuring Frederick II the throne of the Holy Roman Empire, and joining Flanders to France.

The second high point is more interesting: the creation of the image of Louis IX, later St. Louis, as the ideal Christian monarch, both in his life and after his death on crusade in 1270 and his canonization in 1297. In the early years of his rule Louis IX showed a practical as well as an ethical side, but in his later years he almost bankrupted France on two disastrous crusades, the last one of which resulted in his death. The first part of his reign saw the extension of Capetian power into the southern part of what is now France, first with Louis's marriage to Marguerite de Provence, which effectively removed that region from the Holy Roman Empire. He then arranged the marriage of his younger brother, Alphonse of Poitiers, to the heiress Jeanne de Toulouse and, by treaty, had his youngest brother, Charles of Anjou, named heir to the Latin Kingdom, that is, the crusader states established in Palestine. Because these were steadily shrinking as a result of expanding Islamic power in Palestine, Charles had little prospect of reigning there. That did not curtail his ambitions, however; he instead redirected them toward other prizes. Charles is generally thought to have encouraged his brother's crusade in 1270, for example, and after Louis's death to have decided to mount an all-out assault in the east with the aim not only of recapturing the crusader states but also of replacing the emperor in Constantinople with himself. In these delusions he was encouraged by Pope Martin V, who had his own agenda: to reunite the Christian west and east under his own jurisdiction. All these grandiose dreams came crashing down with the 1282 revolt in Sicily, commonly called the Sicilian Vespers, after the tolling of the church bells at Vespers in Palermo that signaled the uprising against the hated French oppressors. The slaughter of the French occupiers crippled Charles's efforts to mount an expeditionary force, and shortly thereafter he lost Sicily to Pedro of Aragon, whose Mediterranean ambitions had been deliberately encouraged by the successor to Martin V in order to derail Charles.

The entry of the kings of Aragon on the international political scene is the end result of efforts begun in the later eleventh century to drive Islam out of the Iberian Peninsula. A series of strong kings, such as Sancho the Great, began to unite the smaller counties into larger and more powerful states that could successfully defeat a weakened Islam kingdom that suffered invasions on both sides, from León and Castille in the north and from the Moorish Almoravids of Morocco in the south. Toledo passed to the Christians in 1085, and in the mid-twelfth century the Almohads replaced the Almoravids. In spite of the efforts of such fabled Spanish kings as Alfonso X, known as the Wise, and heroes like El Cid, the Moors held on to the enclave around Granada until the combined efforts of the Catholic kings, Isabella of Castile and Ferdinand of Aragon, drove them out in 1492.

The fourteenth century is one of the most difficult of the entire Middle Ages because of the numerous problems, both political and social, that effectively wiped out almost half the population. Political instability in Italy, brought about by the political intrigues of the old papal families, the German emperors, as well as a number of the popes themselves, resulted in the French pope, Clement V, fleeing Rome in fear of his life. He transferred the papal court to Avignon, in southern France, where he was, in effect, a captive of the French king. The papacy remained in Avignon from 1305 to 1378, a period referred to as the Babylonian Captivity (a reference to the Old Testament story of the Jews held in slavery in Babylon) by the Romans.

From 1315 to 1322, seven years of rainy summers and generally inclement weather led to the Great Famine all across northwestern Europe. The economy was severely disrupted by the lack of food and by the high cost of whatever was produced or imported, and thousands starved. The situation was worsened, barely a generation later, by the Black Death (bubonic plague), which appeared in Genoa in 1347 and ravaged Europe for that year and the next, sometimes going so far as to wipe out whole villages (Document 53). In the meantime, the best of French and English knighthood was systematically slaughtered in the Hundred Years War, which lasted from 1337 to 1453, a war fought over the succession to the French throne. The fighting, hardly continuous over the entire period, was sufficiently frequent that neither side had the opportunity to recover fully. This war was unlike any other fought in the Middle Ages in that the English army was made up mostly of hired mercenaries, whereas the French clung to the outmoded methods of war developed centuries earlier. A large part of the English army, hired only for wartime, turned into roving marauders pillaging the countryside, even as far afield as Italy, in times when battles were not being waged. In spite of the slaughter of the French nobility in a series of epic battles, the English were defeated and lost all their continental possessions, except for the city of Calais, by the time the war was finally settled.

Needless to say, there was little building during the Hundred Years War, which, coming so soon after the Great Famine and encompassing the Black Death, decimated agriculture year after year. Recovery on the continent was slow and consisted simply of repairing almost to the end of the fifteenth century what had been damaged in whole areas of France, such as Picardie and Champagne, and even in Paris itself. Although there was no physical damage in England itself because the war was fought exclusively on French soil, the English economy suffered as much as the French economy.

Until the devastations of the fourteenth and fifteenth centuries, much of the conflict of the Middle Ages centered on developing power and amassing wealth in the process, both by kings and by popes, because that wealth facilitated the growth of greater power. The episode in 1296, when Pope Boniface VIII attempted to force the kings of England and France to accept papal intervention by issuing a bull that forbade clergy to pay taxes to secular rulers without papal consent, ended badly for the pope when Phillip IV of France answered with an embargo on the export of gold and Edward I of England outlawed the clergy, entitling him to confiscate all their holdings. This one episode in which a pope so obviously indicated his greed for power and gold undid several decades of papal success in stemming the rising nationalism of Europeans. The papacy would never again exert a dominant influence over European political developments. The full impact of this event was delayed by the disasters of the fourteenth century, but by the time of the recovery in the fifteenth century the papacy was notably diminished. A new world order was emerging.

CHAPTER 2

PATRONS, BUILDERS, AND ARTISTS

PATRONS

From the early period of Christianity, large-scale church construction was a cooperative enterprise, even though there might not be universal agreement among those directly or indirectly involved. A leader, be he religious or secular, might have inspired and encouraged the building, but the day-to-day responsibility lay elsewhere. In the early fourth century the emperor Constantine not only gave the bishop of Rome the Lateran palace as his residence, but he probably also paid for the construction of the bishop's church, the cathedral of S. Giovanni Laterano (St. John Lateran) (Documents 1–3). The *Liber pontificalis*, the history of the early popes, records many imperial donations, as well as gifts from high-ranking Christian officials and aristocrats. This is likely the pattern repeated in the other great cities of the empire, from those in the east, such as Constantinople, Jerusalem, Antioch, and Alexandria, to those in the west at Milan, Ravenna, and Trier. Aside from sporadic royal endowments for specific cathedrals, such as Theodoric in Ravenna or Childebert in Paris, few reliable records of patronage exist prior to the later eighth and ninth centuries when Charlemagne and his successors actively supported cathedral construction through donations. One such early record is of the lavish gifts of the later sixth-century bishop Desiderius, a kinsman of the Frankish queen Brunhild, to the churches of Auxerre (Document 9). But the later Carolingian kings were much more inclined to use Benedictine monastic foundations as centers for conversion, Christianization, and acculturation than cathedrals. While much work remains to be done reevaluating questions of early patronage, some patterns do emerge.

In the early centuries of the spread and growth of Christianity, as well as the establishment of early bishoprics, it was likely the personality of the bishops themselves that attracted and even encouraged donations to be used for construction. Early records often imply that the bishop himself was responsible (in the practical sense) for the construction, when, in fact, it was most likely one of his assistants, or someone else in his entourage, or even a member of the congregation with the appropriate skills. The most likely candidate was the person in charge of the financial operations. That the bishop's role was emphasized can be attributed to the manner in which records were kept. Just as royal history was most often expressed in terms of the year in the reign of a king, so ecclesiastical history was usually measured in the year of the reign of the bishop (or abbot for a monastic community). Thus, a reference to a cathedral having been constructed during the episcopacy of a bishop is more a factor of record keeping than a reliable indication of episcopal involvement.

In this examination of royal patronage, let us consider the example of St.-Etienne (St. Stephen), the earliest known cathedral of Paris. With its multicolored marble columns and white marble capitals (fragments of both have been recovered in excavations), St.-Etienne, which survived until the middle of the twelfth century, must have been an impressive building. The archeological evidence indicates that its facade was scarcely twenty feet less wide than the facade of the present cathedral of Notre-Dame. Needless to say, we know nothing of its builders, nor can we be certain of its date. Scholars are split in their opinions as to a date in the late fourth century or a date in the sixth century that was marked by a significant royal donation from King Childebert. Given its impressive size and splendorous interior—fragments of mosaic floors have been found—it was one of the largest cathedrals outside of Byzantium and the Italian Peninsula at either date and would have been a vivid reminder of the still extant Early Christian tradition in Constantinople and Rome. The sixth-century date is based on references to a "founding" by Childebert, but this might be nothing more than a significant royal donation to the cathedral, since the bishopric itself had been founded in the later third century by Dionysius (St. Denis). We have no evidence of a cathedral building on this site prior to these fragments and no way to put a firm date on these finds. Even in later centuries, recognition of an important gift or gifts resulted in the donor being designated the "founder," which might have nothing to do with the actual date of the cathedral construction. In fact, there is another such "founder" in the history of the cathedral of Paris: Bishop Maurice de Sully. In 1196, this bishop's will left the considerable sum of 100 *livres* (pounds) specifically to pay for the lead covering of the roof of the nave, which was nearing completion. As a result, Bishop Maurice was deemed a "founder," which one early twentieth-century French scholar insisted was an indication that the bishop had begun the construction of the new church when he took office in 1160. The same scholar latched on to a suspicious thirteenth-century sermon that suggested, "according to tradition," that the pope had laid the cornerstone and argued that could only have happened in 1163, a spurious date that is still repeated in some textbooks, even though the document was carefully analyzed and declared useless as early as 1881! In truth, we do not know when the building of Notre-Dame was actually begun—a date in the 1150s is supported by the archeology—but we can be sure that it was begun at the orders of the cathedral chapter and not the sitting bishop. These two examples from the same cathedral illustrate the difficulties facing scholars in the absence of precise documentation concerning royal donations. In the nineteenth century the interpretation of other such documents resulted in a number of patrons and donors even being labeled master builders. Actually, royal "donations" usually took the form of confirmations of properties and income already held by monasteries and churches, rather than new gifts. Most medieval rulers were more intent on gathering wealth *from* churches than in dispensing it *to* them. Even Louis IX, St. Louis, famous for having paid for the construction and endowment of the sumptuous royal chapel known as the Sainte-Chapelle in Paris, was not above leaving bishoprics vacant, often for several years, because in the absence of a bishop occupying the see its revenues reverted to the king.

The role of queens in royal patronage is finally receiving appropriate scholarly attention, and a number of these royal ladies are now recognized as influential patrons, usually in the lands that they were given as part of the marriage dower. Adelaide de Maurienne, wife of Louis VI, king of France, exceptionally founded a nunnery on Montmartre, in 1134, with at least the cooperation of her spouse, who arranged property trades to acquire the church, in addition to sponsoring several churches on her lands around Compiègne, north of Paris.

Because bishops were more often regarded as rivals in local power struggles, even donations from the nobility were unlikely to support cathedrals. The Duke of Burgundy, for example, kept his cathedral cities on the periphery of the duchy, well away from his bases of power. In 1157, Henry the Liberal, count of Champagne, founded the collegiate church of St.-Etienne as the family and dynastic burial church in Troyes. It was to be staffed by nine dignitaries (priests and chapter officials) and seventy-two canons. Granted, the prestige and independence only lasted until the early thirteenth century when it came under the control of the bishop of Troyes, but until that time, the enormous wealth and power of St.-Etienne surpassed that of every cathedral in the county of Champagne except Reims, which also had seventy-two canons.

On the whole, royal and noble patronage was used as a political tool and was dependent on the aims and personalities of kings and nobles. Charlemagne, who built the royal palace and chapel at Aachen (Document 15), established a number of Benedictine monasteries in his ever-expanding realm as a means of acculturation, but even he was rather hesitant to support bishoprics by direct financial contributions. In Anglo-Saxon England, minor kings financed church building, but by the eleventh century that support was directed toward monasteries as dynastic burial grounds. After 1066, William the Conqueror replaced the Anglo-Saxon bishops with a whole roster of new appointments, but his financial energy was devoted to castle building rather than church construction.

In the Holy Roman Empire we find a similar situation, save that these kings did use cathedral foundations and construction to create dynastic burial grounds. The Ottos favored Magdeburg, their newly created archbishopric, whereas the Salian emperors were all buried at Speyer. The reconquest of the Iberian Peninsula, which lasted from the eleventh century to the end of the fifteenth, led to a number of new cathedrals, often built right over or even into the mosques that had themselves after the eighth century replaced Visigothic cathedrals. But here, too, the pattern of royal patronage in support of dynastic burial sites was the rule, from the ninth-century kings of Asturias at Oviedo to the kings of León and the royal pantheon at San Isidoro, rather than in support of cathedrals. There are exceptions, of course—Alfonso the Wise at León and Burgos in the thirteenth century—but cathedrals would never have been constructed had they depended on the largesse of rulers and nobles.

Doubtlessly, the actual responsibility for construction grew out of the financial management of the repairs and maintenance of early cathedrals.

By the later ninth century, when the idea of an independent clergy organized into chapters of canons had become the rule, and when the chapter had become sufficiently independent of the bishop to manage their own finances, the responsibility of the day-to-day workings of the cathedral extended to include not only cleaning, repairs, and maintenance but also construction. By that time it is clear that chapters, usually through an agent directly responsible to the treasurer, played the major role in managing the financial aspects of construction, so it is hardly surprising that they were also responsible for what we might call the program of the cathedral. That is, they decided such things as size, internal divisions, and decoration. Ultimately, of course, the program was executed by the master builder working in close contact with the programmer, who was acting on behalf of the chapter and with the approval of the bishop. Since it required approximately seventy-five to eighty-five years to complete a large-scale project, it is hardly surprising that the program was frequently changed, sometimes in significant ways, from that envisioned at the outset of building, as we will see at Reims. All in all, it is probably more accurate to speak of cathedral construction as a series of interactive, ongoing decisions between the builders/artists (creators in the physical sense) and the clergy/users (creators/audience in the spiritual sense). Thus, the bishop had little actual involvement in the day-to-day activity of construction after the eleventh century although he bore the ultimate legal responsibility. The rising mercantile and middle class used patronage as a way to bolster their social status from the later thirteenth century on, but with the exception of Italian and Netherlandish civic involvement in the construction of new cathedrals in the fourteenth and fifteenth centuries, the activities of the middle classes were once again focused on family burial chapels rather than entire cathedrals.

For much of the Middle Ages we have few facts about the costs or financing of cathedral construction. The first solid information that has been found comes from the eleventh century, and the one truth that seems to have been universal is that appropriate fiscal planning was nonexistent. Even when a project began under "royal sponsorship," as was the case of the cathedral of Orléans after the fire of 989, the estimates of time and cost were far too low. Like most projects, Orléans Cathedral was begun auspiciously with royal donations from Hugh Capet and later his son, Robert the Pious, but the project dragged on for more than one hundred years, even with the miraculous finding of a treasure of gold dur-

ing the excavation of the nave foundations. And this was at the time
that Orléans was the chief residence of royalty, which one might think
would have been a financial boon to the canons. In fact, aside from these
specific royal gifts, the influence of royalty was mostly negligible. Simply
put, this early instance of financial problems is an indication of the history of cathedral financing, even repeating itself at Orléans: the Gothic
cathedral was begun on 11 September 1287 but not inaugurated until 8
May 1829!

FINANCING

Cathedral construction proved to be an enormous drain of financial
resources in almost every case. The usual pattern at the beginning would
be a pledge of resources from the chapter, either in the form of an outright sum or in terms of an annual percentage of their individual incomes
for a period of years. This was often matched by the bishop in what
amounted to an endorsement of the chapter's efforts. The length of time
varied from example to example, sometimes as little as three years, sometimes ten years. When those funds were depleted, other resources were
explored. In order to solicit donations the canons at Laon sent their relics
on tour through the diocese, into neighboring dioceses, and finally even
to England. Special dispensations, usually indulgences that entitled the
donor to exemptions from time spent in purgatory, were a frequently used
means of raising monies. Special taxes on the people who lived under
the jurisdiction of the canons were levied at Reims; at the same time the
archbishop raised the price for cases heard in his courts. The situation
seems to have been the same for less prosperous chapters as for large
wealthy chapters like that at Laon, which derived enormous income from
taxes on local wine production at a time when this region was the major
wine-producing area in northern France. As we will see in the discussion
of Canterbury, when there was no money, there was no work. Occasionally there are exceptions, as at Reims, when work apparently continued
even without the ready funds to pay for it; but these are rare exceptions.
The bottom line is that the workers had to be paid; construction was
their livelihood.

The most important study of cathedral financing is that by Wilhelms
Vroom (1981) written and published in Dutch, and even he concentrated
more on who paid rather than what they paid. Vroom believed it was the

office of the bishop that provided most of the impetus to construction in the eleventh and twelfth centuries, with the chapter assuming the responsibility only in the thirteenth. This may be true for the Netherlands and Italy, but in England, and from Flanders through northern Spain, chapters had taken over the financial responsibilities by the twelfth century. In spite of the proliferation of communal charters, there was almost never any municipal participation in funding a cathedral before the later fifteenth century precisely because it was to get out from under episcopal and noble domination that cities and towns sought charters from the king. Those same citizens would hardly have been willing to support their original oppressors and certainly not a project that led directly to their increased oppression.

Although Vroom found that most of the records for Utrecht date from the fifteenth century, he was, nevertheless, able to extrapolate backward into the fourteenth century for some information. For example, fiscal responsibility for cathedral construction in cases of shortages, according to canon law, actually did rest first with the bishop, then the chapter, the lesser clergy, diocesan clergy, and, finally, the people of the city and diocese. In the long run, beginning in the twelfth century, however, contributions by the chapter were the most important in terms of assuring success in completing a building. Although the initial impulse might have been encouraged by the bishop, there were occasions when the chapter had to resort to the courts to force the bishop to honor his commitment. And, finally, Vroom cautioned that we must not underestimate the offerings of the common people through their desire to worship the relics of the saints and to buy indulgences.

BUILDERS

The master builder, a term preferable to "architect," was the designer, structural engineer, site manager, and general contractor all in one. Since the middle of the fifteenth century in Florence, the roles have changed and have been separated. Then and there, the "architect," in the modern sense of the term, emerged as the designer, someone different from the actual builder (or contractor). The change is evident in the generational difference between Filippo Brunelleschi, who was the master builder par excellence of the early fifteenth century in Florence, and León Battisti Alberti, who was the most famous "paper architect," meaning the designer, of the middle of the century. Alberti had no experience with the actual building process, whereas Brunelleschi oversaw every aspect of his projects, from design through construction. When the division between architect and builder occurred in northern Europe remains unclear, but it was most likely near the end of the fifteenth century.

Spiro Kostof (1977) identified three periods in the development of the architectural profession in the west, based on the perceived changes in thinking he observed. Kostof's three periods, noted here, are characterized by increasing responsibilities for the master builder as the complexities of design and construction expanded:

1. 300–800. During the first period the vast building industries that had supported the extensive architectural programs of the Roman Empire came to an end. In short, this was a period of transition from Late Roman forms to medieval forms. The ancient conception of the architect as humanist planner gave way to the medieval concept of the master builder. Aside from churches, and to a lesser degree castles, there was little large-scale construction undertaken in the western Empire, and the churches that were built could hardly compare in complexity with the great Roman civic complexes of previous centuries. Nonetheless, the prestige of Rome and of Roman Christian buildings still stood high: Bishop Wilfrid of Hexham (in the far north of England) brought builders from Rome to build the cathedral at Hexham in the seventh century. More than a century earlier, the pope had given similar support to Augustine at Canterbury (Documents 7, 8, and 10).

2. 800–1150. The ninth-century architecture of the Carolingians represented a conscious revival of the architecture of Early Christian Rome, on the one hand and, on the other, a period of great originality and invention that established the general direction of medieval architectural thought until the advent of the Gothic. That is, the period saw the development of new forms and building techniques, as well as new iconographies (meanings).

3. 1150–c. 1550. This is the period of the Gothic, in which new forms as well as new approaches changed the architectural profession. In fact, all categories of the building trades were throughly professional. Kostof argued that Gothic was the product of architectural imaginations so complex and so dazzling that it can have been created only by extraordinary thinkers; thinkers able to conceive with faultless precision giant shells of masonry that rose to dizzying heights and that were composed of myri-

ads of parts all integrated into total designs. From the latter part of this period we begin to have records of the names of these imaginative thinkers; hundreds of names survive as a testament to their achievements. Education in the art of architecture through participatory experience was the norm throughout this period.

Kostof's divisions need to be refined in ways that reflect changes in architectural thinking as we now understand it. His characterization of the first phase, 300–800, can stand, if we recognize that as in every human endeavor there are extraordinary exceptions to the general rules. But his other two divisions need further clarification and subdivision. His characterization of the second period, 800–1150, fails to take into account the significant changes in thinking that occurred around the year 1000. His definition stands for the period 800–1000, but the succeeding period, 1000–1150, is characterized not only by significant architectural invention but also most importantly by major new exploitation of geometry in planning and by a shift in thinking that recognizes the modular unit as a generating idea that can both simplify and revolutionize conceptual planning. This period saw the development and full flowering in all its variety of Romanesque architecture, western Europe's first pannational (even pan-cultural) style in building. Scholars have spent nearly two centuries dividing the period into "bite-size" bodies of information and thus fragmented the approach to the buildings by insisting more on differences, all in the name of creating more manageable bodies of information. The end result of their efforts, however, has made it much harder to find the unity of thought that characterizes Romanesque architecture.

Likewise, Kostof's characterization of the Gothic, from 1150–c. 1550, privileges the great achievements of the thirteenth century without seeing the experimentation that led to them. For this and other reasons, it is preferable to divide this period into at least three phases. The first, 1130–1230, includes the years that Robert Branner (1961), over forty years ago, characterized as filled with an almost bewildering number of experiments in structure and design. As scholars and architectual historians have explored greater numbers of buildings in detail, Branner's characterization rings even truer. At the same time, however, the period is defined by what amounts to almost a direct reversal of thinking from the Romanesque that preceded it. The major achievement of this first phase of the Gothic, or "Early Gothic," is the change in emphasis from the additive character of the Romanesque to the unified quality in the Gothic. That is, instead of an additive number of units creating a total, the Early Gothic is characterized by a sense of the total design in which every part is subordinated to the sense of the whole. We can think of it as roughly analogous to the revolution in thinking that accompanied the introduction of Arabic numerals from Spain in the early twelfth century. Simple computational skills, such as adding and subtracting, can be accomplished with Roman numerals, but Arabic numerals suddenly make the next stages, multiplication and division, easier and more comprehensible. The thinking of master builders in the twelfth century underwent a change not unlike that wrought by Arabic numerals. For the first time, architectural vocabularies are juggled and combined so that their individual characteristics are secondary to the unity of the overall design. The experimentation that drives this change included all aspects of design and structure. Builders appear to have exchanged ideas freely, and the knowledge of technology spread rapidly across Europe.

A second Gothic phase began about 1230 and lasted until about 1300. It is characterized by a renewed interest in design and the full exploitation and application of the design potentials inherent in geometry. One of the first indications of the new change of direction is the realization at Reims, as we will see, that the window is not just a mere hole punched through a wall, but a design surface in itself that can now be integrated into the total conception. The interest in structural experimentation characteristic of the previous period is replaced by the interest in design. For all intents and purposes, structural experimentation ceased because Reims presented the ideal solution to structural problems, and because the Reims scheme could be adapted to fit just about every need. This is also the period when multiple regional variants of the Gothic style developed all over Europe, even as Paris emerged as the driving force, as well as the source of Gothic design and style that was emulated from southern Spain to Scandinavia, from England to Bohemia and beyond. Because of the enormous variety, the style goes by different national names, Rayonnant in France, Decorated in England. But despite the many variations, the style is always characterized by the total unity of the designs and the overwhelming interest in geometric ornament in lacy stone screens that not only surround and top windows but actually compose and order their surfaces as well.

The last phase, from 1300 until 1550 (and in some of the more remote areas even later), can be termed the Late Gothic, provided there
are no perjorative associations with the word *late*. As with the previous
phase, it is characterized by an enormous variety of styles. Their unify-
ing factor is a renewed interest in illusionary spatial effects. Small buildings are made to look illusionistically larger and more expansive; large
buildings appear to be still larger and more mysterious. There are many
ways these effects were achieved, but all of them have one aspect in common: the expected architectural limits are challenged and even discarded.
Thus, instead of firm, solid, architectural bases on which the piers rest,
the bases become collections of tiny, thin shafts sometimes with many
little bases at different heights, sometimes with no bases at all. Capitals
are treated the same way as bases; that is, they disappear completely leaving the wall ribs flowing directly and smoothly into the vaults. In these
ways the traditional visual divisions represented by bases and capitals disappear, and there is no possibility for the eye to discern size or changes
in direction. Walls, windows, and vaults are covered by the same fine lacy
designs so that changes in the shape and directions of surfaces are all but
invisible. The spaces take on a visionary, otherworldly aspect that is often
heightened by the use of color and pattern. It is a period characterized
by extreme virtuosity in design, as well as by illusionistic experiments
with space.

In the Gothic period builders began to take on distinct personalities
that were expressed in their designs, so it is not surprising that names
begin to appear, tentatively in the twelfth century, but rapidly increasing
in number during the thirteenth. This is interesting but dangerous for
scholarship because of the inherent desire to attribute everything to a
"name." For this reason, we must be careful to avoid the nineteenth- and
early twentieth-century "cult of the name," which all too often took mea-
ger evidence from documents and manufactured fantastic careers for
those master builders whose names are known. Reading such texts one
could easily assume that the thirteenth-century Parisian master builder
Pierre de Montreuil had a hand in every building constructed in Paris
between 1230 and 1270. In fact, it is remarkable that his name can be
associated with even three buildings or major parts of buildings: the south
transept facade of Notre-Dame of Paris, as well as the refectory and the
Virgin Chapel at the Abbey of St.-Germain-des-Prés. This is no small

feat because most master builders are rarely identified with more than a single building project.

THE ROLE OF THE MASTER BUILDER

The master builder was the one person, almost always a man, in charge of every aspect of planning and constructing the cathedral. His design was the response to the demands of the patron or patrons, but his work extends beyond the design. The master builder was responsible for hiring all the workers and their assistants, in every category, beginning with the quarryman and concluding with the makers of the stained glass and the interior furnishings of the church. On occasion, his expertise also extended to the additional structures needed by the chapter and the bishop, but our discussion will only focus on the church itself.

The chronicle of Gervase of Canterbury, one of the most famous texts from the twelfth century, is particularly useful in any discussion of the role of the master builder because it is the only year-by-year record of medieval construction that has been found (Document 39). Gervase was a monk at Canterbury at the time of the destructive fire on 5 September 1174 when the east end of the cathedral, usually referred to as Conrad's choir, burned. The choir was severely damaged, but not totally destroyed, which presented a dilemma for the monks, as Gervase explained. They hoped to preserve the choir but were aware of its damaged condition— Gervase described columns so damaged that they were scaling. The monks tried first to find a master builder who would repair the old choir, but failed to do so. So they summoned French and English builders in what amounted to a competition, but even these men could not agree. Gervase said that the monks were presented with a variety of solutions, ranging from those master builders who proposed only to replace the damaged columns and, thereby, preserve the superstructure, to those who indicated that the entire east end was too damaged and had to be pulled down and completely rebuilt for the sake of safety.

In the end they hired a French master builder, William of Sens, said to be skilled in building both in wood and stone and to possess a lively genius and a good reputation. In fact, William of Sens was hired because he told them what they wanted to hear, as Gervase noted, rather than the truth. William resided with the monks for some time and systematically inspected all the surviving parts of the choir but did not tell them that the whole superstructure had to be destroyed until he had won their confidence and their trust. Only then did he admit that if they wanted to have a safe choir, most of the old one had to be destroyed. In fact, the crypt and outer walls that had survived the fire were ultimately incorporated in William's new design.

Gervase then recounted that William prepared for the new construction in two ways that provide a sense of the range of responsibilities of a master builder in such a situation. Because the building stone was to be imported across the English Channel from quarries along the Orne River near Caen in Normandy—a source of quality limestone still in use—William designed and oversaw the construction of "machines" for loading and unloading stone from ships and for moving the stone from the harbor to the building site. In addition, Gervase reported that William delivered molds for shaping the stones to the assembled sculptors. This probably meant that he delivered molds, templates, profiles, and other devices for measuring and cutting the stones to the masons (the word *sculptor* being reserved for the more specialized task of capital carving). It also implied that William's design for the new choir (Figure 24) had been prepared; but as an examination of the details erected during the first three building seasons indicates, not all the decisions about the handling of details along the aisle walls had been finalized. In fact, William tried three different designs before he was satisfied. A careful examination of other buildings indicates that William of Sens was hardly alone in beginning construction before all the final design details were settled. In fact, this was more often the case than has been recognized.

In short, William spent the majority of the first year, that is, from September 1174 until the winter rains and after winter's end until September 1175, preparing for the new construction. The site was cleared of the damaged materials, new stone was ordered and shipped from France, the machines for loading, unloading, and moving the stone were built, and the design was created to the extent that the masons could be given the necessary patterns so that work could begin. Gervase made no mention of architectural drawings, and, indeed, there may have been none in the sense that we understand drawings as tools for construction.

We tend to think of drawings as encompassing the whole scheme, whereas the use of drawings was probably more often limited to the working out of details. The use of architectural drawings, whether as tools for design or for working out problems, began in the thirteenth century if not before. The earliest surviving examples on parchment, both as free sketches and as scaled drawings, date from c. 1225 to 1250. But drawings on paper or parchment did not become standard procedure for nearly a century after these first isolated examples. Many buildings, however, have drawings engraved at real size on walls and floors, often adjacent to the executed work shown in the drawing. There is, for example, a drawing engraved on the wall surface in the gallery of the south transept of Soissons Cathedral that shows at real size the design and geometric analysis of the circular window immediately adjacent to it. The most complex series of large-scale drawings are those drawn on the roof slabs over the ambulatory of the cathedral at Clermont-Ferrand in central France. Misarranged during the nineteenth-century restorations, they have been recomposed photographically to show that they were used to lay out the elaborate designs for window tracery and for the gables of tracery that surround the adjacent clerestory windows. These are among the largest and most complex drawings at full size to survive from the Middle Ages, but they are by no means the only ones.

The preponderance of known architectural drawings on parchment date from the late fourteenth and fifteenth centuries, and they give ample evidence of the widespread use of drawings as planning and building aids by that time, but the complexity of the majority of architectural designs would suggest that drawings must have been used regularly from the 1220s on. Since they were useful only during the construction of particular buildings or parts of buildings, the parchment must have been either destroyed or scrapped down and used anew so many times that it was simply used up. For instance, the very complexity of the design at Reims would suggest the use of drawings, even though almost nothing has survived. The exceptions, however, might be the so-called Reims palimpsest drawings, several sheets of parchment that once contained inked architectural drawings, but that, c. 1260–70, were carefully scraped to remove the ink and then recycled as pages in the cathedral martryology. In spite of the removal of the inking, the drawings can still be read using infrared light and raking light that reveals the incised lines made by a drawing tool. Among the drawings are two incomplete designs for facades, one of which might even be an early proposal for the facade of Reims itself. This drawing even appears to have been drawn to scale, meaning that it could have been enlarged to become a guide to construction. This is the earliest surviving example of a scaled architectural drawing and should probably be dated to the 1240s or 1250s.

In addition to drawings, which may, in fact, represent the last and most developed phase of building diagrams, there is evidence of molding patterns and profiles made of leather or possibly thin pieces of wood that served as guides for the stonemasons in cutting architectural details. For instance, in modern examples, there are collections of templates and profiles cut from sheet metal in the workshops of the Episcopal Cathedral of Saint John the Divine in New York and the National Cathedral in Washington, D.C., from the late nineteenth and early twentieth centuries. The materials may be different, but the purpose is precisely the same as it would have been in medieval construction. These are just like the "molds" William of Sens prepared for the masons at Canterbury in 1174–75.

In one sense William of Sens was fortunate because the crypt and outer aisle walls of the old choir survived the fire at Canterbury, so he did not have to prepare foundations, as did his successor. Indeed, Canterbury Cathedral is of modest height compared with some of the later gigantic cathedrals in Europe. In those cases, foundations were of the utmost importance for the stability of the structures; yet foundations are the aspect of medieval construction about which we know the least, even in those buildings like Reims and Cologne that have been thoroughly excavated as a result of war damage. There is no known ratio of depth of foundation to height of building. All that is known is that the foundations usually were dug down to bedrock or some other nonmovable underground layer, which is eminently practical and suggests longtime experience and practice. The foundations of the choir and nave of Notre-Dame in Paris go down over thirty feet, and are wider at the base than at the top, according to nineteenth-century reports. Recent new investigations of the foundations at Reims have revealed that those in the area of the crossing are more than twelve meters (nearly forty feet) thick, convincing evidence that a massive crossing tower was planned at one time (see Chapter 5).

Gervase of Canterbury provided other important insights into the rebuilding of Canterbury, particularly in his description of the events after William of Sens's accident. In 1178, probably shortly after 13 September, Gervase noted that the master builder was up on the scaffolding in the crossing of the eastern transept, preparing to erect the great rib vault over the crossing, when the scaffold collapsed. William, accompanied by timbers and stones, fell some fifty feet to the floor. Gervase described him as "sorely bruised," whereas it would probably be more accurate to say he was lucky to have survived. In any case, William remained bedridden and showed little sign of recovering. He managed to complete the crossing vault by making "a certain ingenious and industrious monk"—some scholars have suggested that this monk was Gervase himself—his go-between and overseer of the masons, but Gervase's lack of command of the vocabulary of building makes such a suggestion untenable. Using the monk, William sent precise instructions that enabled the masons to complete the vault. Shortly after, however, showing no sign of improvement, William of Sens gave up his position and returned to France. This passage is particularly informative because it indicates the critical importance of the master builder on the work site, not merely as a director, but as a constant participant. Gervase, for example, noted that William was the only one on the scaffolding preparing for the erection of the vault. In a period well before we have records of the use of drawings, the participation and active direction of the master builder was the only factor that permitted the continuation of construction. The master builder was much more than simply the coordinator of the project. It is also interesting that William of Sens did not have an assistant, but had to use a monk (one supposes for reasons of intelligence and understanding) as a go-between while he was bedridden.

When William of Sens gave up the direction of the works at Canterbury, he was replaced by another master builder, described by Gervase, as "William by name, English by nation . . . acute and honest," hence known as William the Englishman. To him fell the tasks of completing the transept arms and of designing and building the other three successive parts of the choir: the presbytery, Trinity Chapel, and the Corona. It is, in fact, a tribute to the superb organizational skills of his predecessor that William the Englishman was able in five years to complete nearly three times as much work as William of Sens had in five years. The reason is that William of Sens had spent that first year organizing and preparing for the whole construction. The presbytery, like the monk's choir to its west, included the old crypt, outer aisle walls, and the two chapels flanking them that also survived the fire. Trinity Chapel replaced an early chapel of that designation and was intended as the site of the shrine of

Canterbury's martyred archbishop, Thomas à Becket. Again, Gervase's account is a straightforward listing of the parts built year by year and includes no observations about the design, other than citing the dark-colored purbeck stone shafts that decorate and emphasize the crossing piers. Gervase does not even mention the obvious changes in the floor level that he experienced several times every day in the church.

Trinity Chapel was a completely new design by William the Englishman that served as the focal point for the entire eastern end of the cathedral. At the juncture where it joined the presbytery, several archeological remains have led to speculations that what was finally constructed may not have been what was initially intended. More important than speculation about earlier schemes for Trinity Chapel is the pattern of progressively richer materials that culminates in this chapel, although Gervase mentioned none of these. Interestingly, he did add one final, important point: in the year 1183, the year before completion, no work was done for lack of funds, an unexpected reminder of the fiscal precariousness of major construction, even at a site like Canterbury, seat of the most important ecclesiastical figure in England.

Master builders like the two Williams and the countless others, both named and anonymous, who built the great structures of the Middle Ages, were all trained in the same way. Constructing and decorating churches, like almost all occupations in the Middle Ages, demanded specialized skills that could be learned only by experience and participation. Later medieval guild records are very specific about the learning stages from apprenticeship to journeyman to worker and, ultimately, to master. They may be roughly understood as follows: the apprentice did menial tasks while learning the basics; the journeyman assisted the worker in the actual work and may, nearing the end of his term of service, have been allowed to do less complex preparatory and finish work (such as roughing out the basic shape of a capital or smoothing the surface of a block); and the worker executed most of the work and often assisted the master, the director of the works. This system existed in antiquity and continued right through the Industrial Revolution. In many cases, a less formalized system of training still exists in the building trades and related industries because there is no substitute for experience.

The length of service at each stage was also carefully codified. The list of trade regulations compiled by Etienne Boileau in mid-thirteenth-century Paris specified the length of apprenticeship for various building professions (Document 47). One was apprenticed to a carpenter for four years, but to a stonemason for six. Apprenticeship usually began in the teen years, followed by varying years of service as a journeyman, so that one became a skilled worker in one's twenties. Andrea Palladio, the sixteenth-century Italian architect who worked in and around Venice, was apprenticed at the age of thirteen. He ran away after three years and spent the next fourteen years as an apprentice and journeyman mason to another master. Only at the age of thirty was he sent to direct, independently and on his own, renovations to a house. Fortunately for him, that designer and patron recognized his abilities and saw to his formal education, beginning with his learning to read. Palladio, Western history's most influential architect, was a "late bloomer" and enjoyed a long career. No records remain from the Middle Ages that inform us when a talented builder might advance to master builder status, although practice suggests that talent was probably recognized and nurtured from an early stage. Even in the later periods when hundreds of names are recorded, the texts never speak of the age of the master builder, except to record his death and burial. For example, Pierre de Montreuil, the Parisian master builder mentioned earlier in connection with Notre-Dame and so forth, had a career that stretched from 1239 until his death in 1267. Hugues Libergier began the now-destroyed church of St.-Nicaise in Reims in 1231 and worked there until his death in 1263. Thus, both master builders had nearly thirty-year careers, but we do not know the age at which they became masters nor their ages at death.

THE MASTER ARTIST

As with master builders, the names of others engaged in such aspects of the building trades as sculpture, stained glass, or even carpentry are scarcely known. A few names are haphazardly preserved on late eleventh- and early twelfth-century capitals, probably not as a mark of ego or pride, but as an indication for payment. In fact, we cannot even be certain when the sculptor, the carver of decoration for the cathedral, became a specialized profession. It seems to have happened rather gradually in the first half of the twelfth century, but there is no hard and fast division between masons and sculptors even then. Certainly in those areas of western Europe where the taste for large sculpted portals became the norm in the twelfth century, the specialized artist who carved the figures must have been distinguished from the architectural mason rather early. This is demonstrably true in northern Spain, southern and southwestern France (Languedoc and Aquitaine, to use the medieval political designations), northern and far southern Italy (Lombardy and Apulia), Burgundy, and beginning in the Early Gothic period, the Ile-de-France (the area around Paris). In these regions there are probably more names of sculptors preserved than of master builders. Occasionally, master builders are even noted for their sculptures. Wiligelmo at Modena in northern Italy is certainly now more renowned for his portal decorations and sculpted friezes on the west facade (Figure 9) than Lanfranco is for the architecture of the cathedral of Modena.

On large projects several sculptors would have been involved, just as there would have been several masons. Exact numbers are difficult to come by, but as a rule of thumb we can expect that the number involved is directly related to the master builder's ability to direct the shop: too many and it gets out of control, too few and nothing happens. Those documents that speak of hundreds of people piously involved, sometimes spontaneously, can only be literary exaggerations by those who had little experience with actual construction.

One medieval church renowned for its sculpture and for the artist who carved it is St.-Lazare (Lazarus) at Autun in Burgundy, begun c. 1120 as a church separate from the old cathedral of St.-Nazaire, possibly to allow lepers to venerate the saint without disrupting regular cathedral functions. St.-Lazare was built on land donated by Hugh II, Duke of Burgundy (reigned 1102–43) because there was no space for another church in the cathedral precinct and because the canons did not want lepers seeking to venerate the saint to disrupt their regular observances. Lepers were drawn to Lazarus because they confused the saint with the poor leper Lazarus of the parable (Luke 16:19–25). Thus, the main public entry to St.-Lazare was through the north transept portal located just across a narrow square and slightly west of the entry to St.-Nazaire, the old cathedral. The new church, elevated to cathedral status in 1195, is notable because most of the capitals and both major portals were the work of a single sculptor who worked in a very distinctive style. His name, Gislebertus, was inscribed at the feet of Christ in the enormous Last Judgment tympanum that dominates the west door (Figure 15). The fact that the canons had his name prominently inscribed is an indication of the respect in which he was held, as well as a tribute to his work because the location of the inscription makes it a plea for his salvation. Might the figure just below the inscription, who appears to be reading it, be the artist himself? It is a tempting suggestion but cannot be proved. Because the capitals at the lowest levels in the choir of the church are the work of another sculptor, scholars have surmised that Gislebertus arrived only after the church was begun, probably c. 1125; however, he remained at Autun until the church was finished in the early 1140s. The translation of the relics of Lazarus from St.-Nazaire in 1146 probably indicates the end of major construction, although work continued on the exterior porch. The elaborate tomb monument of Lazarus that housed the relics, said to have been carved by the monk Martin, was not completed until the 1170s.

That we have a single sculptor producing two portals and ninety-plus capitals, all of them in a remarkably consistent and homogeneous style characterized by an expressive abstraction, a lively sense of action and gesture, and a linear sophistication, that stand apart from contemporary Romanesque sculpture in Burgundy, makes it possible to assess the work of the artist. There is little sense of change in his style between the earliest and latest works, which would suggest that he was a recognized master sculptor when he was hired to decorate the most visible and important areas of the church. Since the architectural details as a whole changed when he arrived, some scholars have suggested that he might have been the master builder. Although there is no way to know the answer to this question, it is a doubtful proposition. It is much more likely that he arrived with a new master builder. We can note, however, that Gislebertus's fame as a sculptor has far overshadowed that of the anonymous master builder.

And then there is the question of assistants. In St.-Lazare there are three capitals in the south aisle of the nave that are thought to be the work of an assistant, rather than the master experimenting with a different style. Our knowledge of workshop practice suggests that a master sculptor might have had two or three assistants. They would have been in charge of roughing out the capitals from the blocks that arrived from the quarry and performing other preparatory tasks. It is not unreasonable to think that a talented assistant might have been permitted to finish secondary decoration in some of the capitals or allowed, even encouraged, to carve capitals in less prominent locations. On the other hand, almost all the capitals in the upper two stories of the church, which we

might be tempted to assign to an assistant, are more related to the style
of the architectural details, which suggests they are the work of the masons charged with carving architectural ornament. This agrees with the
prominence accorded to the works of Gislebertus, which (except for
those formerly in the crossing and now in the museum), are positioned
to be seen from the ground.

Even more interesting, all the capitals, figural, and foliate, are based
on the same abstract schema. For the many biblical and symbolic capitals, Gislebertus adapted the narrative composition to fit his capital pattern. They present the stories with a telling eloquence and human
immediacy that transcends the formal patterning. In fact, the standard
compositions are usually subtly altered to emphasize the human element
of the biblical narratives.

His two great masterpieces would have been the portals dominated by
large tympana crowded with sculpted figures. Unfortunately, the north
transept portal, which had been conceived as the principal public entry
to the church, was dismantled in 1766, and the stones sold as building
material. Some few pieces have been recovered, including several angels
and the famous figure of Eve from the lintel (Figure 16). The location of
the remainder is known, and these other pieces from the portal will,
eventually, be removed from their basement "prison." In the meantime,
we can appreciate the western portal (Figure 15), which originally served
two purposes. Not only was it the exit from the church that led directly
to the cemetery, but its porch was probably constructed to provide a
chapel for lepers so that they might venerate the saint without entering
the church. Recent consolidation of the stone porch has revealed indications that there was a timber porch prior to its rebuilding in stone. Appropriate to these functions, the theme of the portal was the Last
Judgment. Centered around a gigantic but serene figure of Christ presiding at the end of time, is a dramatic swirling composition of the saved
being pushed through the gates of heaven and the damned being tor-
mented as they are dragged off to hell. On the lintel below the tympanum the dead are rising from their graves, awaiting the moment when
their sins will be weighed on the scales so that they may be saved or
damned. With the exception of the Supreme Judge, this is a tympanum
teeming with action and emotion and full of all-too-human details, such
as the figures hiding beneath the robe of St. Michael in an futile attempt
to avoid judgment. Justifiably the western portal at Autun is recognized

as one of the supreme achievements of French Romanesque sculpture and one of the finest of all works of medieval art.

Scholars have sought to find the places Gislebertus might have worked before coming to Autun, especially since it is obvious that he was already a recognized master. Their searches are, in the absence of documentation, based only on comparative stylistic analysis. That he might have previously worked at the abbeys of Cluny and Vézelay is certainly possible and, in the case of Cluny, plausible, but the evidence is inconclusive. The huge abbey church at Cluny was reduced to fragments after the French Revolution, making comparisons difficult. We do not know what happened to the artist after his work at Autun was completed. He seems simply to have disappeared. His very distinctive style was not influential beyond Autun. A statue in wood of the Virgin and Child (now in The Cloisters in New York) is known to have been in Autun and was obviously carved by a sculptor heavily influenced by Gislebertus, but it is the sole example of the impact of his style to have survived.

In the final analysis, Gislebertus is that rarity: a specialized master sculptor whose name is known and to whom we can safely attribute a number of works of art. It seems almost ironic, given the paucity of recorded names, that we even have the name of a second sculptor working at Autun later in the twelfth century. It was probably in the 1170s that "Martin the monk" directed the workshop that produced the monumental marble tomb of Lazarus that once occupied the place of prominence in the church. The tomb is destroyed, but there are enough major pieces surviving to see the hand of another master sculptor at Autun.

With few exceptions the names of master sculptors are not as numerous as those of master builders until much later. Beginning in the fourteenth century the recorded names of sculptors and artists are more plentiful, and in some cases, bodies of work can be assembled. Although it is important, for example, to show that an artist like Andre Beauneveu worked for a number of influential patrons in Paris, Dijon, and Bourges in the last third of the fourteenth century, it is even more interesting that he was both a painter and a sculptor and that he created both large-scale works in stone and miniatures in ivory. Such versatility is common right through the end of the Middle Ages and the beginning of the Renaissance.

Major projects like cathedrals required many more specialists than just master builders and sculptors. Carpenters, for example, played significant roles from the very beginning of construction. And when their scaffolding was no longer needed, it might well have been turned into the all-important roof timbers. Painters and mosaicists played important roles in the completion of many cathedral projects where the walls were painted with extensive cycles of biblical subjects and floors inlaid with elaborate decorative patterns and mosaics. Early Christian and Byzantine churches favored large-scale wall and ceiling mosaics, especially in important Italian cathedrals. Wall paintings gradually replaced the more expensive mosaics after the ninth century, but they were themselves displaced by the later Romanesque and Gothic predilection for stained glass windows, especially outside of the Italian Peninsula. Stained glass, like the various enamel and metalwork decorations of shrines and altars, required specialized knowledge and experience in thermal technology. While there are a few fragmented sixth- or seventh-century windows containing images of standing saints in the British Isles, the earliest continental examples of stained glass that survive date to the late tenth century, but given the continuous production of lavish jeweled and enameled reliquary shrines, altar ornaments, and the liturgical utensils necessary for the performance of liturgy, there is little reason to doubt that stained glass might already have been used in Carolingian times or even earlier. Roman Early Christian churches and cathedrals had large glass windows, some, apparently, even used colored glass. Therefore, painted ornament on glass is almost a certainty, even though the actual concept of stained glass as the pictorial medium we know appeared only in the twelfth century.

CONCLUSION

The patterns that we have seen in the categories of patrons, builders, and artists discussed in this chapter are remarkably parallel in their development. From rather uncertain, clearly amateur beginnings in the Early Christian period we have witnessed the creation of a whole series of professions, many of them quite as complex as modern professions by the end of the Middle Ages. One thing they all have in common is the importance of experience. That is, increasing experience in building results in more competent builders, and so forth. We must be careful not to see this as a strictly linear development and to remember that all these artists, patrons, and builders were human beings and just as prone to error as in any human undertaking. Nor should the developments be thought of as deterministic. Certainly there were as many failures as successes, but it is the successes that are remembered or that have survived. With the clear understanding that we are seeing the works of people, it is nonetheless remarkable that a great many of humanity's most outstanding achievements were created during these so-called Middle Ages.

CHAPTER 3

PLANNING AND CONSTRUCTION, EARLY MEDIEVAL TO ROMANESQUE

One of the major concerns in cathedral construction from the earliest period has to have been the planning and laying out of the building. With the great churches constructed in the major cities of the Roman Empire, there is clear evidence that the planning techniques of antiquity, and the building industry that supported and carried them out, were still in use. The major difference was that the cathedrals of the Early Christian period were almost always associated with a particular locus, or place, and the major impetus in planning was the reverence for that spot. Although we do not know the generating locus of St. John Lateran in Rome, that of Old St. Peter's, for instance, was the very specific burial site of the Apostle Peter himself. The principal focus was the altar erected over the niche associated with that site. The entire plan of the church was generated from that single locus. And so it was with many, if not most, of the churches and cathedrals that followed. Although there is no particular burial site of a saint associated with the location of the altar in St. John Lateran, nevertheless, the main altar, as the focus of all services, was still the generating point in the planning and lay out of the building. This continued to be standard practice throughout the Middle Ages.

There is no hard and fast rule for fixing the position of the altar. In the early period the altar would be placed adjacent to, often directly over the tomb of the saint (or whatever else was the defined locus), but the relics of the saints themselves could be, and often were, moved over time, usually with no change from the original locus. Frequently there was a good reason for moving the holy relics; the threat of destruction during the pe-

riod of the Viking invasions spurred the moving of the bodies of any number of saints to more protected locations that were often hundreds of miles
away from the places of burial. Then too, there was the threat of theft.
Patrick Geary (1990) has collected numerous stories of the theft of relics
from monasteries and cathedrals alike. The construction of a number of
eleventh- and twelfth-century crypts can be directly related to concerns
for the safety of the holy relics. At Canterbury the bodies of saints were
raised high in the air to prevent theft, as Gervase (Document 39) noted,
while the crypt was used for archepiscopal burials.

Whatever the chosen locus, a traditional site or a new site, it usually
served as the generating point for the plan. At Reims, for example, the
plan of the thirteenth-century cathedral was based first on the square of
the crossing of the ninth-century Carolingian cathedral, which itself was
based on the square that defined the liturgical space around the altar of
the first cathedral on the site. Hence the very first altar was still the locus
in the Gothic cathedral, but the unit used to generate the plan was the
side of the square that defined the liturgical space. The plan of the entire chevet of the cathedral was conceived at once, even though it was
not all constructed in the same campaign.

After the determination of the locus, the entire plan was laid out on
the site using cords and stakes. Around this linear plan the masses, such
as the width of foundations and walls, would have been worked out.
When excavation of the foundation trenches began, the cords and stakes
were obviously displaced. After the completion of sections of the foundations, the plan would have had to be laid out again to mark the limits of the walls. Construction always began along the perimeter and then
worked its way toward the interior. One reason for this was that if the
part being built was an addition or expansion, as much construction as
possible would be carried out before it joined the parts already in place.
The continuity of services took precedence over everything else; the regular liturgical life of the church should be disrupted as little as possible.
At Canterbury, for example, while the new east end was being erected,
the monks kept their regular daily observances in the old nave. Gervase
explained precisely how they set up the temporary liturgical space there
after the fire in 1174.

Our knowledge of the actual planning procedures is largely hypothet-
ical and based on the knowledge gleaned from geometric analysis of the
plans as built. In the Early Christian period, as the old Roman con-

struction industry ceased to exist, so too the techniques used by Roman builders to plan their great complexes were abandoned. That is not to say there was no systematic planning; quite the contrary, but the simple geometric ratios used were drawn not from the learned principles of ancient theorists but from craft practice and the manipulation of such simple ratios as the square root of 2, which is expressed in the ratio of the side of a square to its diagonal. Much of the planning was expressed in the geometry, rather than in the use of numbers, for the simple reason that there was no standard unit of measure. In fact, the idea of standard units of measure can be credited to Napoleon in the nineteenth century. And, of course, the units established by Napoleon were not accepted in all countries, as the enduring conflict between the meter and the foot demonstrates.

One of the most extraordinary documents to survive from the Carolingian period is the idealized monastery plan known as the "Plan of St. Gall," after the monastic library in which it was found. Made to accompany a written document, now lost, that described and laid out the necessities for a new monastery, the plan seems to have been laid out on a square module. This remarkable document shows all the monastic and support buildings necessary for a completely self-sufficient community of seventy-seven monks, down to and including the vegetables planted in the garden, the herbs grown in the physician's garden, and the fruit trees planted in the cemetery. Rather than the actual plan of a specific site, the "Plan of St. Gall" should be regarded as one of the most important intellectual documents of the time. Its thorough and complete sense of planning, even its use of geometry, are unparalleled indications of the organizational skills emanating from the royal court circles at Aachen in the early ninth century.

From the simple geometric ratios of the earlier Middle Ages came the increasing geometric complexity that accompanied more complex spaces. By the twelfth century, master builders were often using several geometries simultaneously in their efforts to find both the ideal plan and the soundest plan from the standpoint of structural stability. It is, of course, appropriate that more complex plans and interpenetrating spatial units were believed to require more complex geometries to plan pier placement, and the like. But it was also still the dictates of practice that the desired visual and spatial effect would take precedence over geometric regularity, which may also explain the difficulties that modern scholars have in identifying the geometric systems used. Then, too, there is the problem that the building might have been regularly laid out at the beginning of construction only to have that regularity, perhaps even the entire system, lost after twenty or thirty years of continuous building. The recently published volume *Ad Quadratum*, edited by Nancy Wu (2002), provides a number of interesting test cases, which give a good idea of the range of geometric problems encountered in analyzing standing buildings and in attempting to identify planning procedures.

Masonry techniques generally followed the same sort of development; that is, the varied masonry techniques of the ancient Romans ceased to be employed, but the more common vernacular tradition of rubble construction continued to be practiced, even in such important buildings as St. John Lateran and Old St. Peter's. In Early Christian and even Carolingian practices all masonry construction was conditioned by the availability of materials and by local traditions, but the loss of Roman concrete construction techniques meant that large-scale masonry vaulting disappeared. The weak mortar used to bond stone construction limited the size of vaults, domes, and half-domes, but the ability to construct these, as well as both barrel vaults and groin vaults, was not lost.

EARLY MEDIEVAL THROUGH ROMANESQUE

Several phenomena affected the church and church building in the period of the early Middle Ages, from roughly the early sixth to the early ninth centuries. The first of these was the general decline in the population that had the most dramatic impact in the old cities. The population of Rome, which at the peak of its power in the second and third centuries had a population of more than one million, dropped to fewer than ten thousand. The result was both fewer and smaller churches. The second was the enormous cultural diversity created in the new kingdoms founded as a result of the great invasions and tribal migrations that began in the fourth century and reached epic proportions in the fifth and sixth centuries. Having little or no tradition of permanent architecture, these new Christians constructed churches that often bore little resemblance to those built earlier. As might be expected, the farther away these peoples were from the old centers, the less their churches, most of which are known only from literary descriptions, resembled the Early Christian buildings of Rome or Milan (Documents 5 and 11). In France, only one building from this early period survives above ground, the baptistry constructed adjacent to the early cathedral of Poitiers. This baptistry is the earliest surviving example of a Christian building with rich exterior ornament. The Early Christian churches of the Mediterranean world had little exterior ornament other than on the facade, whereas the baptistry at Poitiers has a rich and colorful array of patterns alternately derived from Roman architectural sources and from Migrations-era jewelry. In addition to little arcades and gables, there are circular patterns and courses of masonry created from recycled red Roman bricks. The wall ornament at Poitiers seems almost randomly placed, albeit in symmetrical patterns, except where it was used to frame window openings. The cornices at the top of the walls and along the sloping roof gables, however, carefully emphasize those lines. This ornament at Poitiers marks the beginning of what will become a hallmark of Romanesque architecture by the tenth and eleventh centuries, namely, a rich decorative vocabulary of exterior ornament that will articulate openings and surfaces, as for example on the east end of Angoulême Cathedral in the 1120s (Figure 10).

Beginning in the later eighth and early ninth centuries, Carolingian architecture experienced a new wave of influence derived from Early Christian architecture in Rome even as it promoted new features, such as towers, crypts, and cell-like spaces, not common in Late Antique and Early Christian architecture. The renewed, specific focus on Rome led to copies of the plan of the first church of St. Peter's, some even made by reproducing its measurements, just as it led to the creation of a series of central plan structures, chief among them the Palace Chapel at Aachen (Document 15). It also led to greater coherence in planning that manifests itself in the tenth-century buildings of Ottonian Germany, as well as those created in a long crescent stretching from Catalonia in northern Spain around the Mediterranean to Lombardy in northern Italy. Other important regional developments are found in southern Burgundy, a region particularly interested in stone vaulting, as Edson Armi (2004) has convincingly demonstrated in his splendid new analysis. Out of all these varied experiments emerged what we call Romanesque architecture, the first fully multinational manner of building in the Middle Ages. The very term *Romanesque* is a modern (early nineteenth-century) invention, a concept created to fill the void between the styles named by their associations with dynasties (Carolingian, Ottonian, Anglo-Saxon) or geographic regions (Asturian, etc.). Although previous generations tended to regard the Romanesque with all its amazing diversity as one of regional groups or "schools," it is more important to recognize the continuity than the artificial divisions of the past. The architecture that we call Romanesque did, indeed, begin in the ninth century and dominated the European landscape generally until c. 1130–35, although it would still be the dominate mode in the more remote areas almost until the end of the twelfth century.

The central problem of the Romanesque is to comprehend the common characteristics underlying the wide variety of local and international styles. The centuries from the ninth to the twelfth saw increasing experimentation in construction. The common two-story elevation, consisting of lower arcades and upper windows, became three with a variety of features inserted between the arcades and the windows. In the simplest form a second story might be nothing more than a series of decoratively treated openings into the space between the stone-vaulted ceiling over the aisles and the lean-to roof that protects the vaults. Opening the wall area increased air circulation and prevented the buildup of heat that could lead to spontaneous combustion and hence destruction by fire. The desire for increased height and stability also led to the construction of a gallery, sometimes called a tribune, a fully vaulted and windowed story as wide as the aisle below and on occasion even as tall as that aisle. Other examples of second-story elements included internal wall passages that permitted access to the upper stories for cleaning and maintenance. In some case, increasing elaborateness in the liturgy demanded chapels and altars in the second-story zones. Chapels dedicated to the Archangel St. Michael would often be established in these lofty places. In general, the liturgical spaces would also be made more elaborate, particularly in monastic and cathedral churches that needed more altars to accommodate increased numbers of monks and clergy. One particular development characteristic of French-speaking lands was the ambulatory, an aisle space wrapped around the apse, and radiating chapels. As stated in the introduction, the chapels are "radiating" because they look as though they were planned to open off the ambulatory from a spot that corresponds to the high altar in the main apse. This elaborate, often multilevel interior was articulated on the exterior with moldings around the various windows and along the various cornice lines. Although heavily restored, the east end of Angoulême (Figure 10) is one of the few remaining cathedrals where this exterior ornament can be seen.

The rapid technological development in stone construction in the eleventh century can only be explained by the experience and practice of the previous centuries. The churches were now larger and, therefore, required thicker, more substantial walls to support that height. The Carolingian practice of using ashlar masonry, that is, regularly cut rectangular blocks, to articulate the interior piers and to achieve smooth arches and sharp corners would be extended to using ashlar for full walls in those regions with a plentiful supply of good building stone, such as Normandy, northern Burgundy, and the broad area around Paris. Several centuries of shared experience would result in increasingly higher quality construction because builders were able to identify the usefulness of different types and grades of stone, which, of course, translated directly into cost-effectiveness. The harder, fine-grained limestone used for the capitals and portal sculptures created by Gislebertus at Autun, for example, was more costly than the lesser-quality stone used for the non-load-bearing sections of the walls.

Not only were forms and ideas borrowed from the past, but, in many cases, actual marble columns and capitals were deliberately reused in Romanesque buildings because they represented costlier materials that were not readily available and because they represented antiquity. As was the case in Autun, Romanesque churches regularly included more elaborate interior sculptural decoration in the form of historiated (with subject matter rather than abstract) capitals, as well as an enormous variety of foliate capitals and richly carved moldings and other architectural ornament, not to mention the extraordinary sculpted portals on the exterior that for many specialists and tourists alike are the very embodiment of Romanesque art.

Although we must reject the strictness of the old concept of schools of Romanesque art and architecture, we cannot ignore the diversity and must work within a more relaxed concept of regionalism based on available materials, local tradition, and ideas. In the Italian Peninsula, for example, regional groups of buildings are found in Lombardy, Emilia, Tuscany, Apulia, and Sicily. Those in Lombardy are heavily indebted to the Early Christian past in Milan, whereas those in Como celebrate the availability of quality building stone. In Emilia, where the basic building material was not stone but brick, builders would try to re-create an Early Christian past by sheathing the exteriors in marble, as at Modena. In Venice, no doubt because of its location on the Adriatic Sea, patrons and builders re-created a Middle Byzantine church as an appropriate resting place for the body of the Evangelist St. Mark that they had "liberated" from Alexandria. In Apulia, the southernmost province of the peninsula, there are many fine stone churches that often resemble fortresses, no doubt to make them less vulnerable to marauding pirates. In Sicily, especially under the rule of the Norman kings in the twelfth century, we find another kind of Early Christian basilican revival: marble columns and wooden-roofed naves, walls richly decorated with mosaics in the Byzantine manner at Monreale (Figure 23) and Palermo, and stone-vaulted apses, as at Cefalu. In another newly rich maritime city like Venice, but on the western coast of the peninsula, an ambitious attempt was made to create an Early Christian past at Pisa (Figure 8) that never existed. The majority of the churches, including both cathedrals and monasteries, would continue to be timber roofed in the nave, an obvious continuity with the Early Christian tradition, but they were vaulted in the side aisles and in the liturgical spaces, usually with groin vaults. There were a few experiments with rib vaults around Milan, perhaps inspired by Speyer, as both cities were part of the Holy Roman Empire. Generally, despite the grand size, the visual emphasis would continue to be on the horizontal, although by the later eleventh century the bay system, discussed in the next section, was firmly established throughout western Europe as the common conceptual tool for organizing the spaces.

In the early eleventh century a common interest in exploring and perfecting the technology of stone vaulting united Lombardy, Provence, and Catalonia as well as southern Burgundy. The result is that high-quality stone construction continued to be common around the whole of the Mediterranean basin until the end of the Middle Ages. The exteriors of these churches were richly articulated by architectural ornament, continuing a tradition that can be traced back to the sixth and seventh centuries. The Romanesque buildings generally continued to follow the triapsidal plan of the pre-Carolingian type right into the Gothic period.

All the regions across northern Spain, as well as those progressively reconquered from the Arabs and the Moors, also favored long transepts on the Early Christian model, with the difference that their terminal walls often contained the main public entrance. The liturgical importance of the transept probably began in the northern province of Asturias in the ninth century; but reinforced by examples based on Old St. Peter's, such as at Ripoll and elsewhere, it remained a constant feature throughout the Romanesque period, spreading throughout the Iberian Peninsula with the Reconquest. Most of northern Spain was blessed with high-quality building stone and the harder limestone for the rich sculptural tradition that flourished in the later eleventh and twelfth centuries. The great cathedral church of Santiago de Compostela (Figure 12), the goal of a major western pilgrimage that began with the "invention" of the body of the Apostle James, the brother of Christ, in the ninth century, is an excellent example of high-quality stone construction and rich exterior sculptural decoration (Document 33). Indeed, the marble quarries in the Pyrenees that were first exploited by the Romans continued to supply builders and sculptors on both sides of the mountains through the twelfth and thirteenth centuries.

The Germanic lands of the Holy Roman Empire, which included the areas that now make up the modern nations of Belgium, the Netherlands, and Switzerland, as well as other regions such as the Lorraine, Alsace, the Rhineland, and even Lombardy, together with the newly conquered and Christianized lands in the east as far the Oder River, continued to build in the Carolingian tradition, but on a larger scale, just as they also continued to revive and even to imitate the Early Christian and late Roman buildings that still stood in the old Roman cities like Trier, Milan, and Cologne. The Ottonian kings continued the policies of their Carolingian predecessors and passed them on to later dynasties such as the Salians in Speyer. Thus, there are cathedrals like that in Trier that are heavily indebted to the old Roman tradition, side by side with the enormous new buildings in Speyer, Mainz, Bamberg, and Worms, among others, that reflect the political, ecclesiastic, and economic power of important kings and prelates. Speyer, as the largest church constructed outside the Italian Peninsula at the time it was undertaken, is a good reflection of the ambitions of later German kings.

The diverse geographic areas that make up the modern nation of France similarly followed several traditions. Those with Roman and Early Christian traditions continued to draw on them for inspiration, as in the case of the series of large, wooden-roofed basilicas in the Loire River valley from Orléans to Nantes. In Burgundy, the inspiration more often came from Roman monuments, such as at St.-Lazare in Autun, where the elevation was inspired by the Roman city gates, two of which still survive. But at the same time a lively local tradition developed in Burgundy that owed little or nothing to the Roman past. In western France, the hall churches in the Poitou may have been inspired by local Carolingian examples while, in Aquitaine, domed buildings were constructed on the Byzantine model, probably through Venice. In general, Languedoc looked to its Early Christian past; but without a ready supply of good building stone, churches in Toulouse translated that tradition in brick. The tradition of small-stone masonry around Clermont-Ferrand in central France developed into the distinctive exterior decorative patterns of bold originality and striking color contrasts that recall the tradition of the baptistry at Poitiers.

But the most original and the most influential group of buildings for future developments would be those constructed in Normandy and the British Isles from the 1050s to the 1150s. In spite of the lively and rich heritage of Anglo-Saxon building that flourished in the British Isles for several centuries prior to the conquest in 1066, it was almost totally replaced and obscured by the Norman kings and their imported bishops. Thus, Normandy and, after 1066, England developed very distinctive modes of building that tended to use three-story elevations at Durham and Ely (Figure 11), at a time when two stories, aisle arcade and clerestory, were still the norm. In Normandy the three-story elevation was created in a quest for height, especially in those buildings that included a gallery at the second story. The gallery was as wide as the aisle below and, on occasion, even as tall as the aisle. This large second-story zone was often covered with stone vaults. At Durham, in contrast, the second story appears to be a gallery, but there is no finished space behind it, only the lean-to roof that protects the aisle vaults. In other Norman and English examples the second story will simply consist of a few slots opening into the roof space. The other unusual characteristic of these buildings is the creation of a passageway within the thickness of wall at the level of the clerestory windows as part of a system of circulation at the upper level. Never public spaces, these passageways and circulation networks were strictly for purposes of cleaning and maintenance. Lantern towers, so-called for the windows on all sides that brought light to the interior over the crossing are another common feature that, like the clerestory passage, will continue to be used in Gothic buildings. Master builders also developed a system of visual articulation that not only emphasized the bay system but also accented structural lines. England, being one of the richest of all European countries after the Norman Conquest, was the location of some of the largest and grandest Romanesque buildings ever constructed, even surpassing the giant imperial buildings in the Rhineland. Romanesque architecture was also introduced into such newly Christianized areas as Scandinavia, Bohemia, Austria, Hungary, and the western side of the Balkan Peninsula in the later tenth and eleventh centuries. Scandinavia, in particular, preserved and elaborated on the longstanding tradition of building in timber, which has disappeared elsewhere.

THE BAY SYSTEM

So many technological advances took place in the Romanesque period, from the ninth to the twelfth centuries, that entire volumes have been devoted to that topic alone. But several Romanesque features stand out as examples of significant approaches that changed conceptual thinking about architecture. Perhaps the most important of these was the "bay system," first analyzed by Walter Horn (1958) more than fifty years ago. On one level, the bay system involved thinking and conceiving of a building as a series of repeated, additive units; on another, it represented a significant cognitive shift from thinking in terms of the flat planes of walls and ceilings (Old St. Peter's) to thinking in terms of volumes and of volumes of different sizes conceived in relation to each other. Simply defined, the bay system is a series of units, usually the relationship of side-aisle volumes to nave volumes, that became the repeated units that make up a whole building. Horn argued that this first occurred at Speyer Cathedral (Figure 13). Whether or not Speyer was the first is decidedly less important than recognizing that Speyer, indeed, was the most influential example, the one most often viewed as the model. At Speyer the basic unit of volume is the single side-aisle bay, which is delineated by half-columns attached to pilaster strips at all four corners and connected by round arches along the four sides. The exterior side is flanked by the exterior wall that includes the window centered between the framing elements.

Interestingly, the basic units are not squares or cubes, which would have made a relatively simple scheme, but cubic rectangles that make for a more sophisticated scheme in which the basic geometry has not been isolated. Nonetheless, the complexity confirms that the planner or planners thought in terms of volumetric units, as opposed to planar geometry (Figure 1). In the first stage of design at Speyer the "bay" consisted of one side aisle volume on each side and a broad but relatively narrow section across the nave. The aisle bays were covered with groin vaults, while the nave remained timber-roofed. In the second period it was decided to extend the groin vaulting to the nave space, which entailed adding framing elements in every other bay to make each spatial unit of the nave twice as wide and, therefore, easier to vault because, while the unit was still a cubic rectangular, the proportions of the plan were closer to a square. Doubling the nave units for vaulting did not make the resulting cubic rectangle double the proportions of the side aisle units, which again is an indication of the sophisticated conceptual thinking of the master builder. That sophistication is equally apparent in the side aisle units conceived by the first builder. He had worked out the system in the design of the enormous crypt, which basically consists of four great, near-squares, each subdivided into nine groin-vaulted units. Most of the individual units in plan are square, but it hardly matters if the geometry is not perfect because the visual illusion is of identical, cubic, groin-vaulted units conceived in terms of the framing elements that define them.

In addition to the conceptual thinking in terms of repeated volumes, there is the practical side of building a series of repeating units. One significant effect is that the master builder had to work out only the design of a single unit and then have it replicated the appropriate number of times. It also meant that the master builder could effectively manage a larger program because he did not have to oversee each and every unit during the building. For example, at Speyer the core of the crypt consisted of forty-five groin-vaulted units, thirty-eight of which could be constructed using the same timber scaffolding (or several units of the same scaffolding). The scaffolding could simply be moved from unit to unit as each was built. The bay system, then, can be said to represent an advance in conceptual thinking that led to greater efficiency in building simply because it permitted the master builder to control a larger program.

Speyer is certainly the most sophisticated example of the conceptual understanding of the bay system that has survived. It is not, however, unique. In at least two other areas of northern Europe in the early eleventh century, we can identify comparable conceptual thinking. Rather than worrying about which came first, we need to realize that the factors that led to its development and exploitation at Speyer were present in other areas as well. The end results were obviously different because the local architectural vocabularies are not the same as at Speyer, but the conceptual thinking that gave rise to a comparable degree of visual and structural organization and articulation is almost identical in the cathedral at Orléans, begun in the 990s and built slowly over the next century, and in the Catalán church of San Vincente at Cardona in the Pyrenees. Orléans, a vast wooden-roofed basilica with extended transepts, was built atop a groin-vaulted crypt, both revealed by modern archeological excavations. Interior and exterior were articulated with pilaster strips and strip buttresses that defined the carefully organized bay system. Cardona, which survives, stripped of its interior plaster, as a fully vaulted structure of considerable sophistication, was begun c. 1020. It is highly unlikely that there was any professional contact between these master builders, although patronal contact between the Capetian kings and the Salian emperors is a possibility. Contact between them, however, is of no more significance than trying to determine which one was first. On the contrary, it is much more important to realize that changes in conceptual thinking that leap from planar to volumetric ideas can occur at any moment and to recognize that the shift in paradigms took only about a generation to become standard all across western Europe.

GROIN VAULTS

Although fundamentally different from the shift in conceptual thinking represented by the bay system, the mastery of the technique of stone vaults represents another of the more important technological advances of the eleventh century. True, barrel and groin vaults had passed into the experience and vocabulary of medieval builders directly from the Roman past, but the early surviving examples are better thought of as moderately successful attempts to imitate the Roman originals than as examples of technical accomplishment. Speyer is unquestionably the first example to show complete mastery of the process and a full understanding of the technical aspects beyond that of previous examples. In the second phase of its construction, Speyer, along with the great monastic churches at Dijon and Cluny, was among the first large buildings to be fully vaulted throughout.

A groin vault, in the simplest terms, is two barrel vaults intersected at right angles to each other, with the material below the lines of intersection removed. It has innumerable advantages over the barrel vault, not the least that it only requires support at the four corners, as opposed to the continuous wall support required for most barrel vaults. The "groin" refers, of course, to the lines of intersection that roughly trace the diagonals across the square. The actual geometry is more complex (the groin lines should be curving rather than straight), but most builders (and patrons, for that matter) preferred straight groin lines because they suggested lines that could be visually equated with structural solidity. Construction of a groin vault over a square unit was a relatively uncomplicated task that required supporting scaffolding under the four arches that surrounded the square and continuous supporting scaffolding under the surface of the vault until the masonry had hardened. The use of semicircular arches in groin vaults over square spaces meant that the center of the vault was higher than the sides, which was practical from the standpoint of stability. The situation got rapidly more complicated, however, in the rectangular side aisle bays at Speyer with the introduction of a third length, the diagonal, in addition to the short side and the long side. The solution at Speyer was a masterful one in that the longest line, the diagonal, is not a full semicircle but a continuous segment of a circle that is less than half. The result is that the center is only slightly higher than the long side. It is just high enough at the peak to remain structurally stable, but low enough not to disrupt the visual flow between units. In short, the master builder again decided against the dictates of geometry in favor of a visual solution. Such thinking is common in the eleventh century.

Generally, builders tended to use groin vaults over square or rectangular spaces—the nearly square main vaults in the nave at Speyer are the largest ones constructed in the Romanesque period—but there are some extraordinary groin vaults to be found in England, including eight-part groins in chapels at Gloucester Cathedral. Groin vaults quickly became standard in the Romanesque buildings of the Rhineland and of that geographic band that stretches from Lombardy in northern Italy to Catalonia in the Pyrenees, as well as in southern Burgundy. Certainly, by the middle of the eleventh century, groin vaults had become standard in most regions of western Europe, having been introduced in England even before the Norman Conquest of 1066. Barrel vaults were less often used because of problems of piercing windows in the continuous wall necessary to support the barrel vault and because of problems of stability. There are some notable exceptions, particularly in Burgundy (at Autun, for example) and in the Poitou region of western France, but the groin vault, which relied on point support at the corners, proved more popular. Groin vaults were used well into the twelfth century, even in Gothic buildings, but were generally replaced by rib vaults by the thirteenth century.

For most of the Middle Ages builders used the round arches they had inherited from the Roman past. But in the eleventh century they discovered that round or semicircular arches had some visual and practical limitations, as in the nave aisles at Speyer, discussed earlier. Arabic builders in Spain found another solution that produced, as we now know from modern analysis, a more stable form of arch, namely, an arch composed of two segments. The result is often called a pointed arch and is usually considered a characteristic of Gothic architecture. In fact, of course, pointed arches appeared north of the Pyrenees in that band that stretches from Lombardy to Catalonia in the first half of the eleventh century, well before the creation of the Gothic. The old explanation, that the presence of pointed arches at the great Benedictine abbey church of Cluny, begun in 1088, in central Burgundy can be explained by the presence of a builder from northern Spain named Gunzo must be abandoned, however well-established the myth has become. Edson Armi (2004) has documented lots of experiments with pointed arches in groin vaults from Lombardy to Burgundy and demonstrated the expertise and sophistication of the construction that employs both at least two generations earlier than the construction of Cluny. Of late, scholars are also reexamining the possibility that pointed arches might have been introduced at Montecassino, in southern Italy, and spread northward from there in the later tenth or early eleventh century. By the end of the eleventh century, segmental arches and segmental groin vaults were well-established throughout Burgundy. At Durham Cathedral (Figure 14) in northern England, continuous segmental arches (arches composed of continuous arcs that measure less than half a circle) appear in the first phase of construction, beginning in 1093, whereas arches made of two segments (pointed arches) were used in the second phase of construction, after 1104, perhaps the result of renewed contacts with Spain or Italy or both.

RIB VAULTS

Durham Cathedral is also well known for containing the earliest surviving examples of rib vaults (Figure 14), essentially groin vaults to which a large decorative rib molding has been added for visual emphasis. The massive rib vaults appear in the side aisles of the original choir at Durham and are recognized as the earliest remaining examples. Previous generations believed them to be the "first," but the high level of technology and the confident sense of design and construction—there is nothing experimental about these vaults—indicate that the master builder was familiar with earlier examples and profited from this experience. There is no doubt that he understood precisely what the real purpose of the ribs was. Despite many nineteenth-century theories that posited a functional role for the ribs—namely, that they served as supports for the web (or surface) of the vaults—we now know that they never had, nor could they have had, such a role. Instead, the rib has two roles in the rib vault, not necessarily realized in all examples, even those at Durham. The first is that the ribs allowed the master builder to regularize the height of the center of the vault over any space at the beginning of construction because constructing a rib vault required two building seasons. In the first season, the ribs themselves were constructed on top of heavy timber scaffolding. The mortar between the stones that made up the arches of the ribs had to be allowed to settle and to harden before the actual stone surface of the vault, the web, was put in place, again with the aid of timber scaffolding, in the second season. Only after both had been allowed to bond and to settle might the scaffolding be safely removed from both. Removal of the scaffolding revealed the second role of the rib, the purely visual purpose of providing lines for the eye to follow (and thus to ignore the massively thick web that formed the actual ceiling).

The sophisticated understanding of the possibilities afforded by the ribs can be seen at Durham in the way that the builder, using only semicircular and continuous segmental arches, nevertheless managed to triumph over the several irregularities presented by the contrasting designs of the alternating pier forms on the inner side and the uniform wall piers against the outside wall. The plan of each aisle bay is rectangular, as at Speyer, resulting in three different lengths of span, the arcade and wall ribs, the cross ribs, and the intersecting diagonal ribs. Instead of using semicircular arches for the shorter wall ribs, as had the builder at Speyer for the groin vaults, the Durham builder used semicircular arches with short vertical extensions added to raise the arch higher. Both the cross ribs and the diagonal ribs are continuous segments of circles. The result is a rib vault with the height determined by the diagonal cross ribs, which are just slightly less than semicircular. The segment of the diagonal ribs is shortened still more so that the crown, or highest point in the vault, is only slightly above the level of the cross ribs. In other words, the Durham builder already understood how to adjust the lengths of the arcs used for the ribs to achieve a relatively even crown line and a regular rhythm from unit to unit. All the decisions necessary to accomplish the desired effect were made at the beginning of the construction of the vault. That each of the ribs rests on a vertical element to suggest support from the floor proves that rib vaults were planned at the beginning of construction in 1093. The master at Durham exhibited a rather astonishing mastery of the entire design from the beginning. The complexity of the rib vault design and execution indicates that he arrived with a full understanding of how to construct them. They may be the earliest that remain, but they are already very accomplished, which suggests that the Durham builder had prior experience with the process. The rib vaults at Durham are, in fact, more sophisticated and better conceived than the immediate examples that were based on them. The next examples to match them in the degree of understanding are the two enormous square rib vaults installed, possibly c. 1108, over the transept arms at Speyer.

The most important effects of the rib vault, then, are twofold, structural and visual. As at Durham, the ribs regularize the height of the vault and establish its basic form prior to the actual construction of the vault. Second, the rib provides a strong linear accent that attracts the eye. At Durham that linear accent begins at the floor with the visual support that runs up the wall to meet the vault rib at its springing. In spite of the enormous size of the ribs and the thickness of the web, the linear accent appears to lighten the massiveness. In the examples that followed after Durham and Speyer, the size of the rib was progressively reduced and, therefore, made more linear. The eye reads line rather than mass. Romanesque architecture in England and Normandy was substantially altered visually. In the Gothic buildings of the twelfth century the linearity is still more pronounced, resulting finally in that sense of the linear grid, a visual skeleton that ultimately seems to replace the wall.

ROMANESQUE SCULPTURE

One of the more outstanding achievements of the later eleventh and twelfth centuries is the introduction of large-scale stone sculpture, particularly in highly decorated portals. In the Italian Peninsula, doorways were often modeled on Early Christian precedents and consisted of columns that were topped with gables and rested on the backs of lions, references to imperial meaning and to the canopies (*ciboria*) erected over altars. That these were always in marble is an additional association with the past. One of the most elaborate of these is on the west facade of the cathedral at Modena (Figure 9), which is additionally decorated with biblical friezes in marble. The proportions of these panels strongly suggests that Wiligelmo, the sculptor, was deliberately evoking Early Christian carved marble sarcophagi as references to a venerable heritage. Elaborately sculpted capitals, often mixing human figures with fantastic flora and fauna, and friezelike panels around windows are common in Lombardy, from whence they were occasionally exported northward (Speyer), but generally sculpture in the Holy Roman Empire took the form of life-sized images of the crucified Christ suspended above altars or seated figures of the Virgin and Child that served as focal points of devotion.

In Burgundy, Languedoc, southwestern France, and northern Spain, carved portal decoration was elevated to a new high, as at Autun (Figures 15 and 16). The most common theme among these dramatic doorways was the Last Judgment at the End of Time. The imagery is stark and powerfully evokes the wages of sin with dramatic visions of the torments of hell. The visual effect would have been even greater when the decorations were painted in their original, strong colors. Many books stress how such doorways would have looked when bathed in the rays of the setting sun, without regard for the fact that only a few are on the west ends and even many of those, such as Autun, were protected by deep porches that would have barely allowed late afternoon light to reach the sculptures. In addition, many public entrances were situated in the transepts and not in the west ends.

In the imagery on capitals surmounting columns and piers, inside and out, most Romanesque art in northern Europe reveals an awareness of its earlier, pre-Christian past, a vivid reminder that Christianity did not sweep away those older northern traditions. We find this in designs such as serpents bitting their tails and other intertwined creatures. We might expect to find such imagery in the British Isles and Scandinavia, but it is equally strong from the northern frontiers of the Holy Roman Empire to the newly reconquered provinces of Spain.

Many textbooks stress that Romanesque art and architecture was primarily monastic in focus, without realizing how much this idea owes both to the accident of survival and to the patterns of building across Europe. As noted, most cathedral sites had been permanently established by the fourth or fifth century, and their continuous occupation meant a succession of structures one after the other. The evidence suggests that regular rebuilding, usually out of necessity, was a common feature. Thus, there were far more Romanesque cathedrals constructed than actually now survive. The exceptions are England and the Holy Roman Empire. As a result of the systematic rebuilding of cathedrals after the Norman Conquest of 1066, a high percentage of Romanesque buildings still exist in England. In the Holy Roman Empire, many of the great buildings, such as Speyer, have survived the many wars that engulfed the countryside over the ages. Areas that developed later, such as northern France and Spain, saw most of their Romanesque cathedrals replaced in the Gothic era.

CHAPTER 4

PLANNING AND CONSTRUCTION IN THE GOTHIC ERA

The fact that we have high-quality groin vault construction using segmental arches in southern Burgundy in the eleventh century and extraordinarily sophisticated rib vault construction in England, Normandy, and the Rhineland in the decades on either side of 1100 suggests that it is time to lay to rest, once and for all, the definition established almost two hundred years ago that describes the Gothic style as the combination of the pointed arch and the rib vault. The two elements were actually combined in the main vaults of the nave at Durham by 1110, but no expert would call them Gothic. A new definition, one not formulated in terms of the vocabulary of forms, is essential, if only because round arches and groin vaults, characteristics termed Romanesque, in order to contrast them artificially with pointed arches and rib vaults, continue to be used in undeniably Gothic contexts almost to the end of the twelfth century. The difference between Romanesque and Gothic, then, is not a difference in the architectural vocabularies, but a difference in the way those vocabularies were conceived and used. Romanesque architecture, for all its diversity and variety, essentially built on the past. Early elements were constantly being updated and reinterpreted. The borrowing usually consisted of taking features from other schemes and incorporating them almost without change. In such borrowings, as well as in the attempts to link volumetric units into series, Romanesque can essentially be understood as additive.

In Gothic the emphasis is always on the total, unified design; all the parts are subsumed within the whole. The unity of the whole design is more important than its parts. The shift in conceptual thinking is a cognitive shift in the way master builders worked with and within their ar-

chitectural vocabularies. A Gothic design is a totality that may be divided into its many elements, but, at the same time, those elements are
increasingly integrated into a unified design concept. The Romanesque
sense of the repeated volumetric unit is replaced by the Gothic sense of
the unified space with the units contained in and, therefore, contribut-
ing to that totality. The Romanesque struggle to find successful ways to
link volumetric units resulted in additive parts, series of repeating units
that cumulatively add up to a whole; the building is a collection of parts.
Gothic represents an almost opposite conceptual sense; the building is
more about considering the whole design and "juggling" the parts until
they became a coherent, integrated design. In rather oversimplified terms,
Gothic design can be considered as replacing the "addition" practiced by
earlier builders with "division." The numerical analogy may be related to
the introduction of Arabic numerals, imported from Spain in the early
twelfth century, which made the process of division more accessible and
more easily accomplished.

If we are to define Gothic as a shift in cognitive thinking, then we
must also recognize that it was not an absolute solution but, rather, the
result of a series of experiments in a number of different places. It was by
no means preordained that the new attitude was to be "created" in Paris
and the surrounding Ile-de-France. There were contemporary experiments in space formation in areas of western France, particularly Anjou,
and elsewhere, in Burgundy and Normandy, for example. With all these
experiments, architecture moved toward a new emphasis on total spaces
that can be said to "anticipate" what occurred in the region around Paris.
These early experiments defy easy synthesis and suggest that we must appreciate the variety of experimentation, the excitement of discovery, and
the intellectual fervor that resulted in what we recognize as Gothic.

The extraordinary Gothic cathedrals that still dominate European
cities some 600–800 years after their construction, singularly and collectively, represent the greatest achievements of medieval architecture. The
early examples represent a new integration of old and new features and
vocabularies and a new conception of an architectural space of tran-
scendent spiritual power and intimidating episcopal and, by association,
royal authority. Through most of the twentieth century scholars divided
the Gothic era into four periods, largely based (incorrectly) on the or-
ganic model of growth: Early Gothic (c. 1135–95); High Gothic (1195–
1225/30); Rayonnant (France) or Decorated (England) (c. 1225/30–

c. 1400); and Flamboyant or Late Gothic (c. 1400–c. 1525). The four periods were likened to infancy, youth, maturity, and old age. Not only is such incorrectly transposed "Darwinism" singularly inappropriate for understanding Gothic, the first two of these so-called periods do not hold up to scrutiny as distinctly different (or separate) in their achievements. Better that we should consider three periods by combining the first two (c. 1135–1225/30) in a category known simply as Early Gothic. In this way the three stylistic periods correspond to the three stages of the development of the architectural profession in the Gothic period, discussed in the previous chapter. That is, the three relate more closely to shifts in thinking and attitudes toward building that are reflected in different architectural vocabularies, rather than different "styles" per se.

Beginning in the middle of the twelfth century there was almost explosive growth and unparalleled diversity. How did changes in thinking lead to change in building? A question like this permits us to understand how the distinctions made between the types of limestone used for supporting elements (frame) and those used for walls (fill) (which were already well known by the end of the eleventh century in Romanesque buildings), in combination with the exploitation of the arch (framing and load-bearing), allowed master builders to enlarge windows in twelfth-century Gothic structures. Finally, in the thirteenth century these ideas inspired the changes in construction techniques seen at Reims, where the supporting elements were built first, with the rest of the bay filled in later. This practice encouraged, and was encouraged by, the development of standardized pieces serially produced and by the new concept of the window as a design surface. Rather than tracing a singular, linear "development," we can analyze different approaches to the same problem. This permits us to recognize that communication between master builders was widespread and almost immediate by the 1150s, and probably even long before. This rapid exchange of ideas and technology continued without change on a pan-European level until the social and political disruptions of the Hundred Years War and the Black Death.

THE FLYING BUTTRESS

The flying buttress is one of the visually defining characteristics of Gothic cathedrals (Figure 20). It consists of two parts: the uprights, heavy vertical piers constructed at the outer limit of the exterior wall and set perpendicular to that wall; and the flyers, the arch (or arches) that rise from the upright pier to abut the clerestory wall to be braced. The flying buttress is the last major structural device created in the period. In this two-part form it appeared c. 1165–75. In the 1220s, a third part, in the form of a pinnacle placed at the top of the outer edge of the pier, was introduced at Reims (Figure 4). Model testing has confirmed that the pinnacle, which had previously been dismissed as simply decorative, plays a stabilizing role in a major windstorm. The function of the buttress was thought to be to relieve the outward pressure (thrust) in a tall building that resulted from the sheer weight of the stone vaults and from the distribution of the resulting forces that would cause the arches of the vaults to spread outward. This opinion, first developed in the nineteenth century, prevailed through most of the twentieth century. But in the 1970s, photoelastic and computer modeling revealed that, beginning in the 1220s, the role of the flying buttress as a vault support shifted to function as a wind brace. Thus, we can now speak of two "moments" in the history of the flying buttress. The first was about 1175, a date that emphatically does not mark the invention or creation of the flying buttress, but the date when the most influential early examples, the nave buttresses of Notre-Dame in Paris, could be seen. We do not, in fact, know the first example of the flying buttress, although a number of possible "candidates" have been proposed. As for the nave buttresses of Notre-Dame in Paris, as soon as the two-step solution became visible there, c. 1175, a frantic scramble among master builders began all across northern France and even at Canterbury in England to incorporate flyers into projects already under construction or to add them to recently completed buildings (often to buildings that did not need them). That they were thought to be needed is perhaps the most persuasive evidence that builders believed they were not just necessary but crucial. How else can we explain the enormous cost and effort required to return to an already completed building and to erect a whole new system of scaffolding to reach the most inaccessible parts of a tall building in order to add buttressing, as was the case in a good many examples, including the east end of Notre-Dame in Paris.

A second type of flying buttress was introduced at Notre-Dame c. 1180, most likely as part of the effort finally to vault the upper choir. A long-span flying buttress effectively solved the problem of adding buttresses to the nearly completed east end of Notre-Dame (Figure 20). Because the lower stories were already completed, an intermediate pier at gallery level could not be added, so both flyer arches had to spring from the upright piers added around the periphery. The same situation occurred, perhaps even slightly earlier, when flying buttresses were added to the east end of the abbey church of St.-Remi at Reims. Possibly because it was regarded as a "fix," the long-span flying buttress appeared only rarely thereafter, although one of those exceptions is on the nave of Notre-Dame.

Sometime around 1220–25, an event of which we have no record but most likely a weather incident in connection with the slightly lower winter temperatures that announced what climatologists call a "little Ice Age" occurred in Paris. While we do not know the specific event, we do know the outcome: it was rather suddenly decided to rebuild the nave flying buttresses of Notre-Dame. Since the system was changed from the two-stage to the long-span system, but with a higher point of abutment against the upper wall, the cataclysmic event is likely to have been a storm of hurricane magnitude. No evidence of major damage either in the pre-restoration records or in the fabric survives, which suggests that it might have been more insidious and less dramatic, but potentially more dangerous. Model testing and analysis demonstrated the possible weakness of the first nave system under very high wind conditions. Nothing would have been blown down, but the level of stress on the buttressing system from the action of high winds against the giant nave roof at a higher altitude—30 percent higher than any structure previously built in the region—might have caused the mortar bonding the masonry of the highest walls to crack and fall out. This would have permitted water to reach the stonework. If the slightly colder weather conditions dropped below the freezing point, the expanding water would have caused the stone to fracture and scale as it turned to ice. Thus, the damage could quickly have escalated to the danger point. There is no indication in the building fabric, however, that this was permitted to happen. Furthermore, there was a surge of interest in water evacuation from the upper parts of these tall buildings that can hardly be coincidental.

The builder's solution was to eliminate the stress on the walls by rebuilding the buttressing system. The evidence of the thirteenth-century forms recorded in the pre-restoration drawings at Paris indicates that the new buttressing system consisted of expanding the width and height of the uprights and then of constructing long-span arches above and around the old upper flyer arches, which would have been taken down afterward. The major change is the raised height of the point of abutment indicated in the mid-nineteenth-century drawings. The evidence makes clear that the raised abutment was intended to brace the roof and to guard against the "sail" effect during a major windstorm. This change was rapidly adopted elsewhere, as, for example, in the nave buttresses at Chartres and the choir buttresses at Bourges. The lesson of Paris spread quickly; it even reached the workshop at Toledo (Spain) in a matter of months. The re-alignment of the point of abutment is doubtlessly reflected in the change in the design of the flying buttresses at Reims almost immediately after the dedication in 1221.

At Reims (Figures 2 and 4) the two-tiered flying buttress (the lower flyer arch braced the vaults while the upper braced the roof against high winds) became the new standard; furthermore, the master builder introduced the pinnacle as an additional, lateral wind brace at the same moment. This final "adjustment," as it were, to the technology of the flying buttress, together with the two-tiered flyer became, thereafter, the standard solution. In the aftermath of Reims, the exteriors of Gothic cathedrals were dominated by richly decorated flying buttresses topped with pinnacles. Now we would be hard put to imagine a Gothic cathedral without them; even the Gothic revival buildings of the nineteenth and twentieth centuries prominently feature pinnacles.

EARLY GOTHIC

The first period of the Gothic, which lasted from its creation in the region of Paris c. 1130–35 until 1220–25, was one of extraordinary exploration. Branner defined it as a period of a bewildering number of experiments in design and structure. Together with the emergence of master builders and master artists as professions, the one common factor was the creation of a new sense of spatial volume. In general, the period can be described as one in which the importance of the unified design scheme, whether for a building or a portal or any other work of art, became more significant than the collection of parts that made it up because the parts were subservient to, and integrated in, the whole. The first Gothic cathedral was St.-Etienne in Sens, begun in the 1140s in a local variant of Burgundian Romanesque, but dramatically altered, beginning c. 1145, by the experience of the new choir of the abbey church of St.-Denis, dedicated in 1144.

The decades that followed were filled with innovations, but this does not mean that the "old" was discarded. Structural elements and even architectural vocabularies were borrowed from the Romanesque past and updated or rethought for new applications. Among those elements are tribune galleries, lantern towers, and wall passages, all of which appeared at Laon Cathedral (Figure 22), begun c. 1155. On the other hand, there was a new interest in making the wall thinner. Sometimes that wall consisted of two thin layers held together by slabs or arches at the top. Windows got larger and larger and soon were doubled and even tripled as builders experimented with new solutions to increase the light level. Eventually they introduced large-scaled stained glass windows that lowered the light but created striking visual experiences. All too often the period is seen as having as its singular goal the achievement of height, real or imagined. In fact, it is not height per se but volume that is the focus. While Sens and Laon are both about 75 feet tall on the interior, much is made of the fact that Notre-Dame of Paris is over 100 feet tall on the interior (Figure 21), but few people are aware that it is over 115 feet wide in the choir interior, from one outer aisle wall to the other (before chapels were added around the exterior in the later thirteenth and fourteenth centuries). The sense of lateral spaciousness at Paris was practically destroyed by that added exterior ring of later chapels that blocked much of the light at the level of the aisles. In other words, the interior height of Notre-Dame's vaults would have been balanced by the greater width of the original space at ground level. After Paris, it must be noted, only a few Gothic structures have that lateral spaciousness—Bourges (Figure 25) being the most obvious example. By the middle of the 1190s, the quest for height engendered by the success of the flying buttress overcame the visual balance between width and height that had existed before and, until 1230–35, the emphasis in French buildings was only on height.

Anglo-Norman master builders, however, from the time the new style was introduced at Canterbury (Figure 24), never had that fascination with great height and narrow spaces. Rather, they were interested in spaciousness: big spaces filled with multiple, thin, linear moldings that bend around surfaces, effectively concealing the preference for thick masonry walls that had been started after the Norman Conquest. That English interest in the expansiveness of the interior space, so that it appears to be even larger than it is in reality, may, in part, have resulted from that unusual British combination of cathedrals and monastic communities. The separation of the cathedral/monastic precinct from the rest of the city resulted in large open areas around the churches, open areas that never existed on the continent. Large monastic cathedral precincts meant that the churches were less restricted in area than on the continent and that builders could enhance inner spaciousness as a result.

Canterbury is a prime example of the way in which the Gothic was spread. Originally, the use of Gothic was an importation, either of the master builder himself (William of Sens at Canterbury) or by a native builder who had experienced it firsthand (William the Englishman, the second builder at Canterbury). Shortly thereafter native English interpretations of the Gothic style produced such wonderfully spacious cathedrals as Wells, begun c. 1175, and Lincoln, where St. Hugh's choir was started in 1182. In 1220, one of the most majestic of all English Gothic cathedrals was begun at Salisbury (Figure 28).

The same general pattern of importation followed by local interpretation was repeated all over Europe. Hence such importation is apparent in the cathedral of Avila in Spain, probably the work of a master builder from Burgundy, possibly Vézelay, and in that of Limburg an der Lahn in the Holy Roman Empire, the work of a master builder who had visited Laon and Reims. The second stage, the native interpretation of the new style, is exemplified in Spain by Toledo (Figure 29), begun about 1220, and in the Holy Roman Empire by the new chevet of Magdeburg, begun in 1208. Examples of the Gothic style in the Italian Peninsula were more unusual and were more often associated with the monastic orders that fostered them; the Cistercian church at Fossanova and the Victorine church of S. Andrea in Vercelli—neither of them cathedrals—are appropriate examples.

THE SECOND WAVE: RAYONNANT AND DECORATED, 1230–1300

Interestingly, the moment when the Gothic style truly became international across western Europe was also the moment when the direction shifted decisively from a style that balanced a concern for structure with interest in decoration, which is how we might see the Early Gothic, to a style where decoration, a new and decidedly richer, and vastly more complex form of decoration, suddenly became the central focus of master builders and—it is now appropriate to speak of them as such—designers. The structural solution of Reims, with the well-engineered flying buttresses, became the new norm. Every building, even of moderate height, had flying buttresses with double arches (the lower to brace the vaults and clerestory wall, the upper to brace the roof against the effect of wind) and topped with pinnacles. With structural problems solved, the builders' focus turned to ornament to make their mark.

One interesting aspect of this second phase of Gothic is how closely it seems to coincide with the onset of the "little Ice Age" c. 1220–25. The slightly lower temperatures (climatologists speak in terms of less than five degrees), coupled with longer winters, wreaked havoc on agriculture in the region north of Paris and points farther north. The region northeast of Paris around the cities of Laon and Noyon, which had been the major wine-producing area of northern France during the twelfth and early thirteenth centuries, halted production abruptly c. 1220–25. Loss of wine production meant a substantial loss of revenue, but fortunately the cathedrals in those two towns had already been completed. We can trace the impact of climate change in all those areas dependent on agriculture as they struggled to replace lost crops, whereas the effect was nonexistent in those cities farther north that had developed economies around the cloth trade. Their heavy woolens were suddenly in greater demand; this is the only way we can explain why there are few indications of financial difficulties in Amiens and why, in spite of many difficulties, construction was continued at Reims during the crucial decades 1220–40.

In France this new style is called "Rayonnant" (radiating), after the giant round rose windows filled with seemingly radiating patterns of stone tracery that appear in the west fronts and transept facades of many cathedrals, including Paris, Reims, and Amiens. The style appeared in a number of places in the 1230s, although it is irrevocably associated with Paris. In England the equivalent style is the "Decorated," which suits its character. Basically, the French style is about richly patterned tracery, first created in windows and on walls at Reims but in later examples spread across every available surface, even and especially on the exterior. The decoration takes the form of thin screens of design, obviously based on window tracery, but then extended out of the window to encompass the frame around it and even blossoming into decorated gables and the like. The rise of interest in richly layered patterns happened just as changing economies forced churches to be built at smaller scale, which in turn allowed the complex tracery patterns to be readily seen. One of the more interesting aspects of this style is the decrease in the amount of stone required. If we compare the cross section of a building of 1175 with one of 1235, we discover that the later building, assuming a reasonably close correspondence in height, required no more (and probably less) than half the amount of stone. This quickly translates into a savings in the cost of stone, which might well have been offset by the increased wages of the master mason and his assistants to create the lavish ornament. Furthermore, during the winter months, when actual construction ceased, the carvers could prepare multiples of each element in a repeating design—another innovation of experiments at Reims, Soissons, and other sites in the 1220s. Thus, the Rayonnant and the Decorated changed the financial distribution. Monies previously used to pay for stone at the quarry—usually the single greatest cost in Gothic construction—were now spread among more specialized workmen, who enjoyed year-round employment. Finally, in spite of the changing economy the indications are that these smaller, but infinitely more elegant buildings did, indeed, cost more.

The classic French Rayonnant is emphatically associated with the city of Paris, even if its origins and many of its finest examples lie outside the capital. The most emblematic example is the extraordinary royal chapel, the Sainte-Chapelle, built on orders of King Louis IX in the 1240s to house the relics of the Passion of Christ that Louis bought from his distant cousin, Baldwin of Flanders, who, in the success story of all medieval success stories, went on crusade and ended up as emperor in Constantinople. But the new style made its decisive appearance in the early 1230s in the nave of the abbey church of St.-Denis and in the upper stories of the nave (Figure 27) and in the choir of the cathedral of Amiens. Equally successful from the standpoint of design was the addition of new transept facades of Notre-Dame de Paris in the 1250s and 1260s. So strong is the identification of the style with Paris that as late as the fifteenth century Jean Fouquet modeled his vision of the Temple of Jerusalem on an idealized version of Notre-Dame in Paris (cover illustration).

The Decorated style appeared in England in buildings associated with the court circles of King Henry III in the 1230s and culminated in the rebuilding of the coronation church of the kings of England, Westminster Abbey in London. The king's master builder, Henry of Reynes, was sent to Paris to see the latest examples of the royal style associated with Louis IX, although well before the construction of the Sainte-Chapelle. Henry did, indeed, look at a number of the latest Parisian designs, but when he got back to London, he used the style as he had observed it being employed, to create a quintessentially English interpretation that launched the "Decorated." The style shares a similar attitude to the use of ornament as the French Rayonnant but, at the same time, is uniquely and recognizably English. The style is not uniform throughout England, but like the French Rayonnant, it has a number of regional interpretations that have their own originality; nor does it always have the sheer decorative exuberance of the French variant. Despite differences, both share the complete integration of richly carved ornament in the design.

Although the sources of the English Decorated style lay in imported French tracery patterns, the specifically English contribution was to take the patterns beyond window tracery into the complete sculptural interior, to the lierne vaults and flowing, curvilinear tracery that presaged both the French Flamboyant and the English Perpendicular styles of Late Gothic. The rebuilding of Exeter Cathedral (Figure 32), c. 1279–1360, one of the most precisely documented campaigns in medieval England, is a prominent example of the Decorated style, despite the length of its construction period.

Just as the Rayonnant came to epitomize Paris (and the Decorated, London and the court circles), distinctly regional Gothic styles began to appear even in regions immediately adjacent to the area around Paris, such as Normandy, Burgundy, and Champagne. The Gothic style had appeared in all three by 1160, chiefly in its imported variant: the cathedral at Lisieux in Normandy, for example, where the builder borrowed stylistic elements from Noyon, Laon, and even Paris, all by way of Rouen, and integrated them into traditional Norman thick-wall construction. Analogous situations exist in Burgundy at Auxerre and in Champagne at Châlons-en-Champagne. By the time the Rayonnant style was in full bloom in Paris in the 1230s, regional styles had sprung up in a number of other centers across France. The same is true for the Decorated style in England: west country Decorated is exquisitely embodied in Lichfield Cathedral, whereas York Cathedral charts a new direction for the style in the north.

The cathedral of Cologne (Figure 30), begun in 1248, is perhaps the finest example of the Rayonnant in the Holy Roman Empire. Cologne, with an interior 165 feet high, is often seen as the direct continuation of that quest for great height and size associated with Reims, Amiens, and Beauvais in France. The builder's name, Gerardus in Latin, used to be a point of chauvinistic contention: for French scholars he was "Gérard" and thought to be "French"; to German scholars he was "Gerhard." Like Henry of Reynes, he had probably seen the great buildings of northern France, but an examination of the details of the design indicate that these are all strictly within the local Rhenish tradition. Cologne and the nearby abbey church of Altenburg are practically the only examples in the empire to reflect the direct impact of the Rayonnant. German Gothic buildings of the thirteenth century tend to be less lavishly decorated, even though they include such up-to-date ideas as bar tracery. The Liebfrauenkirche in Trier and St.-Elizabeth in Marburg, both begun c. 1235, are more typical in their concern for visual clarity and geometric unity. In both Trier, with its centralized plan, and Marburg, a hall church, double layers of carefully proportioned, bar tracery windows created light-filled interiors that stand in direct contrast to the heavily shadowed Romanesque interiors of the previous epochs. Both buildings are replete with design details taken from Reims, but both integrate those details in totally different ways that result in astonishing originality.

From the first, Gothic architecture in northern Spain was closely based on French models, as was the case at Avila, c. 1175, but those models were found in Burgundy, rather than Paris. Not until the victory in 1212 at Las Navas de Tolosa were the kings of León and Castile able to extend Christian control to southern Spain. This victory opened whole areas for the construction of new churches and cathedrals. Castile was the first beneficiary with its direct ties with France through the marriage of Louis VIII and Blanche of Castile. In the years following, major cathedrals were undertaken at Toledo, Burgos, and León. Toledo (Figure 29) was closely related to Bourges in its five-aisle plan, pyramidal massing, and pier and window plans, yet it also exhibits influence from Notre-Dame in Paris in the flying buttress system and the inclusion of a transept. But the details of the ornament, the interlaced arches of the wall passage and window tracery, reveal the Islamic and Mudejar past, side by side with the latest technology brought directly from Paris. Burgos is also indebted to Bourges and Paris; and León, begun c. 1255, is the finest example of French Rayonnant in Spain. León was begun by Bishop Martín Fernández, a former member of the administration of Alfonso X, the Wise, with direct royal gifts. The builder had obviously seen most of the important French monuments associated with royalty, so the design at León combines design elements from Paris, Amiens, and Reims, with the plan of the destroyed abbey church of St.-Nicaise at Reims, begun in 1231, in a deliberate effort to lend prestige to the increasingly powerful kings of Castile.

GOTHIC SCULPTURE

Since the examination of the sculpture of Gothic cathedrals is a huge topic, this discussion will be limited to a brief introduction touching on a few of the more important formal and thematic developments. Romanesque sculpture, especially that in northern Europe, generally seems to be reacting in visual terms against the tight limits imposed by the architecture. Often we see, as at Autun (Figure 15), crowded tympana teeming with writhing, twisting figures seeming to push against the limits of the frame. The most common theme in Romanesque portals, the Last Judgment, lends itself to this highly charged atmosphere of dynamic action, especially in those doorways that graphically depict the torments of hell. Gothic sculpture largely eschews this dramatic, threatening tone of swift and just retribution in favor of a reading that presents the viewer with a warning, but, more important, with a choice and the promise of a reward for a virtuous life. Instead of the Romanesque emphasis on threats and punishment, Gothic portals stress salvation related to new intellectual concepts, such as purgatory, that were freshly argued and formulated in the contemporary schools in Paris. The old tradition of diverse cathedral schools in the tenth and eleventh centuries was replaced by the concentration of schools in Paris, schools from which the university of Paris would be formed over the course of the twelfth century.

In addition, at the beginning of the Gothic period, sculptors and builders established a different visual relationship between the sculpture and its architectural framework, which can be seen by comparing the Romanesque portal at Autun (Figure 15) with the Early Gothic royal portals at Chartres (Figure 18), dated c. 1140–55. In the latter, there is no sense of dramatic urgency because a different moment is depicted. At Autun, judgment is in progress; the fates of the rising dead are already determined. At Chartres, Christ is shown in the central portal at His Third Coming, before the end of time and before judgment, when Christians, in spite of their sins, might still choose salvation. The atmosphere is highly charged, but the formal control imparts order, not chaos, largely through the careful visual distinctions between the various parts of the doorways, especially the three tympana and the statue-columns. Over time, this formal, architectural framework became less and less important until it was nothing more than a background against which the sculpture was displayed, as can be seen by comparing the portals at Chartres to the west portals of Reims, erected in the 1250s and 1260s (Figure 7).

The chief new components of the Gothic portal are the larger than life-size statues, called statue-columns, displayed against the door jambs of the portals. At Chartres these Old Testament kings, queens, and prophets are elongated, abstract figures with their arms close to, or crossed over, their torsos so they reflect the vertical aspect of the architectural columns to which they are attached. The Chartrain figures are frequently discussed as the common model for all early statue-columns, when, in fact, they are the exceptions that stand apart from all the others in their abstract organization and in the way they seem suspended in front of the architecture rather than being in it.

At Reims (Figure 7), by their twisting and turning actions the figures, especially those in the central portal, practically ignore the columns to which, however, they are still attached. In the central portal at Reims this is especially noticeable because they are arranged in pairs acting and reacting to one another. The architectural background has become a shallow stage space in which the figures interact.

From the leading intellectual circles in Paris came not only the theological concept of purgatory, that intermediate zone where Christians suffered for their past sins before being admitted to heaven, but other new themes such as the Triumph of the Virgin and Mary as the Queen of Heaven, which appeared in a large portal for the first time at Senlis (Figure 19). Both of these themes emphasized Mary as the example of the first saved soul. So, too, came new roles for saints, especially Mary and John, as intercessors on behalf of humankind. Humanism in the university engendered humane themes that replaced the threats of divine punishment with the choice of salvation.

With Paris firmly established as the intellectual center of Europe came its role as style and fashion leader. Like Rayonnant architecture, mid-thirteenth-century Gothic sculpture soon became the European standard. A flourishing sculptural industry supplied statues of the Virgin and Child for clients as far away as Avignon in southern France while the style itself was imported by and also subjected to a number of important local variants in Normandy, England (principally London), Champagne, and the Lorraine right through the fourteenth century. In the fifteenth century, Parisian art inspired sculptors from Troyes to Bohemia, Austria, and other areas of the empire to create their own elegant, courtly variants. Even at Reims, with its strong identification with antique sculpture, the Parisian style was co-opted by local sculptors as early as the 1240s.

And within the framework of courtly Parisian elegance, other ideas emerged. One of the first individualized portraits, for example, is said to be that of the sainted French king Louis IX, created not long after his death in 1270. Related in idea are a remarkable series of individualized likenesses that create the illusion of portraiture at Naumberg, except that those depicted were long dead when the images were carved and painted. These so-called founders in the eastern choir of Naumberg remind us of the important role of interior sculpture in the Gothic period. Naumberg (Figure 26) is one of the rare buildings in which the original sculpted choir screens—two of them because the church has two apses—are intact and well preserved. Unfortunately, most of the interior sculpture of the Gothic period was swept away and replaced in later epochs. Fragments of the original choir screens, which separated the canons and clergy from the congregation, at Bourges, Chartres, and Amiens are preserved in those cathedrals and in the local museums. The side sections of the choir enclosure of Notre-Dame in Paris are still in place, preserved only because they hid the backs of the eighteenth-century stalls; fragments of the destroyed front section, the choir screen or *jubé*, are now in the Louvre.

By the middle of the fourteenth century, sculpture reflects a heightened sense of emotion and general anxiety felt across a western Europe deeply divided by debilitating wars and by the catastrophic effects of the Black Death. The devastations of the Hundred Years War only added to the sense of unease and impending doom. The stylized beauty of the early fourteenth century gave way to a new sense of threat and impending doom acted out in horrific detail and heightened by a new kind of exaggerated hyperrealism. The themes changed to reflect the psychological dislocation caused by the continuing disasters and famines. Devotion be-

came both more private and more fervent; themes of sorrow and suffering abound. Most of the major cathedral programs of sculpture had been set and executed in the thirteenth century, so the emphasis in later medieval sculpture was on interior monuments, such as tombs and other works. One of the more popular sculptural themes was a large—in size and number—depiction of the Entombment of Christ. Around an open sarcophagus containing the very dead body of Christ are gathered a group of six or more figures in poses of great anguish and deep mourning. Entombment groups generally displace the usual scene of the Three Marys discovering the tomb emptied by the Resurrection of Christ. The Resurrection extended a promise of Salvation through sacrifice central to Christianity; but the Entombment did not offer such optimism to the viewer, only the specter of the finality of death.

STAINED GLASS

One of the most original and important aesthetic developments of the Gothic period was the exploitation of the medium of stained glass. Stained glass was not "invented" in the Gothic period, yet the increasingly larger windows in Gothic cathedrals encouraged the use of it in new ways. Stained glass, so named because the mineral colors are dissolved directly in the molten glass—as opposed to being painted on the surface—was used in windows at least as early as the fifth and sixth centuries. The earliest surviving examples indicate that windows with imagery displayed single, standing figures of Christ, the Apostles, or saints. Several heavily restored seventh-century English examples attest to the type.

Such figural windows with their various colors demanded a sophisticated understanding of the thermal technology involved; that is, different temperatures for each color were necessary because of the varying mineral content needed to obtain the colors. Indeed, the addition of painted details for the patterns in the clothing or the details in the faces required still different degrees of heat. The technology is most closely related to metalworking and enameling, both of which also demand the ability to work with and to regulate the high temperatures required.

Designs for figural windows would have been worked out at full size on a worktable probably covered with the same kind of fine sand used to make glass. Once the design was established, then came the decisions about colors—reds and blues were particularly popular, especially after the discovery of hard blue glass in Rome—and the gathering of pieces that had been cut to fit the design. All glass was still produced the way it had been since its discovery in ancient Egypt, that is, by forcing air through a tube until the molten glass formed a bubble. While it was still hot enough to work with, the glass was cut off the pipe, split, and flattened as much as possible. Since the color was in the glass itself, thickness determined the density of the color. The flattened pieces were then cut into the shapes to fit the design. After they had been laid out on the pattern, those that required details were painted with a special iron oxide paint that allowed the artist to outline the features of the face, to suggest shadows by flicking little drops of paint on the surface, or to indicate the patterns in garments or folds of drapery. These pieces were then put back in the oven with a borax flux so that the paint melted and literally fused to the surface of the glass.

When the painting and firing were completed, the pieces were then assembled into panels using strips of H-shaped lead, called calmes, wrapped around the edges of the pieces and soldered together until the predetermined panel size was reached. Panels could have a variety of shapes, but in early single-figure windows they are usually square or rectangular and rarely more than eighteen to twenty-four inches square, so that the completed panel might be inserted into the iron armature of the window. The iron offered support that the lead calmes did not and was used to frame the panels in the window opening. Even a small window might require several panels of framing to support the weight of the glass. Before the leading was put in place, the panels were attached to a clear sheet of glass, most likely by beeswax, and held up to the light to check the relationships between the colors and the clarity of the composition. It was at this time, before being attached by the calmes, that adjustments to the color balance could be made. In short, working in stained glass demanded not only knowledge of rather sophisticated thermal technology but also experience with light conditions and a variety of other factors. It is hardly surprising that stained glass windows were enormously expensive, highly valued, and greatly appreciated. The glowing, colored light emanating from these windows not only defined the sacred space but must also have been reminiscent of the jewels adorning those richly decorated reliquary boxes behind the altars.

The next stage of the development of stained glass in the Middle Ages seems to have happened almost simultaneously with the creation of the first Gothic buildings and the introduction of proportionately larger windows. The new spatial openness and the increased size of the windows offered the stained glass masters new design possibilities, including the development of many narrative scenes filling in the windows. Although early Gothic spaces and multiscene windows have an almost symbiotic relationship, there is no causal relationship. Rather, it appears to be a mutually beneficial exploitation of the possibilities afforded by the new spatial openness and the new, proportionately larger windows. Multiscene windows rapidly appear in the second quarter of the twelfth century, particularly in the spaces of the building reserved for monks or clergy (patrons). And though it appears most likely that the programmers who chose the subjects took their inspiration from compositions in illuminated manuscripts, there is clear evidence that the window designers creatively adapted compositions to fit the medallion format into which the window scenes were arranged. The window of the Infancy of Christ in the abbey church of St.-Denis is one such example. The three tall lancet windows, illustrating the Infancy of Christ, the Passion of Christ, and the royal genealogy of Mary and Christ in the form of the Tree of Jesse, in the west facade of Chartres Cathedral (Figure 17) are also fine examples of the multiscene format. In their present arrangement, these three windows present problems of visibility from the floor of the cathedral nave. They originally opened into the upper room of a narthex constructed between the two cathedral towers, but it was torn out in the sixteenth century, enormously increasing the viewing distance beyond what was intended.

Single-figure windows by no means disappeared after the arrival of multiscene windows, as the survival of the famous image of the Virgin at Chartres demonstrates. Rather, they simply got bigger as the size of the window increased. Medallion windows, that is, windows with multiple scenes arranged in medallions, whether square, round, rectangular, or even lozenge-shaped (c. 1200), required that the intended viewer be able to get close enough to read the scenes and to understand their messages. Curvilinear armatures in more complex patterns appeared c. 1200 in a number of cathedral workshops. The diversity of armature design was parallel to the iconographic sophistication of the programs, which included many more complex themes drawn from the lives of saints and even sermons. In the first half of the thirteenth century French stained glass windows were comprised of figural medallions set against dense mosaic backgrounds of alternating red and blue. In the course of the thirteenth century the armatures became straight and no longer followed the medallion patterns. After the middle of the thirteenth century the colors were generally lightened to permit an overall higher level of interior light. Simultaneously compositions were also simplified to improve visibility.

Such medallion compositions were not used in clerestory windows, where each image would be impossible to see from the ground level. For that reason, they were used in lower, ground-level windows, even when, in the thirteenth century, such windows rose forty to fifty feet in the air. While the surviving windows themselves demonstrate the ability of the artists to simplify both the compositions and the colors to make the imagery carry over a distance, medallion windows rarely appeared in upper levels prior to the fourteenth and fifteenth centuries.

Clerestory windows, on the other hand, were appropriate places to display single figures or combinations of figures, as in the choir clerestory at Reims, where the upper figures are Apostles and prophets standing over images of bishops paired with representations of their churches. At Bourges the programmer constructed a complex scheme to be read from the position of the priest celebrating Mass at the high altar. Looking upward from that spot, the celebrant beheld the giant figures of Bourges's two most important patron saints, St. Stephen and St. William of Bourges. Visible in the next lower level of windows were the two medallion windows that recounted the history of the two saints. Thus, the iconic images of the saints were visible directly above the windows that explained their respective importance in the history of Christianity at Bourges.

The rich saturated colors of the stained glass created in the first century of the Gothic are without comparison in the history of medieval art; but in those few buildings that retain a high percentage of the original glass, for example, the nave at Chartres, the light level is deliberately so low that the architecture is difficult to read. After the middle of the thirteenth century the colors in the windows were lightened, and white or translucent glass was increasingly employed as a means of setting off the compositions, which were themselves increasingly simplified. Figures were reduced to the minimum number required to tell the story, settings almost completely disappeared, and the rich mosaic backgrounds of color and pattern were reduced in complexity and intensity, all of which served to make the iconography readable. This period also saw the increased use of grisaille (gray glass), which was often filled with pattern, although without color. The band window, also introduced toward the middle of the thirteenth century, mixed accents of color in the grisaille patterning. All these changes increased the general interior light level and made it possible to appreciate the increased complexity and richness of the architectural ornament characteristic of the Rayonnant and later styles. Stained glass continued to be used throughout the fifteenth and sixteenth centuries. Frequently in these later periods, the colors and compositions of the windows reflected the latest stylistic developments in northern panel (oil) painting.

LATE GOTHIC VARIANTS, 1300–1500

Flamboyant (flame-like), based on the sinuous, curvilinear tracery patterns that resemble tongues of flame, is the name given in the nineteenth century to French Late Gothic art from the later fourteenth to the sixteenth centuries. Curvilinear tracery patterns began to appear in the late thirteenth century, side by side with the more generally regular Rayonnant and Decorated patterns. The extraordinary west facade of Strasbourg Cathedral (Figure 31), begun in 1277, is an excellent example of the continuation and development of Rayonnant forms and the love of screens of tracery. These distinguishing stylistic characteristics are here carried right into the Late Gothic in the upper parts of this facade. The development can be followed in the architectural drawings preserved in the Musée de l'Oeuvre Notre-Dame on the south side of the cathedral.

The three basic forms of Flamboyant tracery are (1) the tightly pointed ogee (or reversed curve) arch; (2) the "mouchette" (tadpole-shaped); and (3) the "soufflet" (leaflike). The arcs that define all three of these complex forms were drawn from multiple center points within the form (the traditional position) and now from points outside the form. That is, they are still based on complex geometries and the manipulation of geometric forms. The full vocabulary of Flamboyant forms began to appear with some regularity only at the end of the fourteenth century and persisted, with the exception of the hiatus in construction during the Hundred Years War, until the early sixteenth century.

Through most of the fourteenth century in France the Flamboyant was restricted to window tracery. By the end of the Hundred Years War the style had been extended to a new conception of space in simplified, streamlined, often angular building plans based on interconnecting cells that blurred the distinctions between different parts of the church, as between the ambulatory and the radiating chapels. Those blurred distinctions extended to the architectural elements themselves, where both the capitals and bases of the piers might be eliminated to permit the eye to flow directly from the floor through the vault ribs that now seemed scattered across the vault surface in ways that defied the traditional visual logic in favor of a new kind of spatial illusionism. In addition, there are frequent, jarring contrasts between abstract, prismatic forms and extremely naturalistic foliate ornament populated by identifiable birds and miniature animals. The inventiveness and even whimsy of the Flamboyant are often expressed in these miniature forms, which grace not only the buildings but their furnishings as well.

The English chronological and stylistic equivalent to the Flamboyant is the Perpendicular style that flourished from the later fourteenth to the sixteenth centuries. Specifically, the term *Perpendicular* refers to the style that grew out of the designs for St. Stephen's Chapel (after 1292) in Westminster Palace in London. The essence of the Perpendicular is a regularly repeating sequence of linear, crystalline forms, resulting in a thin, transparent structure exploiting the effects of stained glass on the interior. The Perpendicular was developed from the same sources as the English Decorated and, like it, shared in the taste for thin, attenuated linear forms and exquisite, minuscule decoration; but Perpendicular designers marshaled the forms into repeating oblong grids that covered walls, windows, and even vault surfaces. The English occupation of Normandy after 1416 exposed English builders to the Flamboyant then current in Rouen, which served to reinforce the English taste for curvilinear forms. The nave of Canterbury Cathedral (1377–1423) is one of the largest and most complete examples of the Perpendicular, which is more often associated with an overlay of ornament on an existing structure, such as the choir and transept of Gloucester Cathedral, than with new structures.

As a stylistic term, *Late Gothic* dates from the nineteenth century, but because of the many outstanding examples in Germany, eastern Europe, and the Iberian Peninsula, it has never had the negative, even pejorative associations that, for example, have prevented the Flamboyant from receiving an accurate assessment. For far too long the Flamboyant has, unfortunately, been seen as lacking in comparison with earlier stages of

the Gothic in France, but this has not been the case in Germany, Bohemia, or Spain. Late Gothic in Germany and eastern Europe is dated
to the mid-fourteenth-century development of the new spatial concept
represented by the hall church. This is a building in which the side aisles
are as tall as the central nave and choir, so interior light must come from
the windows, often stacked in two levels, in the aisle walls. The main
space then has a single story of tall, increasingly slender piers. The patterns of the main vaults will likewise be extended to the aisle spaces binding the entire building together under the lightest of webs, but webs of
dynamic, expressive tendencies that often relate to the outer walls. The
works of the Parler family in northern Germany and Bohemia, from
Schwabische Gmund to Prague (Figure 33), are noteworthy examples of
these illusionistic features. The new merchant towns of the north built
cathedral-size churches that, because of their expansive, illusionistic interiors, can be read as expressions of their mercantile power. The plain
exteriors of these churches, from Nuremberg to Nordlingen, give no hint
of their extraordinary, visionary interiors, some of the most original designs in all of Gothic architecture.

While the Flamboyant has not yet enjoyed the recognition it deserves,
the same cannot be said for other European Late Gothic styles, from the
English Perpendicular to the original spatial achievements that distinguish buildings in northern Europe, from Germany, Bohemia, and Austria to the Iberian Peninsula. The Late Gothic of Spain and Portugal
reflects the Spanish preference for variations on elaborate French models, combined with the decorative exuberance of the rich Islamic past,
whereas Catalonia and the off-shore islands of the Kingdom of Majorca
produced highly individual cathedrals. There builders constructed vast
hall-like spaces of great height and width covered by thin vaults of prodi-
gious spans. One of the most striking examples is the cathedral at Girona
(Figure 34), which was begun in 1310 on a conventional plan of a choir
with ambulatory and radiating chapels, but was then, after 1416, revised
with a single nave space significantly taller and wider than the earlier
choir. The cathedral at Palma (Figure 35) is another huge space filled
with tall prismatic piers that lack both bases and capitals and that raise
the aisles to impressive heights. In that sense, Palma might almost seem
a prediction of the cathedral of Milan (Figure 37), begun a century later
as a reflection of the prestige of the Visconti family, several members of
which dreamed of uniting all of Italy under their rule. In northern Eu-

rope, Late Gothic churches of extraordinary vision and originality were built right through the end of the Middle Ages. The cathedral at Antwerp (Figure 36) is not particularly tall, but with seven aisles, slender piers, and the other accoutrements of the Late Gothic creates an impressive spaciousness. The new cathedral at Salamanca (Figure 38), begun in 1512, carried the Spanish Gothic spirit right into the seventeenth century. These illusionistic visions of Paradise gave way to Baroque fantasies in the eighteenth century.

CHAPTER 5

NOTRE-DAME AT REIMS: THE CATHEDRAL OF FRANCE

We discussed Reims Cathedral briefly in the Introduction, and in the chapters that followed examined questions of planning, construction, patrons, and builders. Now it is time to explore this magnificent church in greater depth. As this chapter demonstrates, each cathedral is a set of different problems with individual solutions to suit the needs of the patrons. Like most cathedrals, the cathedral of Reims that we visit today is not the project that was first conceived, nor is it the building that was largely completed by the 1290s. In addition, the intended meanings have changed a number times. This chapter focuses on the history of the construction and some of the meanings that can be recovered through a careful reading of the sculpture, stained glass, and furnishings. We are fortunate because the cathedral of Reims has more sculpture decorating its portals and architecture than any other medieval cathedral and, as a consequence, more opportunities to investigate meanings. Our knowledge of its stained glass is almost adequate, although other buildings (Chartres and Bourges, for example) preserve greater quantities of their original medieval glass. In addition, we know the original locations of the main altar and other furnishings in the cathedral. All these factors make it possible to reconstruct a partial picture of the church as it was intended to look at several important moments in its history.

EARLIER HISTORY

Shortly before 900, Archbishop Fulco wrote that St. Peter himself had sent Bishop Sixtus to Reims and had appointed him primate over all other bishops in Gaul. In reality, Sixtus founded the diocese only in the second half of the third century, but nothing is known of his church. The first known cathedral, which must have been at least the second or third building, was dedicated to the Holy Apostles and built in the fourth century. This structure, which later became a parish church, was located some 300 meters east of the present cathedral. Bishop Nicasius, who moved the cathedral, now dedicated to Notre-Dame, to the present site, was martyred in the doorway of the church in 407 by the Vandals. The archeological evidence suggests that Nicasius's church might have been, not a new construction, but a conversion of two rooms (into church and baptistry) in the fourth-century Roman public bath complex.

The foundations of the original altar in this early church and of the Carolingian high altar, about three meters to the west, are still in place under the present high altar. The limits of the enclosure around the earlier altar site were used as the dimensions of the crossing in the Carolingian church. The foundations of the west door in which Nicasius is said to have died have also been found. West of this entrance was the baptistry, the site of the baptism of Clovis by Bishop Remigius (discussed in the next section).

Largely known through archeology, the ninth-century Carolingian cathedral was a large, aisled basilica with a prominent transept crowned by a tall crossing tower with a painted ceiling. At the west end was an elaborate, multichambered *westwerk* with twin towers and upper chapels. This was torn down and supplanted by a large central tower in the late tenth century. In the middle of the twelfth century, under the impetus of Archbishop Samson de Mauvoisin (1140–60), this tower was replaced by a new, Early Gothic, twin-towered facade. Samson, who had assisted at the dedication of one of the most important Early Gothic structures, the new chevet of the abbey church of St.-Denis in 1144, probably encouraged the building of the new choir at Reims. Excavations have revealed the foundations of this elaborate choir plan with an ambulatory and seven radiating chapels, as well as literally hundreds of architectural pieces, including capitals, molded bases, vault ribs, window moldings, and other decorative elements. There is enough evidence, in fact, to re-create a reasonable image of this important structure and to indicate its influence on the present cathedral.

THE CATHEDRAL AS THE CORONATION SITE

In popular imagination the cathedral of Reims has been best known as the coronation church of French kings for over five hundred years, and it has maintained that distinction right into the present century, even though the last king was crowned there in 1825. The primacy claim of Reims was based on two things: the baptism (and conversion) of Clovis, sometime between 497 and 508, by St. Remigius, bishop of Reims; and the unction, the anointing of Clovis with oil, also performed by Remigius. The first event was recounted in the sixth century by Gregory of Tours, but the second appeared only in the ninth-century account of Bishop Hincmar. He also added the story of the miraculous appearance of a dove (rapidly identified as the Holy Spirit) bearing in its beak a vial of holy oil with which Remigius anointed Clovis. Anointing with oil was a rite reserved in the Old Testament for kings (David and Saul) and high priests of the Temple. For the latter reason it had been adopted by Early Christians for the consecration of bishops. Although anointment during the coronation ceremony may have been borrowed from earlier Anglo-Saxon practice, it gave the king of France a quasi-religious status enjoyed by no other medieval kings. Hincmar was the first archbishop of Reims to crown a king, in 869, but at Metz, rather than at Reims. The first French king crowned in Reims Cathedral by the archbishop was Henry I, in 1027. After Henry I, however, every king of France, save two, was crowned at Reims by the presiding archbishop of Reims until 1825. In all, twenty-nine kings were crowned at Reims between 1027 and 1825.

Until the end of the Middle Ages the actual ceremony was not a public event but took place in private at the high altar in the crossing of the cathedral and was attended only by the six bishops and the six barons who were the peers of France. At the end of the ceremony the newly crowned king was presented to the people from atop the choir screen for acclamation. While the only documented choir screen, known now from the drawing by Jacques Cellier, was constructed in 1416, most likely there was an earlier, possibly temporary, jubè built c. 1241 or before (and copied at Strasbourg c. 1250). Before this date, acclamation by the people may have taken the form of a procession through the city, like the procession that welcomed the king on his arrival for coronation. The surviving coronation texts make it clear that the actual ceremony was developed over the course of the thirteenth century, perhaps even in response to the construction of the cathedral.

THE BUILDING HISTORY, INTRODUCTION

All histories of the construction of the present cathedral have always dated its beginning to the years immediately following the fire of 6 May 1210. This is the date when the composite structure—Carolingian nave and transept framed by an early Gothic facade and choir—is thought to have burned. Older histories assumed that the entire church burned, whereas more modern ones argued that only the choir was damaged. Recent discoveries, based on dendrochronological analysis of the timber plugs left in place when the scaffolding was removed from the main arcade piers and responds, have confounded even this interpretation. Dendrochronological analysis, comparison of the growth rings in timber with an established scale, has confirmed that all of the timbers used in the construction of the new choir do, indeed, postdate the fire of 1210. The timbers in the eastern bays of the nave that correspond to the canon's choir, however, *predate* the fire, which means that construction on the new cathedral probably started there between 1204 and 1208. Freshly cut timber cannot be used in construction until it has dried out and shrunk slightly, a process that probably took about two years. Thus, timbers dated 1205 and 1206 by dendrochronology would have been used in construction in 1207, 1208, or later. In addition, the massive foundations in the area of the crossing, which are over twelve meters (nearly forty feet) deep and almost as wide, suggest that a massive new tower was also being planned.

Two other events might also have had an impact on the starting date of the new cathedral. The first was an eclipse of the sun, which would have been seen as an auspicious omen. Astronomers have calculated that a total eclipse of the sun was visible in Reims between 11 AM and 12 noon on 28 February 1207. The second was the installation of new archbishop, Aubry de Humbert, elected before that date and installed on 1 July 1207. Archbishop Aubry's obituary notice recorded his generosity to the chapter, including assigning the income derived from fifteen altars, a number of churches, and other properties in the diocese, all of which was to ensure funding for the construction. In addition, he ceded to them a substantial parcel of land from the archepiscopal plot for the enlargement of the new choir. The obituary notice, however, does not record the exact dates when these gifts, among others, were made, only that they had been made prior to the archbishop's death on 24 December 1218. Every scholar who has studied the cathedral has assumed the gifts were made in the years after the fire in 1210, but it now seems more likely that they were offered earlier. The assignment of income from altars and churches throughout the diocese might have been made at the time the archbishop took possession of the see in 1207, partly to quell opposition in the chapter to his election.

In addition to the twelfth-century choir, some of the new construction in the nave and crossing area might also have been damaged in the fire, for the first thing that took place after the fire was that the nave was closed off by means of a temporary wall erected across it one bay west of the crossing. Services would have been transferred to the nave because the liturgical life of the cathedral had to continue without interruption, irrespective of damage. Closing off the nave and preparing the area of the old choir for reconstruction must have taken place rapidly after the fire because in the space of a single year not only had the site been prepared, but the stone from the damaged church had been buried to form a great foundation mat on which the new building would rise. And the foundations of the new east end were already constructed up to ground level because on 6 May 1211, one year to the day after the fire, the cornerstone, a ceremonial block laid at ground level (or above) that commemorated (rather than indicated) the beginning of construction, was installed on the south side in the presence of the archbishop and chapter. Analysis of the foundations indicates that whereas their construction was marked by stops and changes, the upper construction was relatively straightforward. It was started in the choir aisle bays on both sides simultaneously and moved eastward until the two sides came together in the axial radiating chapel. While the actual construction started with the outside wall, planning and layout started from the interior, in this case from the position of the high altar in the Carolingian church, which determined the location of the high altar in the new cathedral, and from the dimensions of the crossing that surrounded it. Since the new evidence suggests that the crossing was planned in conjunction with the canon's choir before 1210, then the plan of the new choir could easily have been established from this point after the fire in 1210. The sheer size and scale of the undertaking is an indication of the financial resources available to the chapter.

FOUR IMPORTANT DOCUMENTS

Because of the quantity of archeological and documentary evidence concerning the construction, we will examine four documents that have particular bearing on the building before analyzing the church itself. Other evidence can be gleaned from the records of the now-destroyed labyrinth that was set in the floor of the nave. And we should consider the two major civic uprisings against the chapter and the archbishop, if only because, like the two coronations, they seem to have had almost no discernable impact on the building and its meanings.

The first document is a contract issued on the day of the cornerstone laying, 6 May 1211, in which the archbishop gave his approval to the chapter's purchase of tithes (pledges of income) owned by a German knight, Milo, and his wife, Basilia. The contract specified that the purchased revenues were reserved for the endowment and upkeep of the chapels of St. Nicaise and St. Calixtus. In the completed choir, the chapel of St. Nicaise was the first to the left (north side) of the axial chapel, while that of St. Calixtus is in the south choir aisle, near the cornerstone. This contract is a rare surviving example of advance planning for the upkeep of chapels. Such preparations normally occurred only as construction was nearing completion. For example, when Hugues d'Epernay, in 1220, founded two chaplaincies at the altar of St. Nicholas, the last radiating chapel on the south side, the chapel was probably completed and ready for services.

The second document is a letter from the archbishop giving the chapter permission to celebrate a special Mass in honor of the Virgin at the altar in the chapel of St. James (the center chapel) in July 1221. If this altar was ready to be put in service, it means that the other chapels, as well as the aisles and ambulatory that give access to them, were also completed. The axial chapel could not have been used without interior access for the canons because they could *not* have used areas still under construction. In short, all the chapels, straight bay and radiating, as well as the aisle and ambulatory bays were completed through the vaults and the lean-to roof over them.

The third document is an entry in the chronicle of the abbey of St.-Nicaise at Reims (Document 45) that states that on the vigil of the Nativity of Mary (7 September) in 1241, the chapter of Reims moved into the new *chevet*, the French word for the choir. A systematic examination of the building fabric indicates that much more of the building than the architectural choir was completed. The transept and the liturgical choir (the four eastern bays of the nave that housed the canon's seats) must also have been finished. Also, given the usual sequence of building, the outer walls of several additional nave aisle bays were certainly in place, perhaps even vaulted and roofed. A tall building like Reims was constructed not in vertical slices but in stepped layers. Examination of the lower nave aisle walls indicates that at least four more bays beyond the limit of the choir had been started on both sides, perhaps as early as 1207, as noted.

The last document, dated 1252, indicates that the new west facade has been planned but was not yet under construction. The document is the fulfillment of a contract drawn up in 1230 between the Hôtel-Dieu (hospital) and the renters of two small houses in the path of the new west facade. This 1230 contract stated that the houses would have to be vacated at the time they needed to be destroyed in order to build the new facade. This, in fact, is what happened on 8 April 1252. The evidence is somewhat ambiguous, so the inferences must be carefully drawn. That the houses were to be vacated in 1252 obviously indicates that they were still standing and, therefore, that construction of the new facade had not yet started. So the only solid conclusion that can be drawn from the document is that the new west facade was started after April 1252.

On examining later documents concerning the construction, it is interesting to note that though a number mention construction and, after a point, repairs, no document states that the cathedral was completed. In a sense that is correct because the building has always required constant ongoing maintenance, restoration, and repair. Construction of the western towers dragged on into the fifteenth century, but they never received the tall stone spires that were planned for them. Plans to build the spires were no doubt derailed by the fire that destroyed the roof in

1481, which may also have stopped construction of the four corner towers intended for the transept. Except for the towers and spires, the majority of the church was completed by the early to mid-1290s.

THE LABYRINTH

Another piece of evidence commonly evoked in discussions of the
construction sequence at Reims is the destroyed labyrinth. Originally installed in the floor of the third and fourth bays of the nave (counting
from the west), this design of inlaid dark stone lines had a central octagon and four small octagons on the angled sides to create a full square.
In the center space and the four corner spaces were placed images of
standing figures engaged in operations related to building. The labyrinth
was destroyed in 1778 and is now known only through a drawing made
by Jacques Cellier (c. 1600) that records its worn condition. In addition,
there have been at least five attempts to decipher the fragmented inscriptions. Correlating this information, however, reveals that the
labyrinth contained images of four or five builders—the center image was
too worn to be identified and had no traces of the inscription—paired
with only four inscriptions that included their names, length of service,
and the parts of the building on which each one worked. The fact that
only four are known by name does not preclude the presence of others.
Indeed, after a painstakingly detailed analysis, one French scholar con-
cluded that there may have been as many as eleven different builders, a
good reminder that any analysis of the labyrinth will always remain hy-
pothetical.

In general terms, we can speak of four or five major building periods.
The first is the rebuilding of the canon's choir in the eastern bays of the
nave; that is neither mentioned nor represented in the labyrinth, although it was probably directed by Jean d'Orbais, the first builder named
in the labyrinth. The second building period, however, was associated in
the labyrinth with Jean d'Orbais, the chief designing personality. He was
probably in charge from the beginning of construction, c. 1206–8, until
1221, when the lower level of the choir was turned over to the clergy.
The inscription indicated that he began the "coiffe" (the head, meaning
the apse of the choir) but made no mention of the canon's choir. The
drawing associated with the inscription showed a builder tracing the layout of an apse with its angled divisions indicated. Jean le Loup, the sec-

ond builder recorded in the labyrinth, continued the main lines of the first design, but he also made the most sophisticated engineering and structural decisions in the upper stories. The inscription indicated that he was in charge for sixteen years, which would have him in charge from 1221 until 1237. But if we factor in the four years lost because of the strife between the townspeople and the chapter, then he could have been in charge right up to 1241, when the clergy took charge of the choir.

The third builder named and represented in the labyrinth, Gaucher de Reims, has traditionally been the least well-defined artistic personality because of the problematic interpretations of the inscription that put him in control of the works for either as little as seven years or as many as eighteen years. The inscription added that he worked on the "voussures" (English *voussoirs*, the sculpted arches around the portals) and the portals. Since another document indicates that he was still in Reims in 1256, Gaucher is more likely to have been director for the longer term, eighteen years (1241–1258/9) and, therefore, to have been the first designer of the west facade. The last-named builder, Bernard de Soissons, is said to have been in charge for thirty-five years, to have made five vaults and to have opened the big "O." Thus, Bernard would have been in place until 1293 or 1294. The big "O" is most likely a reference to the west rose window, the centerpiece of the upper half of the facade, which suggests that he may have completed the portals and all the facade above them. Bernard was the builder who installed the gallery of kings at the top of the facade, perhaps in connection with the 1287 coronation of Philippe le Bel. This is the first time that the role of Reims as the coronation church of kings is emphasized in the sculpture, although the eastern nave clerestory windows reflected themes from the texts of the coronation rite.

THE CATHEDRAL OF JEAN D'ORBAIS

It is clear that from the beginning of construction the new cathedral of Reims was intended to surpass all its contemporaries in size and in complexity, as befits the dignity of *the* cathedral of France. This is evident in Jean d'Orbais's pre-1210 work, but especially in his plan for the east end (Figure 1) and in the design for the aisles, radiating chapels, chapel walls, windows, and vaults. As a result of a change in the sequence and the pattern of construction employed in the exterior wall

(Figure 4), it is evident that Jean d'Orbais reconceptualized the process. Instead of the traditional technique of continuous horizontal courses of stone along the length and the entire height of the wall, Jean d'Orbais laid out only the lowest horizontal levels in this traditional manner. Above the plinth (the tall base molding) he first built only the vertical points of support, the wall piers, probably to the level of the window opening, possibly higher. This technique allowed him to mark out the supports in the eastern nave bays and around the entire periphery rather rapidly and then to come back later and fill in the wall between the piers, including the windows. The window is no longer just a hole punched through the wall surface. As a result of the change in building technique, the window is now defined as an opening created by the two vertical wall piers and the arch that connects them.

The way in which Jean d'Orbais conceived and designed the actual window opening is an indication of his advanced thinking. He made the interior and the exterior come together in the window opening and turned it into a design surface using long, thin, carved stone moldings called bar tracery to create a pattern of two tall, pointed lancet openings supporting a round, cusped oculus. This window tracery consists of three separate layers of thin, carved stonework. The inner and outer layers are the carved moldings and thin shafts, identical on both interior and exterior, that give form to the design, while the center layer of thin masonry is that into which the stained glass was inserted. In other words, Jean d'Orbais filled the opening with design to create the window rather than simply punching a hole through a wall surface.

Analysis of other components in his design indicates that Jean d'Orbais also rethought each architectural element with an eye to standardizing the sizes of the pieces of stone and, thereby, simplifying the actual building process. Standardization allowed him to have more of the building under construction simultaneously because it meant he did not have to supervise every step individually. At the same time, it allowed him a greater measure of control over the process. This attitude informs the thinking of all his successors at Reims, each of whom added individual changes to the design and refined the building process. To the visitor's eye the cathedral of Reims exhibits a remarkable unity from beginning to end, whereas the specialist observes a succession of minor changes, all of them within the basic conceptual framework established by Jean d'Orbais.

Figure 4. Reims, Cathedral of Notre-Dame. Exterior of East End. *Photograph: Department of Art History, University of Trier (Germany), photographic archive, bequest Richard Hamann-MacLean.*

JEAN LE LOUP AND THE FLYING BUTTRESSES AT REIMS

If Jean d'Orbais created new standards in design and technology with his reconception of the window with bar tracery, then his successor, Jean le Loup, must be recognized as his equal, especially for his simplification in window tracery technique and his design of the flying buttresses. The change in the tracery was a change not in design but in the technique of creating it. What had been a sandwich of three layers under Jean d'Orbais became under his successor a single piece including all three components.

When Jean le Loup succeeded Jean d'Orbais about 1221, this phase of the construction was marked by a donation of land from the cathedral treasurer in the same year. This has been interpreted as an indication of the intention to enlarge the transept, a decision that would have been among the first made by the new builder. By the end of his tenure in 1241, when the canons took possession of the choir on 7 September, the east end and the transept had been joined to the first five nave bays west of the crossing, and all these areas were completed.

The first two things Jean le Loup accomplished were (1) the completion of the upper stories of the east end and (2) the continuation of the nave aisle bays west of the canon's choir, using the construction technique pioneered by Jean d'Orbais. Since two royal coronations were held at Reims in 1223 and 1226, in the canon's choir bays of the nave, it is doubtful that anything more had been started in the new nave, since Jean le Loup would have first completed the upper parts of the choir and the transept before continuing the nave.

One of the first steps Jean le Loup took toward finishing the choir was the construction of the clerestory wall and the flying buttresses that braced it. Jean d'Orbais had laid out and erected the first level of the buttress piers, but everything above that was finished by Jean le Loup (Figure 5). The evidence suggests that, as discussed in an earlier chapter, flying buttresses were first thought to be braces against the forces resulting from the weight and the pressure distribution of the high vaults. The lower range of flyers at Reims are, indeed, perfectly positioned for this role. The upper flyers, however, may well be the result of firsthand experience with the observed structural behavior of flying buttresses at Notre-Dame in Paris c. 1220–25. Since the upper level of Reims was

Figure 5. Reims, Cathedral of Notre-Dame. Interior of Choir. *Photograph: Hirmer Verlag Fotoarchiv, Munich.*

begun at just that moment, the change was directly incorporated in the design. The experience at Paris indicated that the flying buttress was, in fact, not a necessary support for the high vaults, but during major storms, it was an absolutely essential brace against wind pressure on the roof. As Gothic churches were being built taller and taller—Reims among them—builders had to learn to cope with an increased level of wind pressure and the resulting problems that previous generations had never faced. Interior heights of 100-plus feet with a roof adding another 25–30 feet resulted in an enormous sloping surface at an unprecedented height that was vulnerable to geometrically increased wind pressures. The result of experience with wind pressure is almost immediately visible in the change in flying buttress design to meet the challenge: the upper flyer arch at Reims is raised to counter the effect of wind against the roof. The tall stone pinnacles added on top of the outer perimeter of the buttresses were the final technological and design refinement that confirms this understanding of wind pressure. These pinnacles served as counterweights against lateral wind pressure on the buttresses themselves.

THE CIVIC UPRISINGS IN REIMS

Before discussing the work of the last two named builders at Reims, we should take note of the two civic uprisings that occurred when Jean le Loup was in charge. By all accounts the decades from 1221 to 1241 were not only the most active years of construction at Reims but also the most tumultuous. Two bloody civil uprisings against the chapter and the archbishop resulted in their being driven out of the city on one occasion for two years and two months, during which the cathedral workshop was attacked and shut down, and on the second for nearly a year. The building itself, however, reveals almost no traces of the extraordinary social upheaval that gripped the city both times. This suggests that the cathedral construction was well funded by the chapter, although that seems to be the case for only the first building period. But it does confirm the power of the chapter to raise money from the townspeople, using the very methods the burghers had failed to curtail in their two attempts to form a commune in the twelfth century. During the first decade of construction, the canons tightened their control over the money supply and over justice in their courts. In the second decade, they resorted to longer indulgences and aggressive quests for money in the other dioceses. In addition, these same years saw the archbishop consolidating his courts of secular and spiritual justice and moving them to his fortified palace at the port of Mars, one of the old Roman city gates. Furthermore, there was a marked increase in the number of sheriff's oaths swearing to protect the person and possessions of the archbishop, just as there were an increasing number of instances in which the archbishop directly restrained and curtailed commercial activities. All these were direct attempts to tighten control over the city.

Furthermore, there were the costs of two coronations in rapid succession. Phillip II (Augustus) died in 1223, after a reign of forty-three years, and his son was crowned as Louis VIII in that same year. Louis is described as a man already made old by almost incessant warfare when he died at barely forty after only forty months on the throne. His twelve-year-old son was crowned as Louis IX in 1226 in what chroniclers describe as a "modest ceremony." The costs of the two coronations have been reliably estimated at 9,053 Parisian pounds, and the construction costs for the first decade have been calculated at 10,000 Parisian pounds. Since the costs of the coronation were directly borne by the citizens of Reims, and the costs of construction were raised from the increased taxes levied by the canons on the properties they controlled, it is no wonder that rebellion broke out in 1234. The fear of being attacked as usurers and burned as heretics, as had happened in another French city in 1233, may well have led to the escalating violence against the canons in September and October 1234. The burghers harassed the canons and openly attacked merchants in their employ, some of whom were even thrown in the river. Placing the city under interdict, the canons fled on 9 November 1234. The burghers then turned on the archbishop's men after he tried to collect a 10 percent tax on their loans to the cities of Auxerre and Troyes. Between April and July 1235 the townspeople stormed his fortress at the port of Mars, killed his marshall, and beat his men in street battles. The cathedral workshop was sacked, building stones were taken for street barricades, and the tombs of earlier archbishops were broken open and sacked.

Repeated pleas from the archbishop and even the pope to young king Louis IX, who had reached his majority in 1234, were ignored until he could work the situation to his advantage and appropriate royal justice in Reims at the expense of ecclesiastical power. Only then did he intervene and restore order. The outcome of the rebellion was a huge reparation of 10,000 Parisian pounds to be paid to the archbishop. The clergy combined the reparations with multiple penitential processions, such as forcing the burghers to march barefoot to the port of Mars in January 1237 to greet the returning archbishop and clergy. Reparations were made payable on the feast of St. Remi, and other penances were demanded on those liturgical occasions when the archbishop presided over rites exclusive to his office, such as at Easter. In spite of all these humiliating measures to enforce archepiscopal and chapter rights over the citizens of Reims, or perhaps because of them, the burghers rioted again in 1238. They seized the archbishop's fortress again, this time with the help of eighty hired bowmen. The dispute was only settled by the death of the archbishop, Henry of Braine, in 1240, with reparations, penance, and even public floggings in front of the cathedral.

GAUCHER DE REIMS, BERNARD DE SOISSONS, AND THE WEST FACADE OF REIMS

The labyrinth inscription stated that the third builder, Gaucher de Reims, was in charge for seven (or eighteen) years and worked on the portals. Since the west facade was begun after 1252, the years after 1241 would have been devoted to tearing down the remainder of the old nave and then constructing the upper parts of the three nave bays west of the canons' choir (Figure 6). It is possible that Gaucher also tore down the old facade and began the new one after 1252, but this is dependent on a time span of eighteen years. If Gaucher was in charge only for seven years, 1241–48, then his work was probably restricted to nave construction, and the last-named builder, Bernard de Soissons, the one who installed the labyrinth, would be the designer of the west facade.

If Gaucher de Reims started the facade after 1252, then Bernard de Soissons certainly built everything above the level of the portals (Figure 7). Several significant decisions set this extravagant facade project, the most grandiose of any Gothic cathedral, apart from its predecessors. Chief among them are the decision to replace the usual carved tympana in each portal with stained glass windows and to remove the intended tympanum themes to the sculptures in the gables over the doorways. But the most unusual decision was to do away with the idea of each portal as a distinct entity and to create a sweeping history of Christianity from its beginning

Figure 6. Reims, Cathedral of Notre-Dame. Interior of Nave. *Photograph: After Propyläen-Kunstgeschichte, 1926.*

to the end of time across the entire facade. The difficulty in distinguishing who designed the lower level of the facade is compounded by the fact that it incorporated statue-columns created over a thirty-year period, at least, beginning in the 1220s. All the hundreds of sculptures in the archivolts of the three portals and on the plaques on the faces of the outer buttresses date from the 1250s–60s. Then, too, all the figures on the interior, on the back wall of the three portals, must also date from the 1250s–60s. The idea of a full program on the reverse of the facade is unique to Reims. The schemes of the last two builders must overlap in one of these areas, but it is too complex to sort here. Scholars agree that above the level of the portals, we are looking at Bernard's design, which extended the themes in sculpture all the way to the gallery of kings at the top, making Reims the most complex facade in Gothic architecture.

THE ARCHBISHOP AND THE CANONS

A cathedral was not just a church; it was an entire section of the city that housed two principal groups associated with the church, the archepiscopal household and the chapter community. The two entities were quite separate: the oath that a new canon took as part of the ritual of his acceptance into the chapter stressed his obligations to that body alone. Episcopal rights with regard to the chapter were negligible at best: the archbishop had to approve the election of the two archdeacons. The two bodies had their own officials to administer justice and no jurisdiction in each other's area of the cathedral precinct or of the city. As duke of Reims, the archbishop had secular powers and responsibilities, but, aside from the prestige of his office, his ability to exercise those powers depended largely on his personality. In contrast, the real power in the city rested with the chapter. The institution of the chapter at Reims coincided closely with the elevation of the bishop to metropolitan status in the eighth century.

The chapter at Reims was exceptionally large and numbered seventy-two canons until 1313, when two more were created. The chapter had eight officers elected from among the members in residence, which usually amounted to about a third. The chapter was headed by the provost, while the dean was in charge of discipline. The cantor was in charge of the choir and all services, so he had the services of the succentor, who was directly in charge of the chaplains (numbering thirty-three in 1274) who sang the services. In addition, there were the two archdeacons, the scholaster (schoolmaster in charge of both schools), and the vidame, who managed the lands of the archbishopric and was in charge of administering justice. Finally, there was the treasurer, who not only handled the money and the liturgical utensils but, in the name of the chapter, also was responsible for the construction of the cathedral. The treasurer hired the builder, paid the accounts, and conveyed the chapter's wishes to the master builder. The complex, multivalent meanings in the sculpture and stained glass suggest that a learned ecclesiastic was the planner of this decoration. In addition, the canons of Reims had a right unique among all other chapters: they divided the services of nineteen *francs-sergents*, chosen from among the bourgeoisie to oversee their business affairs and to manage the income assigned to every canon.

THE CATHEDRAL PRECINCT

Equal in importance in the cathedral precinct were the archepiscopal palace and the canon's cloister. The palace, including the thirteenth-century archepiscopal chapel, survives on the south side of the church. The underground rooms of the palace are built right into the ancient Roman bath complex, but we know nothing of its early form. In addition to the chapel and living quarters of the archbishop and his staff, the complex would have contained various offices for the archepiscopal administration.

The ninth-century cloister and all its surrounding buildings on the north side of the church have disappeared, but the chapter lived together as a community in the cloister until the end of the twelfth century. From old views and documents we know that the central portal of the cathedral's north transept opened into the first of two successive courtyards, one beyond the other. The first, the "little" cloister, was a rectangular garden surrounded by an arcaded gallery, around which were arranged the other core buildings. These included on the west side the chapter house with the archives above it, and on the east side the school of theology, with the cathedral library in the room above it. The north gallery of the cloister was flanked by the parish church of St.-Michael (the original communal dining hall) to the east and the brewery and food storage cellar to the west. Around this inner ring were the necessary support buildings, such as the canon's bakery, the brewery, and the storage cellar. The barn, the grainery, the forge, and the stables were nearby, although their precise locations are no longer known.

In the center of the second courtyard on the north side, known as the canon's court, stood the prison. Grouped near it were those buildings in the precinct that also served the neighborhood beyond, such as the grammar school, a second bakery that furnished bread to those employed by the canons, and the bailiff's office. To the east of these was the long north-south street that crossed the entire precinct, the *rue du Cloître* (Cloister Street). East of it lay the area divided into individual houses and gardens for the canons in residence. Including those to the south and west, there were twenty-six private houses occupied by canons. Initially they were privately owned, but during the thirteenth century ownership passed to the chapter. The treasurer had a private house on the north flank of the nave, as well as offices and a separate structure that housed the cathedral treasury. Further west and bordering the north side of the cathedral facade was the Hôtel-Dieu, the hospital administered by the chapter.

READING REIMS: THE SEARCH FOR MEANINGS

Reims was particularly rich in sculpture and stained glass. We can recover some of the meanings of these sculptural and stained glass programs at Reims, but some cannot be fully explained because of the absence or destructions of texts. Both the sculpture and the stained glass were started when construction of the building was begun. The initial design of Jean d'Orbais would have included both, but that first program of stained glass, in the aisle and radiating chapel windows, was systematically destroyed in the eighteenth century.

THE CHAPEL BUTTRESS FIGURES

The first program of sculptural decoration at Reims remains intact and indicates the sophistication of planning in the multiple meanings that can be read from the figures. It was comprised of twelve figures carved in high relief on the exterior of the radiating chapels just below the cornice at the top of the lower level of the flying buttress piers and on the chapel wall buttresses (Figure 4). The series begins on the northernmost buttress pier adjacent to the first radiating chapel and continues around the east end through the first chapel on the south side. (The last chapel on the south side, as well as the two buttress piers flanking it, has no figures and was never intended to have any.) The twelve figures include Christ carrying a book, preceded by five angels with processional objects (censers, incense burners of several types, a scepter or mace, and a crown) and followed by six angels carrying books, reliquaries, a holy water bucket, and a processional cross. In short, the group has the look of a liturgical procession, similar to that which would have performed the dedication of the east end. The figure of Christ is placed not at the center of the axial radiating chapel but on the pier buttress to the north of it, which means, in effect, that he is looking to the east of the cathedral in the direction of the Roman city gate, which still existed in the thirteenth century. Thus, the procession could also be waiting for the arrival of the new Messiah, who would be expected at sunrise on Easter Sunday. At the same time, Christ and the eleven angels might also stand for the archbishop of Reims and his eleven suffragan bishops, all of them in their pastoral roles, a theme much emphasized in the contemporary diocesan councils that met in the east end of the cathedral. All these meanings, and others still, could easily coexist in these sculptures. The meanings proposed thus far all relate to salvation and to the role of the archbishop and bishops in leading the Christians of the archdiocese to salvation through the church of Reims. But the figures might also represent the archbishop of Reims and the other eleven peers of France who participated in the coronation rites, an interpretation less likely because the figures are looking east and north, whereas the king arrived from the south and west, and it seems unlikely that the six secular peers would be shown as angels. On the other hand, secular participants in the religious processions so frequent in Reims could have carried censers and some liturgical objects, but not the sacred books and the reliquaries, which would have been reserved for the clergy.

THE ANGELS ON THE FLYING BUTTRESS PIERS

In addition, statues of angels were set into niches at the outside ends of the flying buttress piers. Surrounding the cathedral ramparts with angels transforms the entire cathedral into the image of the Heavenly Jerusalem, that vision of paradise described in the Apocalypse. The Gothic cathedral is often described as a vision of paradise, but only Reims was given the imagery that confirms the meaning. The flying buttress angels are not to be confused in meaning with the lower and smaller group of angels and Christ on the radiating chapels. The buttress angels are the guardians of the ramparts, precisely as in St. John's vision.

THE STAINED GLASS PROGRAM IN THE CHEVET CLERESTORY

The theme of the archbishop of Reims and his suffragan bishops, suggested here as one possible interpretation of the twelve figures on the radiating chapels, returns again at Reims in the stained glass of the choir clerestory. The huge clerestory windows pair standing Apostles and prophets in the top tier above labeled representations of bishops standing beside the labeled facades of their churches in the lower tier. In the axial window, the upper tier shows the Virgin and Child beside the Crucifixion above the facade of Reims Cathedral and its archbishop, the only figure whose name, *Anricus* (Henry of Braine), was included. Flanking Reims and its archbishop are the facade and bishop of Soissons on the right and the facade and bishop of Laon on the left. Soissons and Laon are, respectively, the second and third cathedrals in the hierarchy of the archdiocese. The series continued with images of the other bishops and cathedrals in the archdiocese around the chevet clerestory, but owing to destruction is no longer complete. It has been credibly suggested, however, that the figures and churches were in the order in which the bishops sat in the diocesan councils that were actually held in the center space of the choir directly below these very windows. The choir space was apparently only used for these meetings. The synods were held with regularity in the later twelfth and thirteenth centuries, and the records indicate that the most frequent topic was the pastoral role of the bishops, which might be reflected by the fact that in the stained glass all the bishops have their croziers, the symbolic pastoral staff. The program as a whole stands for the power of the Church. The program was begun during the tenure of Jean d'Orbais, but it was completed and installed by Jean le Loup, along with the stained glass in the transept, including both enormous rose windows, and, most likely, the glass of the liturgical choir in the nave, discussed below. The south transept rose window was destroyed by a storm in 1580, but we can speculate that its original program focused, at least in part, on the archbishops who entered the cathedral from that side, since nineteenth-century descriptions indicate that the north rose contained scenes relevant to the canons, whose ceremonial entrance to the cathedral was directly below it. But both transept rose windows had larger meanings in terms of the church of Reims. Together their scenes span the history of the world from the beginning (Genesis) in the north rose to the End of Time in the south rose, symbolized by either the Last Judgment or the Apocalypse. The Last Judgment seems more likely if only because the archbishop of Reims was often considered a type for Christ in various liturgical ceremonies documented at Reims. The remaining windows in the transept were filled with grisaille glass so that more light would fall on the main altar in the crossing, the primary site of the coronation rite.

THE NORTH TRANSEPT PORTALS

Jean le Loup also oversaw the planning and installation of the sculptures in the north transept portals. There are now three portals in the north transept at Reims, whereas the initial plan may have called for only two. The little doorway on the west end of the north transept, misnamed the "Romanesque door" (*porte romane*), was planned from the beginning. Originally, it was the door into the cathedral from the corridor that led to the chapter room. The sculpture now in this doorway not only does not fit the location, but it is obviously reused from a tomb, so it is reasonable to assume that it was installed after the end of the civic revolt in 1236. Recent cleaning has revealed the colorful painting of the sculpture, including a seated Virgin and Child, two large angels, an arch of much smaller angels, the uppermost pair of which are raising a little soul heavenward, and two corner fragments of the sarcophagus showing priests performing the funerary rites.

The central portal of the north transept was the principal ceremonial entrance of the canons from the cloister. Logically, the sculpture celebrates the most important early papal and episcopal saints of Reims. On the trumeau is the figure of St. Calixtus, the first bishop of Reims to be elevated to the papacy (third century). The large statue-columns on the left side include St. Nicasius, the bishop martyred in the doorway of the cathedral by the Vandals, accompanied by his martyred sister, St. Eutrope. On the right side, the central figure is St. Remigius, shown receiving the Holy Ampoule, the little bottle of sacred oil, from the descending dove. The figure next to him is Clovis, whose bejeweled royal crown was partially chiseled off after the French Revolution. Only a small section of the jeweled band remains on the back side. The outer figures on each side are unidentified and may have been added when the plan of the portal was expanded. The very large tympanum, which blocks the lower sections of the windows behind it, has two scenes on the lowest level that refer to the statue-columns. On the left side Nicasius is being beheaded in the doorway of his church and then offering his head at the high altar, and on the right Remigius baptizes Clovis. The upper registers have carefully chosen scenes from the life of St. Remi that include not only the standard miracles but also two chosen for their penitential meanings, as well as a prominent scene from Job, another penitent. The emphasis of the "beginning" of Reims through its early saints makes this portal a counterpart to the great rose windows above it with its themes of the beginning of Time.

The eastern portal presents more complex problems because it was obviously crowded into a space for which it was never intended and because its theme was both truncated and expanded for this placement at the time of installation. It has often been argued that this portal, devoted to the Last Judgment, is a vestige of one planned for the west facade. At the top of the multiregistered tympanum Christ presides over the End of Time, which is shown occurring in a number of stages simultaneously, from the dead rising from their tombs to be judged, to groups of the already saved, taken by angels to their reward in the bosom of Abraham, and the damned, led off to the torments of hell. The presence of Mary and St. John the Baptist flanking Christ, in their roles as intercessors on behalf of humanity, confirms that, contrary to Romanesque visions of the Last Judgment, such as that at Autun, in which every soul's destiny is predetermined, at Reims salvation is still possible for the repenting soul right to the very last moment. This possibility is reinforced by the doorpost (trumeau) figure of the Blessing Christ. In the present arrangement, Christ is accompanied by only six Apostles because the straight, cramped door jambs allowed for only that many.

THE STAINED GLASS OF THE NAVE

The clerestory windows in the nave must be studied as two groups, the first and more important being the windows above the liturgical choir. These windows consisted of paired representations of enthroned kings *above* archbishops and bishops. The recent "discovery" of a series of au-tochromes (color photographs on glass plates) of the Reims glass made before World War I confirm that the lancet windows were filled with en-throned kings and archbishops, one of which is identified by inscription as "Karolus" (Charles, presumably Charlemagne, but Charles the Bald is also possible), another of which was seated on a throne modeled after a famous fifth-sixth century folding bronze throne, called the throne of Dagobert, kept in the treasury of the abbey of St.-Denis. The royal na-ture of these windows is confirmed by other autochromes (1914) pictur-ing King Solomon, a frequently invoked model for the kings of France, in the upper oculi.

Meredith Lillich (2005) has recently analyzed the autochrome images together with the pre-World War I descriptions of other scenes, which has allowed her to piece together the program of these windows and to identify the source of the program in the writings of Archbishop Hinc-mar and in the text of the 1250 coronation *Ordo*. Not only has she iden-tified scenes in the upper occuli of the windows, but she has demonstrated that the progression of scenes from east to west followed the precise tex-tual sequence of the ceremony leading up to the climactic moment, the acclamation of the newly crowned king. In the last part of the ritual, just prior to acclamation, the archbishop of Reims removed his episcopal miter and kissed the king. The king then mounted the choir screen and sat enthroned to the acclamation of the people.

The second group of nave windows suffered the most destruction of any group of windows at Reims from the World War I bombardments. Lillich was able to demonstrate that, unlike the eastern clerestory win-dows that were certainly finished and installed by 1241, this last group was completed c. 1290. The theme of kings over bishops seems to have been repeated, sometimes even reusing the cartoons prepared for the first series, but the program was misunderstood and garbled in organization.

THE WEST FACADE

On the west facade (Figure 7) the theme of the lower level, meaning the buttress plaques and the statue-columns, is nothing less than the whole history of Christianity from its beginnings to the End of Time. The story begins around the corner (on the north face of the left pier but-tress) with scenes from the life of St. Paul, viewed as the founder of Chris-

Figure 7. Reims, Cathedral of Notre-Dame. West Façade. *Photograph: bednorz-photo.de.*

tianity. The west face of this same buttress has scenes of the Proof of the True Cross. The two faces of the buttress on the right (south) side con- clude the story with scenes from the Apocalypse. This sweeping panorama includes the Crucifixion (in the gable of the north portal) and the Last Judgment (in the south portal gable), while the gable of the cen- tral portal is reserved for the Triumph of the Virgin. The large statue- columns in and between the three portals are treated as a continuous frieze of huge figures running across the whole facade. The three door- ways are no longer three separate, discrete portals with different themes but a continuous ensemble that runs across the entire west facade.

This sweeping sequence is interrupted in the center portal with scenes from the life of the Virgin, to whom the cathedral is dedicated. The as- sociation with the Virgin had already been affirmed in the stained glass of the choir axial clerestory window, directly opposite the facade portal, in which an image of the church of Reims was linked to the image of Virgin and Child. A huge statue of the Virgin, now crowned Queen of Heaven, holding the Child is on the doorpost, flanked to the right by groups of statue-columns showing the Annunciation and the Visitation and to the left by the Presentation in the Temple. The lintel above the doorpost had additional scenes from the life of the Virgin that were chis- eled off after the French Revolution. The gable of the central portal shows the Virgin being crowned Queen of Heaven by Christ.

With the exception of the statue-columns in the central portal, grouped in the Marian scenes, all the rest are intentionally separated from their usual groups. In the panorama of church history represented by these figures, we can recognize Old Testament figures like David, Solomon, the queen of Sheba, Apostles, local saints, including at least one pope, and possibly even St. Denis. Only the final series on the right side of the south portal form a group of Old Testament figures that can be specifically identified by the attributes they hold or display. These six figures are part of the group, called the Christophores, that illustrates Sal- vation through sacrifice and, therefore, constitute the liturgical ancestry of Christ, as they had at Senlis. As a group these figures always and only accompany the scene of the Triumph, or Coronation, of the Virgin. This group has more in common with the sculptures now installed in the north transept portals than with the figures on the west facade, all of which suggests that they, too, are vestiges of an earlier plan that remained in- complete and were later installed on the new west facade.

While this sweeping panorama of the history of the Church was being created across the west facade, another entire program of sculpture was being created for the interior wall on the reverse of that same facade. Except for Reims, sculpture on the interior wall of the west facade is unheard of in medieval sculpture. The decision to create an interior program that extended the entire height of the inner wall may also explain why large stained glass windows replaced the sculpted tympana in the portals. Without these additional sources of light, however subdued, interior sculpture would have been utterly lost in darkness.

That sculpture repeats, reflects, and amplifies the themes of the western portals, even as many of the scenes can be understood as paradigms of the good behavior of kings and thus as lessons for the newly crowned king. The scenes are presented in a strict grid of horizontal, trilobed arcades and vertical frames, with each containing a single figure. Each band of figures is separated by exquisitely carved panels of foliage. Across the bottom of all three portals are panels of deep, hanging folds of drapery, mirroring the drapery beneath the facade figures. The scenes in each portal reflect, relate, and even repeat the scenes on the exterior. On the verso of the north portal, for example, above several rows of prophets and the martyrdom of St. Stephen on the lintel, are the salvation miracles of Christ balanced with Old Testament scenes of salvation. The central portal verso intertwines scenes from the life of the Virgin and scenes from the life of John the Baptist. The south portal verso wall has, above the prophets, scenes from the life of St. John that focus on the writing of the Apocalypse. The sequence of scenes, in other words, follows the panoramic sweep of Christianity depicted on the west facade itself. The figures on the verso walls are the work of several artists, yet they all have the courtly elegance that marks them as creations of the middle of the thirteenth century. They are additional evidence that the aim of the clergy at Reims was to have an all-encompassing panorama of Christian history reflecting the most up-to-date ideas of style and fashion from Paris.

Sculpture on the facade of Reims is not confined to the level of the portals but continues right to the top of the facade, which was probably completed in the later 1280s. Four giant figures adorn the piers of the buttresses above the level of the portals, reading left to right, St. John, Christ as the Pilgrim to Emmaeus, Mary Magdalen, and St. Peter. Scenes from the lives of David and Solomon, regarded as the ideal kings and models for earthly sovereigns in the Middle Ages, are arranged around the great rose window, while above it were the scenes of David confronting and slaying Goliath. Lastly, across the top of the facade is the gallery of kings in which we finally see a deliberate association of the Baptism of Clovis with the rite of coronation. The king in the center of the composition, shown half immersed in a baptismal font, is flanked to his left (viewer's right) by St. Remigius, dressed in full archepiscopal regalia, accompanied by a deacon carrying a processional cross. To Clovis's right (viewer's left) stand Queen Clotilde, holding out the royal crown, and a count or baron, no doubt meant to be one of the peers of the realm. Prior to this sculptural group, one of the last to be put in place on the building, nothing in the planning and organization of the spaces, nor in any of its decoration, indicated anything about the coronation ceremony. The two early representations of the Baptism of Clovis, on the north transept portal, present it only within the context of the legend and miracles of St. Remigius because royal coronations were one-time affairs and had little effect on the daily life of an active diocese like Reims. Everything in the Gothic cathedral, from the earliest to the latest programs in sculpture and stained glass, consistently stressed the pastoral role of the clergy and the archbishop in the life of the church. The decorated niches in which the figures stand are repeated continuously across the entire facade and around the massive tower bases. Kings standing in niches were used on the four tower bases of the transept; but in comparison with the series of giants across the west facade, these earlier images of royalty are practically lost. The contrast between the two groups is a good metaphor for the growing importance of the royal coronation at Reims.

CONCLUSION

The great French historian Jacques LeGoff described four stages in the development of what he termed the "myth" of Reims. The first is what he called the "prehistory" of the myth, namely, the history of Reims up to the time of the baptism of Clovis. The second stage, the "creation" of the myth, reaches a triumphant conclusion with the gallery of kings across the top of the facade of Reims. The third stage represented the propagation of the myth, during which time Reims came to be identified in terms of the coronation of the kings of France. The final stage,

the "destruction" of the myth, or better, its "dislocation," began with the
French Revolution and except for short interludes in the times of
Napoleon, Charles X, and Napoleon III, continued through the nineteenth century. The systematic deconstruction of the myth began in
earnest in 1870, after the departure of Napoleon III in exile, with the
establishment of the Third Republic. The massive government effort to
replace Reims as the site of national memory was, in effect, undone by
the German bombardments of World War I. While the popular association of Reims with kings and coronation continues even today, long
after the last king of France has disappeared, the myth has entered a fifth
phase, that of historical memory. Reims Cathedral is a magnificent relic
of the past that has seen its role as the first church of French Christendom, like its mission to minister to the faithful, altered and overtaken
by history.

CHAPTER 6

EPILOGUE

In the world of the twenty-first century the medieval cathedrals of Europe are fascinating artifacts, fragments of an era of powerful growth and expansion when Christianity played a central, organizing role in the lives of the people. Today, the actual participation, like their attendance, of Christians, Roman Catholic or Protestant, has sharply declined, according to an analysis published in the *New York Times* (13–14 October 2003). The great buildings, however, are still centers of attraction, but more for tourists than for worshipers. Notre-Dame in Paris ranks just below the much larger Louvre museum as the destination for visitors to the "City of Light." Visitors marvel at its size, its beauty, and its age, as well as at the richness and elaborateness of the sculptural and architectural decoration on the west facade and the dazzling color of its stained glass windows, without realizing that most of what they see is the result of extensive nineteenth-century reconstructions and replacements, only a few of which were faithful to the originals. Indeed, many visitors recall Victor Hugo's immortal story of Quasimodo and Esmeralda, not from the original book, but from the Disney animated film. Still, they flock to the cathedral by the busloads to be assaulted by postcard vendors hawking overpriced souvenirs and to be warned of pickpockets as they enter, more often than not wondering why they are there. The cathedral has become a museum populated by grouchy, unpleasant ecclesiastical curators who rudely resent the presence of visitors as an intrusion, yet they are dependent on these same visitors and on the city of Paris for the revenues that are absolutely essential for the maintenance of the building.

Under such rather adverse conditions it is difficult to recapture the excitement, the feeling of awe on entering the sacred space of the cathedral. Modern visitors cannot re-create what it must have been like to enter the largest single architectural space that the medieval worshipers experienced. Opening to vast length and rising to unprecedented height, the cathedral was literally a towering experience that expressed the power and authority of the church and the extraordinary financial commitment of the community that made its construction possible.

A sense of the powerful effect of cathedral space can still be found, however. A recent travel article on the sites of New York City quite correctly touted the wonders of the newly restored great hall of Grand Central Station, noting that if the city installed an altar at one end, people would flock to it as to a cathedral. This addresses the problem in another way. In the modern world the cathedral has many competitors for the title of grand architectural space. From Grand Central Station we might branch out to include even the "Cathedral of Commerce," New York's landmark Woolworth Building in Lower Manhattan, at one time the tallest building in the world. Cass Gilbert's masterly adaptation of the Gothic style to promote the heroic age of the high-rise building ranks as one of the great achievements of twentieth-century American architecture.

Although there is much to enjoy and even more to marvel at in the great European cathedrals of the Middle Ages, they remain but skeletons of their formerly glorious selves. Most now stand isolated from the richly layered urban contexts in which they were created, their surroundings destroyed, reduced, or adapted to new, even competitive uses. The former archbishop's Palace at Reims, for example, is now a museum that openly competes with the cathedral for the visitor's attention. In addition to liturgical objects from the cathedral treasury, the museum displays a few of the thousands of pieces from the earlier buildings on the site that were recovered in the extensive excavations after World War I, as well as fragments of the present church salvaged after the savagely destructive German bombardments of 1914 and 1918. Finally, the museum is home to the enormous tapestries that used to be displayed in the cathedral and to a number of pieces of original medieval sculpture removed—and replaced by copies—before they were totally destroyed by the ravages of time and industrial pollution.

Most cathedrals are not so financially fortunate as Cologne or Paris or even York in northern England. Cologne Cathedral, for instance, benefits from the parking tariffs and fines imposed on the adjacent municipal parking lot. After an accidental fire destroyed the timber vaults in the south transept at York, an immediate plea for help appeared in the cathedral, although the public was not informed that the building disaster was covered by government insurance. Restoration work proceeded quickly, especially after the Queen graciously donated some gigantic trees from royal forests to supply the wood with which to reconstruct the vaults. Still, there are cathedrals in perilous straits. Some years ago the problem of maintenance was made clear by a chance encounter in Paris. I was upstairs at Notre-Dame studying some architectural details when I was stopped and questioned by a young worker in mason's coveralls because that area of the building is off limits to the public. When I explained what I was doing, he asked if I was a professor. I answered yes, and he announced that I should tell my students in America that the cathedral was started in the twelfth century and was not finished yet! Many churches are in grave danger because the cities and towns that now own them no longer have the millions necessary for restoration, repair, and the constant maintenance that is required. At Beauvais in France and Tournai in Belgium, for example, the danger of imminent collapse is so great that the church buildings are frequently closed to the public as civic and state governments desperately seek the funds necessary to save them. Hopefully, Beauvais will not collapse a third time! The first collapse, in 1285, resulted from a change in construction; the second, in 1573, from the weight of the crossing tower and its very tall spire. We can only hope that a third will not be the result of neglect.

But the great cathedrals have not lost their ability to impress and to inspire. Technologically and aesthetically, they represent some of humanity's most extraordinary efforts, some of which are only recently understood. In the mid-1980s when Robert Mark, the Princeton professor and engineer, put together a program for the *Nova* science series on public television, he titled it "The Master Builders." The show began with a lengthy analysis of Gothic cathedral construction in thirteenth-century France. In fact, more than half the show was devoted to his detailed analysis of these marvelous feats of architecture and engineering. And when David MacCauley, the artist and author, was queried by the *New York Times Magazine* on the eve of the new millennium for his opinion on the greatest achievements of the second millennium, he unhesitatingly chose the great Gothic cathedrals of Europe as the most magnificent feats of design and engineering.

Nor have cathedrals lost their power to fascinate and to enthrall us with these feats of daring engineering, design, and construction created in the preindustrial age. Beginning with the analyses of architect-restorers and theoretical engineers in the 1860s, nearly a century was spent arguing over the functioning of rib vaults and flying buttresses, often with considerable acrimony. It was not until photoelastic model analysis and, slightly later, computer imaging model technology of the 1970s and 1980s that scholars working together with engineers were able to pool their expertise to understand how these features of Gothic buildings really worked, and even then the answers provided by these newest techniques were not universally accepted when they first appeared. The controversy is over, but the fascination lingers.

To step into a building like Speyer, Amiens, Salisbury, Toledo, Palma, or most of the buildings discussed here is to be awestruck by the power and majesty of great architecture, to be overwhelmed by the space that seems otherworldly and almost infinite in its seeming expansion, and to be enthralled by the beauty of the decoration and the colors of the stained glass. It is difficult to believe that these huge stone structures were built without the cranes, elevators, and other electrical and mechanical heavy equipment that we now have. What we do know is that they were constructed hundreds of years ago by people with extraordinary expertise and remarkable vision.

CHAPTER 7

MEDIEVAL CATHEDRALS: SELECTED EXAMPLES

The illustrations of cathedrals in this chapter have been arranged more or less chronologically in four stylistic groups: Romanesque (Figures 8–16), Early Gothic (Figures 17–26), Rayonnant/Decorated Gothic (Figures 27–32), and Late Gothic (Figures 33–38). Within these divisions, they have been arranged by types of views. General exteriors are followed by facades and east ends (choirs); over all interiors are followed by views of parts, such as naves, choirs, aisles, and ambulatories. Examples of Romanesque and Early Gothic facade portals have been grouped together to facilitate comparisons and contrasts. The aim is to present a broad spectrum of medieval cathedrals in a few illustrations. The bibliography (pp. 259–265) directs the reader to the more recent survey volumes and picture collections. Many cathedrals now have their own Web sites with multiple images of the buildings, and their decorations and furnishings, as well as their treasured liturgical implements.

Figure 8. Pisa, Cathedral of Santa Maria, begun 1063. View from the West. The cathedral complex at Pisa, which includes the church, the baptistry, the bell tower (the famous leaning tower), and the covered cemetery, is a classic example of the re-creation of an early Christian style in a new city that had no early history. *Photograph: Robert G. Calkins.*

Figure 9. Modena, Cathedral of St. Geminianus, begun 1099. West Façade, c. 1100. The west facade of Modena deliberately evokes its Early Christian past through the use of marble in the small, gabled portal and in the many sculpted friezes, the proportions of which resemble early sarcophagi. *Photograph: bednorz-photo.de.*

121

Figure 10. Angoulême, Cathedral of St.-Pierre, begun 1120s. View of Choir Exterior. This east end is articulated by carved architectural ornaments around the windows and along the cornices that is typical of Aquitaine and the Languedoc in the west and south of France. *Photograph: After Propyläen-Kunstgeschichte, 1926.*

Figure 11. Ely, Cathedral of Sts. Etheldreda and Peter, begun 1082. Nave Interior. The long, narrow, and tall proportions of the nave of Ely are characteristic of building in England after the Norman Conquest in 1066. The painted timber ceiling is a rare surviving original medieval example, although it is later than the nave walls. *Photograph: Malcolm Thurlby.*

Figure 12. Cathedral of Santiago de Compostela, begun 1075–80. Interior of Transept. The great, continuous barrel-vaulted nave means that the windows are removed to the aisles and galleries, which makes the interior dark. Santiago de Compostela is still the object of an annual pilgrimage to the shrine of St. James, brother of Christ, whose tomb was "discovered" in the ninth century. *Photograph: After Propyläen-Kunstgeschichte, 1926.*

Figure 13. Speyer, Cathedral of Sts. Mary and Stephan, 1030–61, 1082–1106. North Aisle of Nave. The development of the bay system, which can be seen here in the nave aisle, is one of the most notable and influential features of this giant church, one of the largest Romanesque cathedrals in Europe, which was built as the dynastic funerary church of the Salian emperors. *Photograph: William W. Clark.*

Figure 14. Durham, Cathedral of St. Cuthbert, begun 1093. North Aisle of Choir. The choir aisles of Durham preserve some of the earliest surviving examples of rib vaults in Anglo-Norman Romanesque architecture. The quality of their construction demonstrates the builder's mastery and suggests previous experience with rib vaulting on his part. *Photograph: Private Collection.*

Figure 15. Autun, Cathedral of St.-Lazare, begun 1120–25. West Façade Portal. The west Portal of Autun is one of the most famous examples of the Last Judgment in medieval sculpture. The sculptor, Gislebertus, based his depiction on the liturgical service for the dead, since this portal led directly to the canon's cemetery. *Photograph: bednorz-photo.de.*

127

Figure 16. Autun, Cathedral of St.-Lazare, begun 1120–25. Eve. Lintel fragment from the North Transept portal, now Autun, Musée Rolin. The famous figure of Eve at the moment of her temptation, one of the most extraordinary images of a woman from the Middle Ages, is also one of the few pieces of sculpture known from the original entrance portal carved by Gislebertus for the north transept, which was the main entrance to the cathedral. *Photograph: William W. Clark.*

Figure 17. Chartres, Cathedral of Notre-Dame, begun after 1134. West Façade. The west façade of Chartres consists of two towers, each originally standing in front of the eleventh-century façade. The three portals were inserted between the towers, rather than farther back on the old front, when the canons realized they would have been blocked by the towers. *Photograph: William W. Clark.*

Figure 18. Chartres, Cathedral of Notre-Dame, begun after 1142 Royal Portals. The three sculpted portals most likely represent the three comings of Christ: the Incarnation (the birth of Christ) on the right; the second coming (at the moment of Transfiguration) on the left; and Christ coming to judge the saved and the damned at the End of Time in the center. *Photograph: William W. Clark.*

Figure 19. Senlis, Cathedral of Notre-Dame, begun 1150s. West Façade, Central Portal, 1160s. This is the earliest known portal devoted exclusively to the Virgin Mary as the Queen of Heaven, the exemplar of the first saved Christian and the Intercessor on behalf of humanity. The complexity of the iconography suggests it was formulated in the schools of nearby Paris. *Photograph: William W. Clark.*

Figure 20. Paris, Cathedral of Notre-Dame, begun 1150s. East End in 1851. This detail from a rare, unpublished 1851 photograph shows the choir of Notre-Dame prior to the restorations of Lassus and Viollet le Duc that included redesigning and rebuilding the flying buttresses. Such early photographic images reveal the many differences that are the result of almost continual rebuilding over nearly 200 years, differences that were softened by the restorations. *Photograph: Private Collection.*

Figure 21. Paris, Cathedral of Notre-Dame, begun 1150s. Interior. One of the largest and tallest churches begun in the twelfth century, Notre-Dame was planned to be not only the largest clerical space in any cathedral but also the tallest structure in Paris, deliberately surpassing the seventy-five-foot tower on the royal palace west of the cathedral. *Photograph: Gerard Boullay.*

Figure 22. Laon, Cathedral of Notre-Dame, begun c. 1155. Nave Interior. The four-story elevation and narrow proportions at Laon were intended to suggest height greater than seventy-five feet, just as the lantern tower above the main altar was to add to the illusion of great length in the church, an effect heightened by the flat-ended choir. *Photograph: Hirmer Verlag Fotoarchiv, Munich.*

Figure 23. Monreale, Cathedral of Sta. Maria Nuova, begun by 1174. The intention at Monreale, one of the rare monastic cathedrals outside of England, was to combine the Early Christian basilica with the lavish mosaic decoration of the Middle Byzantine aesthetic as a tribute to the Norman royal founder William II, king of Sicily. *Photograph: Scala/Art Resource, New York.*

Figure 24. Canterbury, Christchurch Cathedral, 1174–84. Choir Interior. The spectacular east end of Canterbury contains spaces for three functions, the monk's choir, the cathedral presbytery, and the shrine of the martyred archbishop Thomas à Becket. Each change is marked by a rise in floor level and progressively richer building materials and more elaborate architectural ornament. *Photograph: Malcolm Thurlby.*

136

Figure 25. Bourges, Cathedral of St. Etienne, begun c. 1195. Choir Interior. The key to understanding the magnificent spatial experience at Bourges lies in recognizing that the triangular section emphasizes the expanse of the space as much as its height and that the builder used very tall piers to open up the elevation and make the windows visible at each of the three levels. *Photograph: William W. Clark.*

Figure 26. Naumburg, Cathedral of Sts. Peter and Paul, begun before 1213. Naumburg is one of the few medieval churches to preserve intact its original, contemporary choir screens. This is the west screen decorated with carved and fully painted scenes of the Passion of Christ. The larger sculptures of the Crucifixion flank the doors in the gabled entrance. *Photograph: After Pindar.*

Figure 27. Amiens, Cathedral of Notre-Dame, begun 1218–20. Nave Interior. At 148-feet tall and 474-feet long, Amiens is the largest completed Gothic cathedral in France. The uninterrupted horizontal band of foliage divides the nave elevation in half with the two upper stories revealing the decorative complexities of the new Rayonnant style. *Photograph: Hirmer Verlag Fotoarchiv, Munich.*

Figure 28. Salisbury, Cathedral of the Blessed Virgin Mary, begun c. 1220. Nave Interior. With its exceptional length, strong horizontals and spatial width, Salisbury is the classic example of the early English Gothic style. The use of darker stone emphasizes the linear aspects of the design that deliberately conceals the thickness of the walls. *Photograph: Malcolm Thurlby.*

Figure 29. Toledo, Cathedral of Nuestra Señora, begun c. 1220. Ambulatory Interior. The design of Toledo is based on Bourges, but with ornamental details borrowed from the Moorish architecture that it replaced. Like Bourges, Toledo is an exceptional building in the boldness of its statement of the new Gothic Christian architecture in Spain. *Photograph: bednorz-photo.de.*

Figure 30. Cologne, Cathedral of St. Peter and Notre-Dame, begun 1248. Cathedral under construction in 1852. Cologne reached the unprecedented height of 165 feet on the interior. The gigantic scale and complex Rayonnant design are among the reasons that construction dragged on—Cologne was only completed in 1882—but the design is remarkably consistent throughout. *Photograph: Dombildarchiv Köln, Matz, and Schenk.*

Figure 31. Strasbourg, Cathedral of Notre-Dame, begun c. 1190. West Façade, begun 1277. This extraordinary west façade, one of the finest and most sophisticated combinations of Rayonnant and Late Gothic designs, includes the tallest towers built in the Middle Ages. The adjacent museum preserves several original architectural drawings of the façade. *Photograph: Propyläen-Kunstgeschichte, 1926.*

Figure 32. Exeter, Cathedral of St. Peter, begun 1279. Interior View. Despite minor differences, the interior of Exeter is the most consistent example of the Decorated style in England, although it was constructed over nearly eighty years (1279–1360). The overwhelming linearity and the dazzling tracery designs contribute to the sense of fantasy. *Photograph: Private Collection.*

Figure 33. Prague, Cathedral of Sts. Vitus, Wenceslas, and Adalbert, begun 1342. Choir Interior. The initial, French Rayonnant design, created by Matthew of Arras, was subtly altered by Peter Parler, a member of the illustrious north German family of builders, through the undulating tracery screens and the illustionistic vaulting patterns. The result is an appropriately rich and original design suitable for the shrine of the national saint of Bohemia. *Photograph: Robert G. Calkins.*

Figure 34. Girona, Cathedral of Nuestra Señora, begun 1310; nave after 1416. Interior of Nave and Choir. The inventive originality of Late Gothic builders in Catalonia is evident in the contrast between the conventional choir with ambulatory and radiating chapels and the extraordinary nave of exceptional width and height added to it after 1416. *Photograph: bednorz-photo.de.*

146

Figure 35. Palma de Majorca, Cathedral of Sta. Maria, begun 1296. Nave from South Aisle. The enormous cathedral at Palma exploited the Catalán technique of thin vaulting to achieve tall, structurally light, unified space intended both as the national and the burial church of the Balearic kings. *Photograph: bednorz-photo.de.*

Figure 36. Antwerp, Cathedral of Onze Lieve Vrouw, begun 1352. Interior. With its seven-aisle plan the Church of the Virgin in Antwerp is the most expansive spatial scheme in Belgium and also one of the most important examples of the Brabantine Gothic style. The two-story elevation was ultimately derived from Gothic in Normandy but here has a refined linear elegance that contributes to the expansive illusionism. *Photograph: bednorz-photo.de.*

148

Figure 37. Milan, Cathedral of Sta. Maria Maggiore, begun 1385. Interior. The enormous size of the Late Gothic cathedral at Milan is both a tribute to the ambitions of the Visconti family and a constant source of problems for the Lombard builders, who were unaccustomed to building on this scale and resistant to the Gothic of northern Europe. *Photograph: Robert G. Calkins.*

Figure 38. Salamanca, New Cathedral, begun 1512. View of Choir from Transept. Built beside the Old Cathedral of Nuestra Señora, rather than replacing it, the New Cathedral is a brilliant Late Gothic fantasy, as well as one of the most elaborate and beautiful cathedrals in Spain. The tall clustered piers lead the eye to the splendid linear designs spun out across the surface of the vaults. *Photograph: bednorz-photo.de.*

PRIMARY
DOCUMENTS

The primary documents included in this section consist of two types: historical documents concerning important events or social situations pertaining to cathedrals or to ecclesiastical officials, such as bishops and popes; and descriptive documents about cathedrals. In most cases these are selected excerpts from much longer texts. They are arranged in chronological order, rather than by type, and are intended to add another level of understanding to the text, where they are cited by the numbers used in this chapter. All these primary sources have been translated into English from their original languages. Every effort has been made to use the best available translations, but occasional "modernizations" have been undertaken for the benefit of the twenty-first-century reader. Added information is enclosed in brackets.

DOCUMENT 1
Emperor Constantine's Gifts to St. John Lateran and Old St. Peter's (313–37)

In his time Constantine Augustus built the following basilicas and adorned them: the Constantinian basilica [St. John Lateran], where he offered the following gifts: a ciborium of hammered silver, which has upon the front the Saviour seated upon a chair, in height 5 feet, weighing 120 lbs., and also the 12 apostles, who weigh each 90 lbs., and are 5 feet in height and wear crowns of purest silver; further, on the back, looking toward the apse are the Saviour seated upon a throne in height 5 feet, of purest silver, weighing 150 lbs., and 4 angels of silver, which weight each 105 lbs. and are 5 feet in height and have jewels from Alabanda in their eyes and carry spears; the ciborium itself weighs 2025 lbs. of wrought silver; a vaulted ceiling of purest gold; and a lamp of purest gold, which hangs beneath the ciborium, with 50 dolphins of purest gold, weighing each 50 lbs., and chains which weigh 25 lbs.; 4 crowns of purest gold with 20 dolphins, weighing each 15 lbs.; a covering for the length and breadth of the apse vault of the basilica of purest gold, weighing 500 lbs.; 7 altars of purest silver, weighing each 200 lbs.; 7 golden patens, weighing each 30 lbs.; 16 silver patens, weighing each 30 lbs.; 7 goblets of purest gold, weighing each 10 lbs.; a single goblet of coral set all about with prases and jacinths and overlaid with gold, which weighs in all 20 lbs. and 3 ounces; 20 silver goblets, weighing each 15 lbs.; 2 pitchers of purest gold, weighing each 50 lbs., and holding each 3 medimni; 20 silver pitchers, weighing each 10 lbs. and holding each one medimnus; 40 smaller chalices of purest gold, weighing each one lb.; 50 smaller chalices for service, weighing each 2 lbs. For ornament in the basilica: a chandelier of purest gold before the altar, wherein burns pure oil of nard, with 80 dolphins, weighing 30 lbs.; a silver chandelier with 20 dolphins, which weighs 50 lbs., wherein burns pure oil of nard; 45 silver chandeliers in the body of the basilica, weighing each 30 lbs., wherein burns the aforesaid oil; on the right side of the basilica 40 silver lamps, weighing each 20 lbs.; 25 silver chandeliers on the left side of the basilica, weighing each 20 lbs.; 50 silver candelabra in the body of the basilica, weighing each 20 lbs.; 3 jars of purest silver, weighing each 300 lbs., holding 10 medimni; 7 brass candlesticks before the altars, 10 feet in height, adorned with figures of the prophets overlaid with silver, weighing each 300 lbs.; and for maintenance of the lights there he granted. . . .

At the same time Constantine Augustus built the basilica of blessed Peter, the apostle, in the shrine of Apollo, and laid there the coffin with the body of the holy Peter; the coffin itself he enclosed on all sides with bronze, which is unchangeable: at the head 5 feet, at the feet 5 feet, at the right side 5 feet, at the left side 5 feet, underneath 5 feet and overhead 5 feet: thus he enclosed the body of blessed Peter, the apostle, and laid it away.

And above he set porphyry columns for adornment and other spiral columns which he brought from Greece.

He made a vaulted apse in the basilica, gleaming with gold, and over the body of the blessed Peter, above the bronze which enclosed it, he set a cross of purest gold, weighing 150 lbs., . . . and upon it were these words:

"CONSTANTINE-AUGUSTUS AND HELENA AUGUSTA . . . THIS HOUSE . . . SHINING WITH LIKE ROYAL SPLENDOR A COURT SURROUNDS," inscribed in clear letters of niello work.

He gave also 4 brass candlesticks, 10 feet in height, overlaid with silver, with figures in silver of the acts of the apostles, weighing each 300 lbs.; 3 golden chalices, set with 45 prases and jacinths, weighing each 12 lbs.; 2 silver jars, weighing 200 lbs.; 20 silver chalices; weighing each 10 lbs.; 2 golden pitchers, weighing each 10 lbs.; 5 silver pitchers, weighing each 2 lbs.; a golden paten with a turret of purest gold and a dove, adorned with prases, jacinths and pearls, 215 in number, weighing 30 lbs.; 5 silver patens, weighing each 15 lbs.; a golden crown before the body, that is a chandelier, with 50 dolphins, which weighs 35 lbs.; 32 silver lamps in the basilica, with dolphins, weighing each 10 lbs.; for the right of the basilica 30 silver lamps, weighing each 8 lbs.; the altar itself of silver overlaid with gold, adorned on every side with gems, 400 in number, prases, jacinths, and pearls, weighing 350 lbs.; a censer of purest gold adorned on every side with jewels, 60 in number, weighing 15 lbs.

Source: Louise R. Loomis. *The Book of the Popes*. Records of Civilization 3. New York: Columbia University Press, 1916.

DOCUMENT 2
Prudentius's Descriptions of St. John Lateran and Old St. Peter's (c. 400)

People are gathering more than is usual for rejoicings. Tell me, friend, what it means. All over Rome they are running about in exultation.

Today we have the festival of the apostles' triumph coming round again, a day made famous by the blood of Paul and Peter. . . .

The Tiber separates the bones of the two and both its banks are consecrated as it flows between the hallowed tombs. The quarter on the right bank took Peter into its charge and keeps him in a golden dwelling, where there is the grey of olive-trees and the sound of a stream; for water rising from the brow of a rock has revealed a perennial spring which makes them fruitful in the holy oil. Now it runs over costly marbles, gliding smoothly down the slope till it billows in a green basin. There is an inner part of the memorial where the stream falls with a loud sound and rolls along in a deep, cold pool. Painting in diverse hues colours the glassy waves from above, so that mosses seem to glisten and the gold is tinged with green, while the water turns dark blue where it takes on the semblance of the overhanging purple, and one would think the ceiling was dancing on the waves. There the shepherd himself nurtures his sheep with the ice-cold water of the pool, for he sees them thirsting for the rivers of Christ.

Elsewhere the Ostian Road keeps the memorial church of Paul, where the river grazes the land on its left bank. The splendour of the place is princely, for our good emperor dedicated this seat and decorated its whole extent with great wealth. He laid plates on the beams so as to make all the light within golden like the sun's radiance at its rising, and supported the gold-panelled ceiling on pillars of Parian marble set out there in four rows. Then he covered the curves of the arches with splendid glass of different hues, like meadows that are bright with flowers in the spring.

There you have two dowers of the faith, the gift of the Father supreme, which He has given to the city of the toga to reverence. See, the people of Romulus goes pouring through the streets two separate ways, for the same day is busy with two festivals. But let us hasten with quickened step to both and in each get full enjoyment of the songs of praise. We shall go further on, where the way leads over Hadrian's bridge, and afterwards seeks the left bank of the river. The sleepless bishop performs the sacred ceremonies first across the Tiber, then hurries back to this side and repeats his offerings. It is enough for you to have learned all this at Rome; when you return home, remember to keep this day of two festivals as you see it here.

Source: H. J. Thompson, *Prudentius: Crowns of Martyrdom*, II. Loeb Classical Library. Cambridge: Harvard University Press, 1953.

DOCUMENT 3
Description of Constantine's Three Great Churches in Rome (12th c.)

During the days of Pope Silvester, Constantine Augustus built the Lateran Basilica, which he adorned beautifully. He put there the Ark of the Covenant, which Titus had carried from Jerusalem with many thousands of Jews, and the Golden Candlestick of Seven Lamps with vessels for oil. In the ark are these things: the golden emeralds, the mice of gold, the Tablets of the Covenant, the Rod of Aaron, manna, the barley loaves, the golden urn, the coat without seam, the reed and garment of Saint John the Baptist, and the tongs that Saint John the Evangelist was shorn with. Moreover he also put in the basilica a ciborium with pillars of porphyry. And he set there four pillars of gilded brass, which the consuls of old had brought to the Capitoline from the Campo Marzio and set in the Temple of Jupiter.

He also made, in the time of the pope and after his prayer, a basilica for the Apostle Peter before Apollo's Temple in the Vatican. The emperor first dug the foundation, and in reverence to the twelve apostles he carried out twelve basketsful of earth. Saint Peter's body is kept as follows. He made a chest closed on all sides with brass and copper, which may not be moved, five feet of length at the head, five at the foot, on the right side five feet and on the left side five feet, five feet above and five feet below. And so he enclosed the body of the Blessed Peter.

He adorned the altar above in the fashion of an arch with bright gold. And he made a ciborium with pillars of porphyry and purest gold. And he set there in front of the altar twelve pillars of glass, which he brought from Greece and which were from Apollo's Temple at Troy. Moreover he set above the Blessed Apostle Peter's body a cross of pure gold weighing one hundred and fifty pounds. On it is written: Constantinus Augustus et Helena Augusta.

He also built a basilica for the Blessed Apostle Paul on the Via Ostiense and put his body in brass and copper just like the body of the Blessed Peter.

The same emperor, after he became a Christian and built these churches also gave to the Blessed Silvester a *Phrygium* [Tiara], and white horses, and all the *imperialia* pertaining to the dignity of the Roman Empire. Then he went away to Byzantium. The pope, decorated with these gifts, went forth with Constantine as far as the Roman Arch, where they embraced and kissed each other, and so parted.

Source: Fr. Morgan Nichols. *The Marvels of Rome*. London: Ellis and Elvey, 1889.

DOCUMENT 4
The Second Creed of Nicaea (381)

I believe in one God the Father Almighty: Maker of heaven and earth, and of all things visible and invisible. And in one Lord Jesus Christ, the only-begotten Son of God, begotten of the Father before all worlds [*God of God*] Light of Light, very God of very God, begotten, not made, being of one substance [*essence*] with the Father; by whom all things were made; who, for us men and for our salvation, came down from heaven, and was incarnate by the Holy Ghost of the Virgin Mary, and was made man; and was crucified also for us under Pontius Pilate; he suffered and was buried; and ascended into heaven, and sat on the right hand of the Father; and he shall come again, with glory, to judge both the quick and the dead; whose kingdom shall have no end.

And in the Holy Ghost, the Lord and Giver of Life; who proceeded from the Father [*and the Son*]; who with the Father and the Son together is worshiped and glorified: who spake by the prophets. And one Holy Catholic and Apostolic Church. I acknowledge one baptism for the remission of sins; and I look for the resurrection of the dead, and the life of the world to come. Amen.

Source: Philip Schaff. *The Creeds of Christendom*, 4th ed. New York: Harpers, 1890.

DOCUMENT 5
Gregory of Tours: Descriptions of
Several Fifth-Century Basilicas (591)

In the city of Tours, upon the death of Eustochius, in the seventeenth year of his episcopate, Perpetuus was consecrated as fifth in succession from the blessed Martin. Now when he saw the continual wonders wrought at the tomb of the saint, and observed how small was the chapel erected over him, he judged it unworthy of such miracles. He caused it to be removed, and built on the spot the great basilica which has endured until our day, standing five hundred and fifty paces from the city. It is one hundred and sixty feet long by sixty broad; its height to the ceiling is forty-five feet. It has thirty-two windows in the sanctuary and twenty in the nave [and] forty-one columns. In the whole structure there are seventy-two windows, a hundred and twenty columns, and eight doors, three in the sanctuary, five in the nave. The great festival of the church has a threefold significance: it is at once a feast of the dedication, of the translation of the saint's body, and of his consecration as bishop. This festival you shall keep on the fourth day of July; the day of the saint's burial you shall find to fall on the eleventh of November. They who keep these celebrations in faith shall deserve the protection of the holy bishop both in this world and the next. As the ceiling of the earlier chapel was fashioned with delicate workmanship, Perpetuus deemed it unseemly that such work should perish; so he built another basilica in honour of the blessed apostles Peter and Paul, and in it he fixed the ceiling. He built many other churches, which are still standing today in the name of Christ.

At this time also the church of the blessed Symphorian, the martyr of Autun, was built by the priest Eufronius, who himself afterwards became bishop of this city. He it was who, in his great devotion, sent the marble which covers the holy sepulchre of the blessed Martin.

After the death of Bishop Rusticus, the holy Namatius became in these days eighth bishop of Clermont. By his own efforts he built the church which still exists, and is deemed the older of those within the town walls. It is a hundred and fifty feet long, sixty feet broad, that is across the nave, and fifty feet high to the ceiling: it ends in a rounded apse, and has on either side walls of skilled construction; the whole building is disposed in the form of a cross. It has forty-two windows, seventy columns, and eight doors.

There is felt the dread of God, and the great brightness of His glory, and verily there often the devout are aware of a most sweet odour as of spices wafted to them. The walls of the sanctuary are adorned with a lining of many kinds of marble. The building being completed in the twelfth year, the blessed bishop sent priests to the city of Bologna in Italy to bring him relics of the saints Vitalis and Agricola, crucified, as is known of all men, for the name of Christ our Lord.

The wife of Namatius built the church of the holy Stephen outside the walls. As she wished it to be adorned with paintings, she used to hold a book upon her knees, in which she read the story of deeds done of old time, and pointed out to the painters what subjects should be represented on the walls. It happened one day, as she was sitting reading in the church, that a certain poor man came in to pray. And when he saw her clad in black, for she was advanced in years, he deemed her one of the needy, and producing a piece of bread, put it in her lap, and went his way. She did not despise the gift of the poor man who did not perceive her quality, but took it and thanked him, and put it by, afterwards preferring it to her costlier food and receiving a blessing from it every day until it was all consumed.

Source: O. M. Dalton. *Gregory of Tours: The History of the Franks*. Oxford: Oxford University Press, 1927.

DOCUMENT 6
Gregory of Tours: The Baptism of Clovis (591)

The queen never ceased to entreat the king to recognize the true God and give up idols, but nothing could move him to believe these things until he was engaged in a war with the Alemanni in which he was compelled by constraint to confess what he had refused to do voluntarily. It came to pass that his army was in danger of being wiped out. Thereupon, lifting his eyes to heaven, with compunction of heart and moved to tears, he cried, "Jesus Christ, who art, according to Clotilde, the Son of the living God, who art said to give aid to those in trouble and victory to those who hope in Thee . . . I beseech, Thee . . . if Thou wilt give me victory over mine enemies I will believe in Thee and be baptized in Thy name: I have called upon my gods and they are far removed from helping me. Hence I believe they are powerless, since they do not succour their followers. I now call upon Thee. Only save me from mine enemies." When he had thus spoken the Alemanni turned their backs and took to flight. . . . Clovis returning related to the queen how he had won the victory by calling upon the name of Christ. Then the queen with haste secretly summoned Remigius, the bishop of Reims, that he should instruct the king in the word of salvation. He then began privately to tell his majesty that he should believe in the true God, the maker of heaven and earth and should give up idols. The king said, "Willingly, holy father, but there is one difficulty. My people will not give up their gods. But I will go and speak to them according to your word." But before he had opened his mouth all the people cried, "Pious king, we reject the mortal gods and are ready to follow the immortal God, whom Remigius preaches." Then the bishop with great joy gave orders to prepare the fount. The church was

resplendent with banners, flickering candles and the scent of wax and in-
cense, so that those present; believed that they partook of the Saviour of
Heaven. The king asked that he be baptized by the pontiff. Like a new
Constantine, Clovis ascended to the laver, putting off his former leprosy.
As he went down into the water the bishop said, "Bow your neck. Adore
what you have burned. Burn what you have adored." Now the holy bishop
Remigius, a man of consummate learning and of great sanctity, may fitly
be compared to the holy Sylvester [who baptized Constantine].

Source: O. M. Dalton. *Gregory of Tours: The History of the Franks*. Oxford: Oxford University Press, 1927.

DOCUMENT 7
Bede: Pope Gregory I Sends Augustine to Canterbury (597)

Having been strengthened, therefore, by the encouragement of the
blessed father Gregory, Augustine, with the servants of Christ who were
with him, returned to the work of the Word and came to Britain. At that
time King Ethelbert in Kent was most powerful. . . . In this island, then,
Augustine landed . . . having received, by the charge of the blessed Pope
Gregory, interpreters from the nation of the Franks; and sending to Ethelbert, he gave orders to say that they had come from Rome, and brought
the best message, which promised, without any doubt, to those who
obeyed it, eternal joys in heaven, and a future kingdom without end with
the living and true God. The king, on hearing these things, commanded
them to remain in the island to which they had come, and that neces-
saries should be afforded them, until he should see what to do respect-
ing them. For before this the fame of the Christian religion had reached
him, inasmuch as he had a Christian wife of the royal family of the
Franks, by name Bertha, whom he had received from her parents upon
this condition, that she might have leave to keep inviolate the rite of
her faith and religion. . . . After some days, the king came to the island,
and sitting in the open air, commanded Augustine with his companions
to come there to conference with him. For being influenced by an ancient superstition, he had taken precaution that they should not come
to him in any house, lest, on their arrival, if they had any knowledge of
witchcraft, they might deceive him by taking some advantage of him. But

they came endued not with demoniac but with divine virtue, bearing a silver cross for a standard, and the image of the Lord and Savior painted on a panel; and singing litanies. . . . When they preached to him the king replied, "Fair indeed are the words and the promises which you bring, but, because they are new and uncertain, I cannot give my assent to them, and leave those which for so long a time I have kept with all the nation of the Angles. . . . But we do not prohibit you from gaining by your preaching all whom ye are able to the faith of your religion." He gave them therefore an abode in the city of Canterbury.

Source: Oliver Thatcher and Edgar H. McNeal. A *Sourcebook for Medieval History*. New York: Scribner's, 1905. No. 39.

DOCUMENT 8
Two Letters of Gregory the Great Concerning the Church in England (601)

1. To Augustine, Bishop of the Angli

Gregory to Augustine, etc.

Though it is certain that for those who labor for Almighty God ineffable rewards of an eternal kingdom are reserved, yet we must needs bestow honors upon them, that by reason of remuneration they may apply themselves the more manifoldly in devotion to spiritual work. And, since the new Church of the Angli has been brought to the grace of Almighty God through the bountifulness of the same Lord and your labors, we grant to you the use of the pallium therein for the solemnization of mass only, so that you may ordain bishops in twelve several places, to be subject to your jurisdiction, with the view of a bishop of the city of London being always consecrated in future by his own synod, and receiving the dignity of the pallium from this holy and Apostolical See which by the grace of God I serve. Further, to the city of York we desire you to send a bishop whom you may judge fit to be ordained; so that, if this same city with the neighboring places should receive the word of God, he also may ordain twelve bishops, so as to enjoy the dignity of a metropolitan: for to him also, if our life is continued, we propose, with the favor of God, to send a pallium; but yet we desire to subject him to the control of your

Fraternity. But after your death let him be over the bishops whom he shall have ordained, so as to be in nowise subject to the jurisdiction of the bishop of London. Further, between the bishops of London and York in the future let there be this distinction of dignity, that he be accounted first who has been first ordained. But let them arrange by council in common, and with concordant action, whatever things may have to be done in zeal for Christ; let them be of one mind in what is right, and accomplish what they are minded to do without disagreement with each other.

But let your Fraternity have subject to yourself under our God not only those bishops whom you shalt ordain, and those whom the bishop of York may ordain, but also all the priests of Britain, to the end that they may learn the form of right belief and good living from the tongue and life of your Holiness, and, executing their office well in their faith and manners, may attain to heavenly kingdoms when it may Please the Lord. God keep thee safe, most reverend brother. Given on the tenth day of the Kalends of July, in the nineteenth year of the empire of our lord Mauricius Tiberius, the eighteenth year after the consulship of the same lord, Indiction 4.

2. To Edilbert, King of the Angli

Gregory to Ethelbert, etc.

On this account Almighty God advances good men to the government of peoples, that through them He may bestow the gifts of His loving-kindness on all over whom they are preferred. This we have found to be the case in the nation of the Anglii, which your Glory has been put over to the intent that through the good things granted to you, heavenly benefits might be conferred on the nation subject to you. And so, glorious son, keep guard with anxious mind over the grace which thou hast received from above. Make haste to extend the Christian faith among the peoples under thy sway, redouble the zeal of my rectitude in their conversation, put down the worship of idols, overturn the edifices of their temples, build up the manners of your subjects in great purity of life by exhorting, by terrifying, by enticing, by correcting, by showing examples of well-doing; that so you may find Him your recompenser in heaven Whose name and knowledge you shall have spread abroad on earth. For He Himself will make the name of your glory even more glorious to posterity, if you seek and maintain His honor among the nations.

For so Constantine, the once most pious Emperor, recalling the Roman republic from perverse worshiping of idols, subjected it with himself to our Almighty Lord God Jesus Christ, and turned himself with his subject peoples with all his heart to Him. Hence it came to pass that that man surpassed in praise the name of ancient princes, and excelled his predecessors as much in renown as in well-doing. And now, therefore, let your Glory make haste to infuse into the kings and peoples subject to you the knowledge of God, Father, Son and Holy Spirit, that you may both surpass the ancient kings of your race in renown and in deserts, and the more you shall have wiped away the sins of others among your subjects, the more secure you may become with regard to your own sins before the terrible scrutiny of Almighty God.

Moreover, you have with you our most reverend brother, Augustine the bishop, learned in monastic rule, replete with knowledge of holy Scripture, endowed by the grace of God with good works. Listen gladly to his admonitions, follow them devoutly, keep them studiously in remembrance: for, if you listen to him in what he speaks on behalf of Almighty God, the same Almighty God will the sooner listen to him when he prays for you. For, if, which God forbid, you disregard his words when will it be possible for Almighty God to hear him for you, whom you neglect to hear for God? With all your heart, therefore, bind yourselves in fervor of faith to him, and aid his endeavors by the power which he gives you from above, that He Whose faith you cause to be received and kept in your kingdom may Himself make partakers of His own kingdom.

Furthermore, we would have your glory know that, as we learn from the words of the Almighty Lord in holy Scripture, the end of the present world is already close at hand, and the reign of the saints is coming, which can have no end. And now that this end of the world is approaching, many things are at hand which previously have not been; to wit, changes of the air, terrors from heaven, and seasons contrary to the accustomed order of times, wars, famine, pestilences, earthquakes in diverse places. Yet these things will not come in our days, but after our days they will all ensue. You therefore, if you observe any of these things occurring in your land, by no means let your mind be troubled, since these signs of the end of the world are sent beforehand for this purpose, that we should be solicitous about our souls, suspectful of the hour of death, and in our good deeds be found prepared for the coming Judge. These things, glorious son, we have now briefly spoken of, that, when the Christian faith shall have been extended in your kingdom, our speech to you may also extend itself to greater length, and that we may be pleased to speak so much the more fully as joy multiplies itself in our heart for the perfected conversion of your nation.

I have sent you some small presents, which to you will not be small, when received by you as of the benediction of the blessed Apostle Peter. And so may Almighty God guard and perfect in you the grace which He has begun, and extend your life here through courses of many years, and after a long life receive you in the congregation of the heavenly country. May heavenly grace keep your Excellency safe, blessed son. Given this tenth day of the Kalends of July, the nineteenth year of the empire of our most pious lord Mauricius Tiberius Augustus, the eighteenth year after the consulship of the same our lord, Indiction 4.

Source: James Barmby, ed. *Selected Epistles of Gregory the Great*, Library of Nicene and Post-Nicene Fathers, 2nd series, v. 13, pt. 2. New York: Christian Literature Co., 1895, pp. 81–82.

DOCUMENT 9
Bishop Desiderius's Gifts to Auxerre Cathedral
(early 7th c.)

He [Desiderius] very splendidly decorated and enlarged the basilica of St. Stephen, his cathedral church. He added a large vault to the eastern half, marvelously decorated with gold and mosaic, similar to that which Syagrius, bishop of Autun, is known to have built. Bringing the old altar there, he held a solemn dedication on the 13th day before the kalends of May, and offered the following gifts: A gilded platter . . . weighing 50 pounds, with seven figures, a man with a bull and a Greek inscription. He also gave another similar platter . . . set with garnets, weighing 40½ pounds with a circle and a wreath around the center and men and beasts around the rim. Also a third platter . . . weighing 35 pounds, with the story of the sun and with a tree and snakes. Also a fourth platter, weighing 30 pounds, with an Ethiopian and other men. Also a gilded bowl, weighing 12 pounds and 2 ounces, with a fisher with a trident and a centaur in a seascape. Also another bowl . . . with circular decorations and niello work,

weighing 14 pounds and 9 ounces. Also another similar bowl . . . with rev-
ellers weighing 13 pounds. Also another bowl . . . weighing 9 pounds, with
a man with horns, a tree and two cupids holding small children. 4 drinking vessels . . . weighing 11 pounds and 2 ounces, with cupids, and beasts:
one of these is gilded. He gave several dishes . . . one of these, decorated
with niello, weighs 4 pounds, it has on it a bear, seizing a horse. Also another one . . . weighing 3 pounds with a lion seizing a bull. Also another
one, weighing 2 pounds and 9 ounces, with a lion seizing a goat. Also another similar dish . . . weighing 2 pounds, with a buck with horns. Also
another one, weighing 1 pound and 7 ounces, with a grazing stag. Also
another one, weighing 1 pound and 9 ounces, with a leopard seizing
a goat. He gave also 4 salt cellars . . . weighing 4 pounds. He gave also
6 deep dishes, weighing 16 pounds, and 1 deep dish of medium size . . .
weighing 3½ pounds, with 4 stamps below and little berries around the
rim. Small drinking vessels, decorated with small heads, weighing 6½
pounds. He also gave 2 decanters, weighing 4 pounds and 3 ounces. Also
3 decanters . . . weighing 5 pounds. He also gave 9 spoons, weighing 2½
pounds. Also one ladle, weighing 1 pound and 10 ounces, with a circular
ornament in niello and a border around its rim. He also gave a mug, weighing 2 pounds, with a lion and a bull, both gilded. Also a trident, already
mentioned, with the head of a lion, weighing 3 pounds. He also gave a
pitcher . . . weighing 4½ pounds. And a waterbowl for the hands, weighing 3½ pounds. Also two gilded cans of like form weighing 5 pounds, encircled with images of men and wild beasts. He also gave a flat platter,
weighing 8½ pounds, with a monogram in the middle encircled by a
wheel. Also another platter, weighing 8 pounds, with a cross and two men
in the center. Also a bowl . . . weighing 10 pounds, with 5 cupids and two
winged beasts. Also another bowl . . . weighing 8 ½ pounds with a rider
and a snake at his felt. Also another bowl with circular ornaments . . .
weighing 7½ pounds, with three tall men in its center and a border of
cupids and wild beasts around it. He gave also deep gilded dishes . . .
weighing 18 pounds, with cupids and fishes. One deep gilded dish of middle size . . . weighing 8 pounds with sea centaurs and fishes in the center.
Also 5 deep dishes ornamented with flowers, all of them alike, weighing
9½ pounds. Also a deep dish . . . of medium size, weighing 3 pounds, with
the head of a bearded man in the center. Also a deep dish of medium size
plain, weighing 2 pounds and 3 ounces with a cock in the middle. Also
a deep dish . . . with a lip, weighing 3 pounds, with a band of cupids and

wild beasts around it. Also a dish, weighing 2 pounds, with a cupid, a goat, and a tree in the middle. Also a dish . . . weighing 2 pounds with two cupids with lances in the center. Also a small dish, weighing 1 pound, with a wheel-like ornament in the center and a niello border. Also a salt cellar . . . weighing 1 pound with a man and a dog in the center. Also a shell . . . weighing 9 pounds, with a man and a woman in its center and a crocodile at their feet. Also a small cross-shaped salt cellar, weighing 9 ounces. Also a saucer . . . weighing one and a half pounds. 12 spoons, weighing 3 pounds and 2 ounces. Also 12 spoons, weighing 2 pounds and 9 ounces. Also 12 spoons, weighing 3 pounds with inscribed handles. Also 3 decanters with lips, each weighing 1 pound. And one decanter, weighing 1 pound and 1 ounce. Also a small drinking vessel, weighing 1 pound and 1 ounce. Also a jug . . . weighing 3 pounds with a handle with berries and the head of a man in the center. A basin for washing the hands, weighing 2 pounds and 9 ounces with a round floral decoration in the center and a man's head on the handle. Also a gilded wine cooler, weighing 2½ pounds with openings at the outside. Also another wine cooler, weighing 1 pound and 9 ounces, with a border and wild beasts in the center. Also a large sieve, weighing 1 pound, with niello work on the handle. Also a smaller sieve, weighing 2 ounces. Together 420 pounds and 7 ounces.

. . . He gave besides to the basilica of the Lord Germanus [the abbey church of St. Germain at Auxerre] these gifts: A silver platter, with the name Thorsomodus on it; it weighs 37 pounds and shows the history of Aeneas with Greek inscriptions. Also another simple platter, weighing 3 pounds. Likewise a bowl . . . weighing 13 pounds with a lion seizing a bear in the center and a border of cupids and wild beasts. Also another bowl, weighing 9½ pounds with a man and a woman and beasts at their feet. Also a dish . . . weighing 5 pounds and 6 ounces, with a rider holding a snake in his hands. Also a dish . . . weighing 3 pounds, with a round decoration in niello work and a wild beast in its center. He also gave 2 deep dishes, of similar shape with floral ornaments at the inside, weighing 8 pounds and 2 ounces. A pitcher . . . weighing 4 pounds, with niello work on the handle and the head of a lion in the center. A washbasin weighing 3 pounds and 9 ounces, with Neptune and a trident in the center.

Source: *Gesta Pontificum Autissiodorensium*, ed. L. M. Duru. Auxerre: Bibliothèque historique de l'Yonne, 1850.

DOCUMENT 10
Benedict Biscop's Imports from Rome

He came to the court of Egfrid, king of Northumberland, and gave an account of all that he had done since in youth he had left his country. He made no secret of his zeal for religion, and showed what ecclesiastical or monastic instructions he had received at Rome and elsewhere. He displayed the holy volumes and relics of Christ's blessed Apostles and martyrs, which he had brought, and found such favour in the eyes of the king, that he forthwith gave him seventy hides of land out of his own estates, and ordered a monastery to be built thereon for the first pastor of his church. This was done, as I said before, at the mouth of the river Were, on the left bank, in the 674th year of our Lord's incarnation, in the second indiction, and in the fourth year of King Egfrid's reign.

After the interval of a year, Benedict crossed the sea into Gaul, and no sooner asked than he obtained and carried back with him some masons to build him a church in the Roman style, which he had always admired. So much zeal did he show from his love to Saint Peter, in whose honour he was building it, that within a year from the time of laying the foundation, you might have seen the roof on and the solemnity of the mass celebrated therein. When the work was drawing to completion, he sent messengers to Gaul to fetch makers of glass, (more properly artificers) who were at this time unknown in Britain, that they might glaze the windows of his church, with the cloisters and dining rooms. This was done, and they came, and not only finished the work required, but taught the English nation their handicraft, which was well adapted for enclosing the lanterns of the church, and for the vessels required for various uses. All other things necessary for the service of the church and the altar, the sacred vessels, and the vestments, because they could not be procured in England, he took especial care to buy and bring home from foreign parts.

Some decorations and muniments there were which could not be procured even in Gaul, and these the pious founder determined to fetch from Rome; for which purpose, after he had formed the rule for his monastery, he made his fourth voyage to Rome and returned loaded with more abundant spiritual merchandise than before. In the first place, he brought back a large quantity of books of all kinds; secondly, a great number of relics of Christ's Apostles and martyrs, all likely to bring a blessing on many an English church; thirdly, he introduced the Roman mode of chanting, singing, and ministering in the church, by obtaining permission from Pope Agatho to take back with him John, the archchanter of the church of St. Peter, and abbot of the monastery of St. Martin, to teach the English. This John, when he arrived in England, not only communicated instruction by teaching personally, but left behind him numerous writings, which are still preserved in the library of the same monastery. In the fourth place, Benedict brought with him a thing by no means to be despised, namely, a letter of privilege from Pope Agatho, which he had procured, not only with the consent, but by the request and exhortation, of King Egfrid, and by which the monastery was rendered safe and secure for ever from foreign invasion. Fifthly, he brought with him pictures of sacred representations, to adorn the church of St. Peter, which he had built; namely, a likeness of the Virgin Mary and of the twelve Apostles, with which he intended to adorn the central nave, on boarding placed from one wall to the other; also some figures from ecclesiastical history for the south wall, and others from the Revelation of St. John for the north wall; so that every one who entered the church, even if they could not read, wherever they turned their eyes, might have before them the amiable countenance of Christ and his saints, though it were but in a picture, and with watchful minds might revolve on the benefits of our Lord's incarnation, and having before their eyes the perils of the last judgment, might examine their hearts the more strictly on that account.

Source: Bede. "Lives of the Holy Abbots." *The Complete Works of Venerable Bede.* IV, *Historical Tracts*, ed. J. A. Giles. London: Whittaker and Company, 1843.

DOCUMENT 11
Two Descriptions of Hexham (late 7th c. and 12th c.)

1. So continually, in the words of the Psalmist, he drew near to God, placing in Him his hope and rendering to the Lord, who had given him all things, his dearest vows. For in Hexham, having obtained an estate from the queen, St. Aethilthryth, the dedicated to God, he founded and built a house to the Lord in honour of St. Andrew the Apostle. My feeble tongue will not permit me to enlarge here upon the depth of the foundations in the earth, and its crypts of wonderfully dressed stone, and

the manifold building above ground, supported by various columns and many side aisles, and adorned with walls of notable length and height, surrounded by various winding passages with spiral stairs leading up and down; for our holy bishop, being taught by the Spirit of God, thought out how to construct these buildings; nor have we heard of any other house on this side of the Alps built on such a scale. Further, Bishop Acca of blessed memory, who by the grace of God is still alive, provided for this manifold building splendid ornaments of gold, silver, and precious stones; but of these and of the way he decorated the altars with purple and silk, who is sufficient to tell?

2. St. Wilfred, then, in the year of our Lord's Incarnation 678, in the fortieth year of his life, in the tenth year after he had been made a bishop, and in the fourth year of the reign of King Egfrith, built in Hexham a church of most elaborate and accomplished workmanship, in honor of God and St. Andrew, in requital for the benefit that had been bestowed on him through St. Andrew's intercession. For when he had first come to Rome; he had often visited that saint's church, imploring that the remission of his sins, for which he constantly prayed, should be indicated to him in the following fashion: that he should as a result of the saint's intervention be liberated from the slowness of his mind and the rusticity of his language. And without delay, through the prayers of his beloved Apostle, God's generosity bestowed such grace on his faithful servant that he knew that he had acquired the quickness of mind most suited to learning and the corresponding fluency of speech most suited to expounding what he had learned. This gift, by the salvation of innumerable souls which he gained for the Lord, he later most successfully manifested.

And so he laid the foundations of this church with great zeal, and made crypts and subterranean oratories and twisting passageways. He also erected walls of vast length and height, consisting of three different storeys and carried by straight [or square] columns variously and skillfully made. He adorned the walls and capitals of the supporting columns and the arch of the sanctuary with histories and images and various figures, sculpted and protruding from the stone as well as painted, and with a delightful variety of colors and marvellous decorations. The nave of the church he surrounded on all sides with galleries and other additions, set off at different heights and with marvelous art by walls and stairwells.

In and above them there were stone stairs and passageways and turning corridors, now leading up and now down. All this he devised so cunningly that it was possible for a large crowd of people to be there and to walk around the nave of the church without disturbing anyone within it. Several secluded and beautiful oratories which he constructed up high as well as further down within those aisles and galleries were dedicated to Mary the Holy Mother of God Ever Virgin, to St. Michael the Archangel, to St. John the Baptist, and to the holy apostles, martyrs, confessors, and virgins, and were furnished in a most dignified fashion. And even today some of these oratories can still be seen rising like towers or ramparts. Our poor words are unable to describe how many and what relics, and what a crowd of monks and ministers devotedly serving God, he brought together there, and with what magnificent, pious, and precious treasures of books, vestments, and all manner of furnishings and ornaments suitable for divine worship he adorned the interior of the church. The forecourt of the temple he surrounded with a thick and powerful wall. An aqueduct of hollow stone moreover ran through the middle of the village to serve the workshops. We will pass by the many and varied structures ruined by neglect and by destruction; many of their foundations can still be seen here and there. Just as the old chronicles and histories testify, among the nine monasteries that the aforesaid bishop and father and patron ruled, this one excelled all the others, as well as all other churches in England in the elegance of its arrangement and in its exquisite beauty. And in fact there was at that time nothing comparable to be found on this side of the Alps.

There are still in the same town two other churches besides. One is close to the main church and a wonderful piece of architecture. It is nearly round and built like a tower. It has wings on four sides and is dedicated to the Virgin Mary. The other church, dedicated to St. Peter the Apostle, stands somewhat further off. There is also an oratory dedicated to St. Michael, towards the north across the river Tyne and on a mountain which is close to its banks and which is called in English Erneshou and in Latin Mons Aquila.

Sources: 1. Eddius Stephanus. *The Life of Bishop Wilfrid*, ed. Bertrand Colgrave. Cambridge: Cambridge University Press, 1927; 2. James Raine, ed. "Prior Richard's History of the Church at Hexham." *The Priory of Hexham*. The Publications of the Surtees Society 44. Durham: Andrews and Co., 1843.

DOCUMENT 12
Carloman Publishes St. Boniface's Decrees on Bishops' Synods and Rules (742–43)

In the name of our Lord Jesus Christ, I, Carloman, duke and prince of the Franks, in the seven hundred and forty-second year of the Incarnation of Christ and the twenty-first day of April, by the advice of the servants of God and my chief men, have brought together in the fear of Christ the bishops of my realm with their priests into a council or synod; namely, Archbishop Boniface, Burchard [of Würzburg], Reginfried [of Cologne], etc. . . .

And by the advice of my priests and nobles we have appointed bishops for the several cities and have set over them as archbishop Boniface, the delegate of St. Peter.

We have ordered that a synod shall be held every year, so that in our presence the canonical decrees and the laws of the Church may be reëstablished and the Christian religion purified. Revenues, of which churches were defrauded, we have restored and given back to them. We have deprived false priests and adulterous or lustful deacons of their church incomes, have degraded them, and forced them to do penance.

We have absolutely forbidden the servants of God to carry arms or fight; to enter the army or march against an enemy, except only so many as are especially selected for divine service such as celebrating Mass or carrying relics—that is to say: the prince may have one or two bishops with the chaplains, and each praefect one priest to hear confessions and prescribe penance. We have also forbidden the servants of God to hunt or wander about the woods with dogs or to keep hawks and falcons.

We have also ordered, according to the sacred canons, that every priest living within a diocese shall be subject to the bishop of that diocese. Annually during Lent, he shall render to that bishop an account of his ministry. . . .

We have decreed, according to the canons, that every bishop within his own diocese and with the help of the count, who is the defender of the Church, shall see to it that the people of God perform no pagan rites but reject and cast out all the foulness of the heathen, such as sacrifices to the dead, casting of lots, divinations, amulets and auguries, incantations, or offering of animals, which foolish folk perform in the churches, according to pagan custom, in the name of holy martyrs or confessors, thereby calling down the wrath of God and his saints and also those sacrilegious fires which they call "Niedfeor," and whatever other pagan practices there may be. . . .

We have decreed also that priests and deacons shall not wear cloaks after the fashion of laymen, but cassocks according to the usage of the servants of God. . . .

. . . The whole body of the clergy—bishops, priests, deacons, and clerks—accepting the canons of the ancient fathers, have promised to restore the laws of the Church as to morals and doctrine and form of service. Abbots and monks have accepted the Rule of the holy father, Benedict, for the reformation of the regular life. . . .

We order also, by the advice of the servants of God and of the Christian people and in view of imminent wars and attacks by the foreign populations which surround us, that a portion of the properties of the Church shall be used for some time longer, with God's indulgence, for the benefit of our army, as a *precarium* and . . . paying a *census*, on condition, however, that annually from each *casata* [of these ecclesiastical estates] one *solidus*, that is twelve *denarii*, shall be paid to the church or monastery which owns it. In case of the death of the persons to whom the property was entrusted as a *precarium*, it shall revert to the Church. Also, if conditions are such that the prince deems it necessary, let the *precarium* be renewed for another term and a new contract be written. But let extreme care be taken that churches and monasteries whose property is granted in *precarium* shall not be reduced to poverty and suffer want; and, if they should thus be distressed, let the whole property be given back to the church and the house of God.

Source: Ephraim Emerton, ed. *The Letters of Saint Boniface*. New York: Octagon Books, 1973.

DOCUMENT 13
Chrodegang of Metz: Prologue of the Rule for His Clergy (744)

If the authority of the 318 holy fathers [Council of Nicaea, 325] and of the canons were observed, and the bishops and their clergy were living in the proper way, it would be quite unnecessary for anyone so humble and unimportant as we to attempt to say anything about this matter [that is, the way in which the clergy should live], which has been so well treated by the holy fathers, or to add anything new to what they have said. But since the negligence of the bishops as well as of their clergy is rapidly increasing; a further duty seems incumbent on us. And we are certainly in great danger unless we do, if not all we should, at least all we can, to bring our clergy back to the proper way of living.

After I had been made bishop of Metz [743] and had begun to attend to the duties of my pastoral office, I discovered that my clergy as well as the people were living in a most negligent manner. In great sorrow I began to ask what I ought to do. Relying on divine aid and encouraged by my spiritually minded brethren, I thought it necessary to make a little rule for my clergy, by observing which they would be able to refrain from forbidden things, to put off their vices, and to cease from the evil practices which they have so long followed. For I thought that if their minds were once cleared of their vices, it would be easy to teach them the best and holiest precepts.

Source: Oliver Thatcher and Edgar H. McNeal. *A Sourcebook for Medieval History*. New York: Scribner's, 1905. No. 265.

DOCUMENT 14
The Coronation of Pepin and His Sons (751–54)

749. Burchard, bishop of Würzburg, and Fulrad, priest and chaplain, were sent [by Pepin] to pope Zacharias to ask his advice in regard to the kings who were then ruling in France, who had the title of king but no real royal authority. The pope replied by these ambassadors that it would be better that he who actually had the power should be called king.

750 [751]. In this year Pepin was named king of the Franks with the sanction of the pope, and in the city of Soissons he was anointed with the holy oil by the hands of Boniface, archbishop and martyr of blessed memory, and was raised to the throne after the custom of the Franks. But Childerich, who had the name of king, was shorn of his locks and sent into a monastery.

753. In this year pope Stephen came to Pepin at Kiersy, to urge him to defend the Roman church from the attacks of the Lombards.

754. And after pope Stephen had received a promise from king Pepin

that he would defend the Roman church, he anointed the king and his two sons, Charles and Carloman, with the holy oil. And the pope remained that winter in France.

Source: Oliver Thatcher and Edgar H. McNeal. *A Sourcebook for Medieval History*. New York: Scribner's, 1905. No. 6.

DOCUMENT 15
Einhard: The Building Activity of Charlemagne (820)

17. Illustrious as the king was in the work of enlarging his kingdom and in conquering foreign nations, and though so constantly occupied with such affairs, he nevertheless began in several places very many works for the advantage and beautifying of his kingdom. Some of these he was able to finish. Chief among them may be mentioned, as deserving of notice, the Basilica of the Holy Mother of God, built at Aachen, a marvel of workmanship; and the bridge over the Rhine at Mainz, five hundred paces in length; so broad is the river at that place. This bridge, however, was destroyed by fire the year before the king died, nor could it be restored on account of his approaching death, although it was in the king's mind to replace the wooden structure by a bridge of stone.

He also began some magnificent palaces, one not far from Mainz, near the village of Ingelheim, and another at Nymwegen, on the river Waal, which flows past the island of the Batavians on the southern side. He was more especially particular in giving orders to priests and fathers to see to the restoration of those churches under their care, which in any part of his kingdom he found had fallen into decay, taking care by his officers that his commands were obeyed. . . .

26. The Christian religion in which he had been brought up from infancy was held by Charles as most sacred, and he worshiped in it with the greatest piety. For this reason he built at Aachen a most beautiful church, which he enriched with gold and silver and candlesticks, and also with lattices and doors of solid brass. When columns and marbles for the building could not be obtained from elsewhere, he had them brought from Rome and Ravenna. . . .

He provided for the church an abundance of sacred vessels of gold and silver, and priestly vestments, so that when service was celebrated it was

not necessary even for the doorkeepers, who are the lower order of ec-
clesiastics, to perform their duties in private dress. . . .

27. . . . He held the church of the blessed Peter the apostle, at Rome,
in far higher regard than any other place of sanctity and veneration, and
he enriched its treasury with a great quantity of gold, silver, and precious
stones.

Source: William Blaister, trans. *Einhard, Life of the Emperor Karl the Great*. London, 1877.

DOCUMENT 16
Two Descriptions of the Treaty of Verdun (843)

1. Charles met his brothers at Verdun and there the portions of the
empire were assigned. Ludwig received all beyond the Rhine, including
also Speyer, Worms, and Mainz on this side of the Rhine; Lothar received
the land bounded [by that of Ludwig on the west, and] by a line following along the lower Rhine, the Scheldt, and the Meuse, then through
Cambrai, Hainaut, Lomme, including the counties east of the Meuse, to
where the Saone flows into the Rhone, then along the Rhone to the sea,
including the counties on both sides of the Rhone; the rest as far as Spain,
went to Charles.

2. 842 (843). The three brothers divided the kingdom of the Franks
among themselves; to Charles fell the western portion from the British
ocean to the Meuse; to Ludwig, the eastern portion, that is, Germany as
far west as the Rhine, including certain cities and their counties east of
the Rhine to furnish him with wine; to Lothar, who, as the oldest, bore
the title of emperor, the part in between, which still bears the name of
Lotharingia, and all of Provence and the land of Italy with the city of
Rome.

Source: Oliver Thatcher and Edgar H. McNeal. *A Sourcebook for Medieval History*. New York: Scribner's, 1905. Nos. 17 and 18.

DOCUMENT 17
Hincmar Refuses to Swear Loyalty to
Louis the German (858)

The churches entrusted to us by God are not royal property, nor benefices of such a sort that the king can give them or take them away as he sees fit, because every thing which belongs to the churches is dedicated to God.

. . . And we bishops, consecrated to the Lord, are not men of such a sort that, like laymen, we should commend ourselves in vassalage to anyone . . . nor should we in any fashion take a solemn oath [of homage] which scriptural and apostolical and canonical authority forbid. It is abominable that hands anointed with holy oil, hands which through prayer and the sign of the cross can make the body and blood of Christ out of bread and water . . . that such hands should be touched in a secular ceremony of oath-taking. And it is sinful that the tongue of a bishop, which by the grace of God is a key to heaven, should pronounce an oath over holy relics like any common layman.

Source: Hincmar. In MGH, Capitularia II, ed. A Boretius and V. Krause. Hannover: MGH, 1897.

DOCUMENT 18
Bishops Fighting the Norse Invasions (885)

883. The Northmen, ascending the Rhine, plundered and burnt many villages. Liutbert, archbishop of Mainz, with a small band of troops, attacked them and, after killing many of them, recovered much of the booty which they had taken. Cologne [which had been burnt by the Northmen in 881] was rebuilt, except its churches and monasteries, and its walls with their gates and towers were restored.

885. The Northmen entered the territory about Liège, collected all kinds of provisions, and prepared to spend the winter there. But Liutbert, archbishop of Mainz, and count Heimrih, with others, fell upon them suddenly, killed many of them, and drove the others into a small stronghold. They then seized the provisions which the Northmen had col-

lected. The Northmen, after enduring a long siege, during which they suffered from hunger, finally fled from the stronghold by night.

Source: Oliver Thatcher and Edgar H. McNeal. *A Sourcebook for Medieval History*. New York: Scribner's, 1905. No. 20.

DOCUMENT 19
On the Election of Bishops (9th c.)

Every election of a bishop, priest, or deacon, which is made by the nobility [that is, emperor, or others in authority], is void, according to the rule which says "If a bishop makes use of the secular powers to obtain a diocese, he shall be deposed and those who supported him shall be cast out of the church."

Laymen have not the right to choose those who are to be made bishops.

No layman, whether emperor or noble, shall interfere with the election or promotion of a patriarch, metropolitan, or bishop; lest there should arise some unseemly disturbance or contention; especially since it is not fitting that any layman or person in secular authority should have any authority in such matters. . . . If any emperor or nobleman, or layman of any other rank, opposes the canonical election, of any member of the clergy, let him be anathema until he yields and accepts the clear will of the church in the election and ordination of the bishop.

Source: Oliver Thatcher and Edgar H. McNeal. *A Sourcebook for Medieval History*. New York: Scribner's, 1905. No. 33.

DOCUMENT 20
The Election of Otto I (936)

After Henry, the father of his country and the greatest and best of kings, had died, all the people of the Franks and the Saxons chose for their king his son Otto, whom Henry had already designated as his successor, and they sent out notices of the coronation, which was to take place at Aachen. . . . And when all were assembled there, the dukes and the commanders of the soldiers and other military leaders raised Otto upon the throne, which was erected in the portico adjoining the church of Karl the Great, and giving him their hands and promising him their fidelity and aid against all his enemies, they made him king according to their custom. Meanwhile the archbishop of Mainz and the clergy and people awaited him within the church. And when he approached the archbishop met him, . . . and went with him to the center of the church; . . . then turning to the people . . . he said: "I bring you Otto, chosen by God, designated by our lord Henry, and now made king by all the princes; if this choice pleases you, raise your right hands." At this, the whole people raised their right hands to heaven and hailed the new ruler with a mighty shout. Then the archbishop advanced with the king, who was clothed with a short tunic after the Frankish custom, to the altar, on which lay the royal insignia, the sword and belt, the cloak and armlets, the staff with the sceptre and diadem. The primate at this time was Hildibert, a Frank by birth and a monk by training. He had been brought up and educated at the monastery of Fulda, and finally was made archbishop of Mainz. . . . Now when there had arisen a dispute as to who should consecrate the king (for the honor was claimed by the archbishops both of Trier and of Cologne, the former because his see was the oldest and had been founded, as it were, by St. Peter, and the latter because Aachen was in his diocese), the difficulty was settled by both of them yielding with all good will to Hildibert.

The archbishop, going up to the altar, took up the sword and belt and, turning to the king, said: "Receive this sword with which you shall cast out all the enemies of Christ, both pagans and wicked Christians, and receive with it the authority and power given to you by God to rule over all the Franks for the security of all Christian people." Then taking up the cloak and armlets he put them on the king and said: "The borders of this cloak trailing on the ground shall remind you that you are to be zealous in the faith and to keep peace." Finally, taking up the sceptre and staff, he said: "By these symbols you shall correct your subjects with fatherly discipline and foster the servants of God and the widows and orphans. May the oil of mercy never be lacking, to your head, that you maybe crowned here and in the future life with an eternal reward." Then the archbishops Hildibert of Mainz and Wicfrid of Cologne anointed him with the sacred oil and crowned him with the golden crown, and now that the whole coronation ceremony was completed they led him to the throne, which he ascended. The throne was built between two marble columns of great beauty and was so placed that he could see all and be seen by all.

Then after the Te Deum and the mass, the king descended from his throne and proceeded to the palace, where he sat down with his bishops and people at a marble table which was adorned with royal lavishness; and the dukes served him. Gilbert, duke of Lotharingia, who held the office by right, superintended the preparations [i.e., acted as chamberlain], Eberhard, duke of Franconia, presided over the arrangements for the king's table [acted as seneschal], Herman, duke of Suabia, acted as cupbearer, Arnulf, duke of Bavaria, commanded the knights and chose the place of encampment [acted as marshal]. Siegfrid, chief of the Saxons, second only to the king, and son-in-law of the former king, ruled Saxony for Otto, providing against attacks of the enemy and caring for the young Henry, Otto's brother.

Source: Oliver Thatcher and Edgar H. McNeal. *A Sourcebook for Medieval History*. New York: Scribner's, 1905. No. 27.

DOCUMENT 21
Pope Leo VIII Grants the Emperor the Right to Choose the Pope and to Invest Bishops (963)

In the synod held at Rome in the Church of the Holy Saviour. Following the example of blessed pope Adrian, who granted to Charlemagne, victorious king of the Franks and Lombards, the dignity of the patriciate and the right to ordain the pope and to invest bishops, we, Leo, bishop, servant of the servants of God, with all the clergy and people of Rome, by our apostolic authority bestow upon lord Otto I, king of the Germans, and upon, his successors in the kingdom of Italy forever, the right of choosing the successor of the pope, and of ordaining the pope and the archbishops and bishops, so that they shall receive their investiture and consecration from him, with the exception of those prelates whose investiture and consecration the emperor has conceded to the pope or the archbishops. No one, no matter what his dignity or ecclesiastical rank, shall have the authority to choose the patricius or to ordain the pope or any bishop without the consent of the emperor, and that without bribery; and the emperor shall be by right both king [of Italy] and patricius [of Rome]. But if anyone has been chosen bishop by the clergy and people, he shall not be consecrated unless he has been approved by the aforesaid king and has received his investiture from him.

Source: Oliver Thatcher and Edgar H. McNeal. *A Sourcebook for Medieval History*. New York: Scribner's, 1905. No. 55.

DOCUMENT 22
Otto I Grants a Market to the Archbishop of Hamburg (965)

In the name of the undivided Trinity. Otto by the favor of God Emperor, Augustus. If we grant the requests of clergymen and liberally endow the places which are dedicated to the worship of God, we believe that it will undoubtedly assist in securing for us the eternal reward. Therefore, let all know that for the love of God we have granted the petition of Adaldagus, the reverend archbishop of Hamburg, and have given him permission to establish a market in the place called Bremen. In connection with the market we grant him jurisdiction, tolls, a mint, and all other things connected therewith to which our royal treasury would have a right. We also take under our special protection all the merchants who live in that place, and grant them the same protection and rights as those merchants have who live in other royal cities. And no one shall have any jurisdiction there except the aforesaid archbishop and those to whom he may delegate it. Signed with our hand and sealed with our ring.

Source: Oliver Thatcher and Edgar H. McNeal. *A Sourcebook for Medieval History*. New York: Scribner's, 1905. No. 302.

DOCUMENT 23
Eadmer on the Church at Canterbury (1067)

6. In the days of Archbishop Odo (the twenty-second) the roof of Christ Church had become rotten from excessive age, and rested throughout upon half shattered pieces: wherefore he set about to reconstruct it, and being also desirous of giving to the walls a more aspiring altitude, he directed his assembled workmen to remove altogether the disjointed structure above, and commanded them to supply the deficient height of the walls by raising them. But because it was absolutely necessary that the Divine Service should not be interrupted, and no temple

could be found sufficiently capacious to receive the multitude of the people, the archbishop prayed to Heaven that until the work should be completed, neither rain nor wind might be suffered to intrude within the walls of the church, so as to prevent the performance of the service. And so it came to pass: for during three years in which the walls of the church were being carried upwards, the whole building remained open to the sky: yet did no rain fall either within the walls of the church, or even within the walls of the city, that could impede the clergy standing in the church in the performance of their duty, or restrain the people from coming even to the beginning of it. And truly it was a sight worth seeing, to behold the space beyond the walls of the city drenched with water, while the walls themselves remained perfectly dry.

7. During the primacy of this good and holy Odo, it happened that in the course of one of his visitations he came to the monastery of Ripon, which had been founded by Wilfrid, and in the church of which his remains had been deposited. But at this time the place was reduced by wars and hostile incursions to a deserted and ruined solitude. Wherefore having opened the ground where the blessed Wilfrid was deposited, he reverently raised his bones and dust, with the intention of conveying them to his church at Canterbury. "Nevertheless, lest the place which Wilfrid had loved above all others while he remained in the flesh, should be utterly deprived of all relics of him, he deposited there in a convenient place a small portion of them, and then, enriched with so great a treasure, returned to Canterbury, where he was received by the whole population with great rejoicing, and accompanied to the house of God with solemn praises. He there placed the relics of the blessed Wilfrid which he had brought with him in the great Altar, which was consecrated in honor of our Lord Jesus Christ."

8. It has been related to me by certain of the seniors of the convent, that in the time of King Edgar, there came to England four clerks, who presented themselves at his court, and asserted that they had brought with them the body of Saint Audoen. And when the king refused to believe this, they appealed to the miraculous power which the relics possessed. Whereupon the king, thinking this to be a matter rather for ecclesiastical judgment than for his own, commanded the attendance of Archbishop Odo. And when he had succeeded in performing several miraculous cures by the contact of the relics in question, the truth of the story was no longer doubted; the king munificently rewarded the bearers

of this treasure, and committed it to the charge of the archbishop, that it might be conveyed to Canterbury, and worthily deposited in Christ Church. As to the four clerks, they accompanied it there, and were so well pleased with the monastery, that they became monks, and ended their days therein.

9. When the sacred bones of the blessed Father Audoen were brought to Canterbury, a precious and handsome coffer (scrinium) was made for them, according to the fashion of those days, in which they were decently laid, and carefully enwrapped in several winding-sheets. This took place about the same time that the venerable Odo had translated the body of the blessed Wilfrid, archbishop of York, from Ripon to Canterbury (as above related).

10. Now on the day of the coming of Dunstan, the successor of Odo, to Canterbury, he was celebrating mass at the Altar of the Saviour, when suddenly the house was covered with a cloud, and that dove which first was seen by John in Jordan, again appeared, and hovered over him. And when the sacrifice was completed, it rested upon the tomb of the blessed Odo, which was constructed in the fashion of a pyramid, to the south of the Altar.

14. After these things, and while misfortunes fell thick upon all parts of England, it happened that the city of Canterbury was set on fire by the carelessness of some individuals, and that the rising flames caught the mother church thereof. How can I tell it?—the whole was consumed, and nearly all the monastic offices that appertained to it, as well as the church of the blessed John the Baptist, where as aforesaid the remains of the archbishops were buried. The exact nature and amount of the damage occasioned by that conflagration no man can tell. But its extent may be estimated, from the fact that the devouring flames consumed nearly all that was there preserved most precious, whether in ornaments of gold, of silver, or, of other materials, or in sacred and profane books. Those things that could be replaced, were therefore the less to be regretted; but a mighty and interminable grief oppressed this Church because the privileges granted by the popes of Rome, and by the kings and princes of this kingdom, all carefully sealed and collected together, by which they and theirs were bound to defend and uphold the Church for ever, were now reduced to ashes. Copies of these documents were sought for, and collected from every place where such things were preserved: but their bulls and seals were irrecoverably destroyed with the church in which they had been deposited.

17. Now, after this lamentable fire, the bodies of the pontiffs (namely, Cuthbert, Bregwin, and their successors) rested undisturbed in their

coffins for three years, until that most energetic and honorable man, Lanfranc, abbot of Caen, was made archbishop of Canterbury. And when he came to Canterbury, and found that the church of the Saviour, which he had undertaken to rule, was reduced to almost nothing by fire and ruin, he was filled with consternation. But although the magnitude of the damage had well nigh reduced him to despair, he took courage, and neglecting his own accommodation, he completed, in all haste, the houses essential to the monks. For those which had been used for many years, were found too small for the increased numbers of the convent. He therefore pulled down to the ground all that he found of the burnt monastery, whether of buildings or the wasted remains of buildings, and, having dug out their foundations from under the earth, he constructed in their stead others, which excelled them greatly both in beauty and magnitude. He built cloisters, celerers' offices, refectories, dormitories, with all other necessary offices, and all the buildings within the enclosure of the curia, as well as the walls thereof. As for the church, which the aforesaid fire, combined with its age, had rendered completely unserviceable, he set about to destroy it utterly, and erect a more noble one. And in the space of seven years, he raised this new church from the very foundations, and rendered it nearly perfect. But before the work began, he commanded that the bodies of the saints, which were buried in the eastern part of the church, should be removed to the western part, where the oratory of the blessed Virgin Mary stood. Wherefore, after a three days' fast, the bodies of those most precious priests of the Lord, Dunstan and Elphege, were raised, and in presence of an innumerable multitude, conveyed to their destined place of interment, and there decently buried. To which I, Edmer, can bear witness, for I was then a boy at the school.

18. But, in process of time, as the new work of the commenced church proceeded, it became necessary to take down the remainder of the old work, where the bodies of the saints just mentioned were deposited. Having prepared, therefore, the refectory of the brethren for the celebration of Divine Service, we all proceeded thither, from the old church in festal procession, bearing with honour and reverence our glorious and sweet fathers, Dunstan and Elphege.

19. When the high Altar of the old church was taken down, the relics of the blessed Wilfrid were found, and placed in a coffer (scrinium); but after some years, the brethren became of opinion that they ought to have a more permanent resting-place, and, accordingly, a sepulchre was pre-

pared for them, on the north side of an altar, in which they were reverently inclosed, on the fourth idus of October. Moreover, when the other altars were destroyed, all the holy places, which the wisdom of the ancient fathers had constructed within them, were discovered; to the truth of which I can bear a faithful testimony, seeing that I was myself an eyewitness of all that was done.

22. Archbishop Anselm, who succeeded Lanfranc, (A.D. 1093), appointed Ernulf to be prior. This Ernulf was a Frenchman, and originally a monk of St. Lucian, in Beauvais. He, then, becoming dissatisfied with that monastery, joined Lanfranc, whose pupil he had been at Bec, and remained with him as a monk at Canterbury. After the death of Lanfranc, he was made prior, as above related, then (in 1107) abbot of Burgh, (Peterborough,) and finally, (A.D. 1114,) bishop of Rochester. While at Canterbury, having taken down the eastern part of the church which Lanfranc had built, he erected it so much more magnificently, that nothing like it could be seen in England, either for the brilliancy of its glass windows, the beauty of its marble pavement, or the many coloured pictures which led the wondering eyes to the very summit of the ceiling.

23. This chancel, however, which Ernulf left unfinished, was superbly completed by his successor Conrad, who decorated it with excellent paintings, and furnished it with precious ornaments. At Burgh, Ernulf pulled down the ruinous old buildings, laid new foundations, and finished them to the roof; to wit, a dormitory, chapter-house, refectory, and necessarium. And at Rochester, he built a dormitory, chapter-house, and refectory.

24. His works at Canterbury, however, originated with Anselm, for that prelate allowed the monks to manage their own affairs, and gave them for priors Ernulf, and then Conrad, both monks of their own monastery. And thus it happened that, in addition to the general prosperity and good order of their property, which resulted from this freedom, they were enabled to enlarge their church, by all that part which stretches from the great tower to the east; which work Anselm himself provided for. For when Duke Robert of Normandy undertook his crusade, (A.D. 1096,) great riches were exacted from the English by his brother King Henry to supply him with funds, and the archbishop being compelled to contribute, drew out a large sum from the treasury of the church of Canterbury. And to make amends, straightway granted to the said church the revenues of his town of Peckham, for seven years, the whole of which were expended upon the new work.

26. The church of Canterbury, thus founded and finished by Lanfranc, but enlarged by Anselm, was dedicated by Archbishop William, with all respect and liberality, on the 4th of May. At this dedication were present, Henry king of England, David king of Scotland, and all the bishops of England. So famous a dedication has never been heard of on the earth since the dedication of the temple of Solomon.

Source: Robert W. Willis. *The Architectural History of Canterbury Cathedral.* London: Longmans and Company, 1843.

DOCUMENT 24
Two Accounts of the Revolt against and the Expulsion of the Archbishop of Cologne (1074)

1. To his beloved brother and fellow bishop, Udo, archbishop [of Trier], Anno, archbishop of Cologne sends his love, etc. . . . You have no doubt heard about the violence and insults which I have suffered from my citizens, although I have said nothing about the matter in my letters to you. And you have also probably heard how I was restored to my place in the city by the help of others. According to the canon law, I should immediately have punished their abominable insolence with excommunication and interdict, but I restrained myself from doing so, because it might have seemed that I did it not out of zeal for the Lord, but for personal reasons. But some of the insolent ones disregarded and despised my gentle treatment of them, and at night secretly collected and threatened me with worse things than they had done before. On this account, with the advice of the bishops whom the pope sent me, I anathematized them a week after Pentecost. I beg you to publish this anathema in your diocese. Do not permit your people to be infected with the leprosy of these excommunicated persons, but keep them out of your territory, lest by their speech they excite your people to do the same things against you. I beg you to inform your bishops of this, in order that my contaminated flock may not infect theirs also.

2. The archbishop spent Easter in Cologne with his friend, the bishop of Munster, whom he had invited to celebrate this festival with him. When the bishop was ready to go home, the archbishop ordered his ser-

vants to get a suitable boat ready for him. They looked all about, and finally found a good boat which belonged to a rich merchant of the city,
and demanded it for the archbishop's use. They ordered it to be got ready
at once and threw out all the merchandise with which it was loaded. The
merchant's servants, who had charge of the boat, resisted, but the archbishop's men threatened them with violence unless they immediately
obeyed. The merchant's servants hastily ran to their lord and told him
what had happened to the boat, and asked him what they should do. The
merchant had a son who was both bold and strong. He was related to the
great families of the city, and, because of his character, very popular. He
hastily collected his servants and as many of the young men of the city
as he could, rushed to the boat, ordered the servants of the archbishop
to get out of it, and violently ejected them from it. The advocate of the
city was called in, but his arrival only increased the tumult, and the merchant's son drove him off and put him to flight. The friends of both parties seized their arms and came to their aid, and it looked as if there were
going to be a great battle fought in the city. The news of the struggle was
carried to the archbishop, who immediately sent men to quell the riot,
and being very angry, he threatened the rebellious young men with dire
punishment in the next session of court. Now the archbishop was endowed with all virtues, and his uprightness in all matters, both of the
state and of the church, had often been proved. But he had one vice.
When he became angry, he could not control his tongue, but overwhelmed everybody, without distinction, with bitter upbraidings and violent vituperation. When his anger had passed, he regretted his fault and
reproached himself for it. The riot in the city was finally quieted a little,
but the young man, who was very angry as well as elated over his first
success, kept on making all the disturbance he could. He went about the
city making speeches to the people about the harsh government of the
archbishop, and accused him of laying unjust burdens on the people, of
depriving innocent persons of their property, and of insulting honorable
citizens with his violent and offensive words. . . . It was not difficult for
him to raise a mob. . . . Besides, they all regarded it as a great and glorious deed on the part of the people of Worms that they had driven out
their bishop because he was governing them too rigidly. And since they
were more numerous and wealthy than the people of Worms, and had
arms, they disliked to have it thought that they were not equal to the
people of Worms in courage, and it seemed to them a disgrace to submit

like women to the rule of the archbishop who was governing them in a
tyrannical manner.

Source: Oliver Thatcher and Edgar H. McNeal. *A Sourcebook for Medieval History.* New York: Scribner's, 1905. Nos. 308 and 309.

DOCUMENT 25
Mutual Assistance of the Bishop of Liège and
the Count of Hainaut (1076)

In assigning all these allods and fiefs to the church of Liège, and in
the liege homage of this great man the Count of Hainaut, it was laid
down that the Count of Hainaut owed his lord the Bishop of Liège service and aid for all purposes and against all men with all the forces of his
vassals, both infantry and cavalry, and that once the Count was outside
the County of Hainaut these forces should be maintained at the Bishop's
expense. If the lord Count came to the lord Bishop for the purpose of receiving his land, the lord Bishop had to pay him any expenses he had
incurred after leaving the County of Hainaut. If the lord Bishop summoned the Count of Hainaut to his court or to any conference, he had
likewise to pay him his expenses. If the lord Emperor of the Romans summoned the Count of Hainaut to his court for any reason, the Bishop of
Liège ought at his own expense to bring him safely to and from the court
and appear on his behalf and answer for him in the court. Furthermore,
if anyone should for wicked ends attack the land of Hainaut, the Bishop
of Liège had to provide the Count of Hainaut with army for army at the
expense of the Bishop. Should the Count of Hainaut lay siege to any
fortress which belonged to his own honor or should siege be laid to him,
the Bishop must at his own expense assist the Count with five hundred
soldiers, whilst the Count must provide the Bishop with means to buy
victuals at a fair price. If there were grass or other fodder necessary to
horses in the fields, the Bishop and his men might take this at the
Bishop's choice. The bishop of Liège owed this assistance to the Count
of Hainaut over three periods in a year, each consisting of forty days.
With the Count, three castellans of Hainaut, those of Mons, Beaumont
and Valenciennes, did homage to the Bishop of Liège. The Bishop of
Liège had to give the Count of Hainaut three pairs of garments at Christ-

mas, each garment to be worth six marks of silver (Liège weight), and he was to give garments also to each of the castellans, again each garment to be worth six marks. Should any allod anywhere in the whole county be given to the Count of Hainaut and subsequently received back from him as a fief, or should he acquire as his property any allod, any serfs or any serving women within the boundaries of his county, he would at once hold them, with the rest of his fief, of the Bishop of Liège. And although many eminent men, such as dukes, barons and counts, and other noblemen and their men of peace had to answer and make amends to the law court of Liège, the Counts of Hainaut and their men of peace were in no way bound to answer to this court.

Source: Gislebert of Mons. *Chronicon Hanoniense*, ed. L. Vanderkindere. Brussels, 1904.

DOCUMENT 26
Five Documents about the Investiture Conflict (1076)

1. HENRY IV DEPOSES POPE GREGORY VII

Henry, king not by usurpation, but by the holy ordination of God, to Hildebrand, not pope, but false monk.

This is the salutation which you deserve, for you have never held any office in the church without making it a source of confusion and a curse to Christian men instead of an honor and a blessing. To mention only the most obvious cases out of many, you have not only dared to touch the Lord's anointed, the archbishops, bishops, and priests; but you have scorned them and abused them, as if they were ignorant servants not fit to know what their master was doing. This you have done to gain favor with the vulgar crowd. You have declared that the bishops know nothing and that you know everything; but if you have such great wisdom you have used it not to build but to destroy. Therefore we believe that St. Gregory, whose name you have presumed to take, had you in mind when he said: "The heart of the prelate is puffed up by the abundance of subjects, and he thinks himself more powerful than all others." All this we have endured because of our respect for the papal office, but you have mistaken our humility for fear, and have dared to make an attack upon the royal and imperial authority which we received from

God. You have even threatened to take it away, as if we had received it from you, and as if the empire and kingdom were in your disposal and not, in the disposal of God. Our Lord Jesus Christ has called us to the government of the empire, but he never called you to the rule of the church. This is the way you have gained advancement in the church: through craft you have obtained wealth; through wealth you have obtained favor; through favor, the power of the sword; and through the power of the sword, the papal seat, which is the seat of peace; and then from the seat of peace you have expelled peace. For you have incited subjects to rebel against their prelates, by teaching them to despise the bishops, their rightful rulers. You have given to laymen the authority over priests, whereby they condemn and depose those whom the bishops have put over them to teach them. You have attacked me, who, unworthy as I am, have yet been anointed to rule among the anointed of God, and who, according to the teaching of the fathers, can be judged by no one save God alone, and can be deposed for no crime except infidelity. For the holy fathers in the time of the apostate Julian did not presume to pronounce sentence of deposition against him, but left him to be judged and condemned by God. St. Peter himself said: "Fear God, honor the king" [1 Pet. 2:17]. But you, who fear not God, have dishonored me, whom He hath established. St. Paul, who said that even an angel from heaven should be accursed who taught any other than the true doctrine, did not make an exception in your favor, to permit you to teach false doctrines. For he says: "But though we, or an angel from heaven, preach any other gospel unto you than that which we have preached unto you, let him be accursed" [Gal. 1:8]. Come down, then, from that apostolic seat which you have obtained by violence; for you have been declared accursed by St. Paul for your false doctrines and have been condemned by us and our bishops for your evil rule. Let another ascend the throne of St. Peter, one who will not use religion as a cloak of violence, but will teach the life-giving doctrine of that prince of the apostles. I, Henry, king by the grace of God, with all my bishops, say unto you: "Come down, come down, and be accursed through all the ages."

2. FROM THE GERMAN BISHOPS TO POPE GREGORY VII

Siegfried, archbishop of Mainz, Udo, bishop of Trier, William, bishop of Utrecht, etc. [a list of names of bishops, twenty-six in all], to brother Hildebrand.

At first when you made yourself pope we thought it better to ignore the illegality of your action and to submit to your rule, in the hope that you would redeem your bad beginning by a just and righteous government of the church, although we realized even then the enormity of the sin which you had committed. But now the lamentable condition of the whole church shows us only too well how we were deceived in you; your violent entrance into office was but the first in a series of wicked deeds and unjust decrees. Our Lord and Redeemer has said, in more places than we can well enumerate here, that love and gentleness are the marks of his disciples, but you are known for your pride, your ambition, and your love of strife. You have introduced worldliness into the church; you have desired a great name rather than a reputation for holiness; you have made a schism in the church and offended its members, who before your time were living together in peace and charity. Your mad acts have kindled the flame of discord which now rages in the churches of Italy, Germany, France, and Spain. The bishops have been deprived of their divine authority, which rests upon the grace of the Holy Spirit received through ordination, and the whole administration of ecclesiastical matters you have given to rash and ignorant laymen. There is nowhere in the church today a bishop or a priest who does not hold his office through abject acquiescence in your ambitious schemes. The order of bishops, to whom the government of the church was entrusted by the Lord, you have thrown into confusion, and you have disturbed that excellent coordination of the members of Christ which Paul in so many places commends and inculcates, while the name of Christ has almost disappeared from the earth; and all this through those decrees in which you glory. Who among men is not filled with astonishment and indignation at your claims to sole authority, by which you would deprive your fellow-bishops of their coordinate rights and powers? For you assert that you have the authority to try any one of our parishioners for any sin which may have reached your ears even by chance report, and that no one of us has the power to loose or to bind such a sinner, but that it belongs to you alone or to your legate. Who that knows the scriptures does not perceive the madness of this claim? Since, therefore, it is now apparent that the church of God is in danger of destruction through your presumption, we have come to the conclusion that this state of things can no longer be endured, and we have determined to break our silence and to make public the reasons why you are unfit and have always been unfit to rule the church as pope.

These are the reasons: In the first place, in the reign of emperor Henry [III] of blessed memory, you bound yourself by oath never to accept the papacy or to permit anyone else to accept it during the life of that emperor or of his son without the consent of the emperor. There are many bishops still living who can bear witness to that oath. On another occasion, when certain cardinals were aiming to secure the office, you took an oath never to accept the papacy, on condition that they should all take the same oath. You know yourself how faithfully you have kept these oaths! In the second place, it was agreed in a synod held in the time of pope Nicholas [II] and attended by 125 bishops, that no one, under penalty of excommunication, should ever accept the papacy who had not received the election of the cardinals, the approbation of the people, and the consent of the emperor. You yourself proposed and promoted that decree and signed it with your own hand. In the third place, you have filled the whole church with the stench of scandal, by associating on too intimate terms with a woman who was not a member of your family [the countess Matilda]. We do not wish to base any serious charge on this last accusation; we refer to it because it outrages our sense of propriety. And yet the complaint is very generally made that all the judgments and acts of the papacy are passed on by the women about the pope, and that the whole church is governed by this new female conclave. And finally, no amount of complaint is adequate to express the insults and outrages you have heaped upon the bishops, calling them sons of harlots and other vile names. Therefore, since your pontificate was begun in perjury and crime, since your innovations have placed the church of God in the gravest peril, since your life and conduct are stained with infamy; we now renounce our obedience, which indeed was never legally promised to you. You have declared publicly that you do not consider us to be bishops; we reply that no one of us shall ever hold you to be the pope.

3. Pope Gregory VII Excommunicates Henry IV

St. Peter, prince of the apostles, incline thine ear unto me, I beseech thee, and hear me, thy servant, whom thou hast nourished from mine infancy and hast delivered from mine enemies that hate me for my fidelity to thee. Thou art my witness, as are also my mistress, the mother of God, and St. Paul thy brother, and all the other saints, that thy holy Roman church called me to its government against my own will, and that I did not gain thy throne by violence; that I would rather have ended my days in exile than have obtained thy place by fraud or for worldly ambition. It is not by my efforts, but by thy grace, that I am set to rule over the Christian world which was specially intrusted to thee by Christ. It is by thy grace and as thy representative that God has given to me the power to bind and to loose in heaven and in earth. Confident of my integrity and authority, I now declare in the name of omnipotent God, the Father, Son, and Holy Spirit, that Henry, son of the emperor Henry, is deprived of his kingdom of Germany and Italy; I do this by thy authority and in defence of the honor of thy church, because he has rebelled against it. He who attempts to destroy the honor of the church should be deprived of such honor as he may have held. He has refused, to obey as a Christian should, he has not returned to God from whom he had wandered, he has had dealings with excommunicated persons, he has done many iniquities, he has despised the warnings which, as thou art witness, I sent to him for his salvation, he has cut himself off from thy church, and has attempted to rend it asunder; therefore, by thy authority, I place him under the curse. It is in thy name that I curse him, that all people may know that thou art Peter, and upon thy rock the Son of the living God has built his church, and the gates of hell shall not prevail against it.

4. THE AGREEMENT AT OPPENHEIM: HENRY IV CAPITULATES TO GREGORY VII

Promise of king Henry to pope Hildebrand, also called Gregory.

In accordance with the advice of my subjects, I hereby promise to show henceforth fitting reverence and obedience to the apostolic office and to you, pope Gregory. I further promise to make suitable reparation for any loss of honor which you or your office may have suffered through me. And since I have been accused of certain grave crimes, I will either clear myself by presenting proof of my innocence or by undergoing the ordeal, or else I will do such penance as you may decide to be adequate for my fault.

5. HENRY IV ANNULS THE DECREES AGAINST POPE GREGORY

Henry, by the grace of God king, to the archbishops, bishops, margraves, counts, and to his subjects of every rank and dignity, greeting and

good will. Our faithful subjects have convinced us that in our recent controversy with pope Gregory we were led astray by certain evil counsellors.
Therefore we now make known to all, that we have repented of our former actions and have determined henceforth to obey him in everything,
as our predecessors were wont to do before us, and to make full reparation
for any injury which we may have inflicted upon him or his office. We
command all of you to follow our example and to offer satisfaction to St.
Peter and to his vicar, pope Gregory, for any fault you may have committed, and to seek absolution from him, if any of you are under his ban.

Source: Oliver Thatcher and Edgar H. McNeal. *A Sourcebook for Medieval History*. New York: Scribner's, 1905. Nos. 75, 76, 77, 78, and 79.

DOCUMENT 27
Trial of William of Saint-Calais, Bishop of Durham, before William II (1088)

The bishop said: "Lord barons and laymen . . . I will answer to the
archbishops and bishops; I have nothing to say to you and I have not
come here to receive your judgment. . . ." Then Roger Bigot, a great
baron, said to the king: "You should tell the bishop why you accuse him,
and if he will answer, we will judge him on his answer; if not, do what
your barons advise." The bishop answered: "I have said, and I repeat, that
I totally reject the judgment of laymen. . . ." Then Hugh de Beaumont,
another great baron, rising by order of the king, said to the bishop: "The
king accuses you of this, that when his enemies were advancing on
him . . . he summoned you, in my hearing, to come to his aid, and you
promised that you would come with seven knights. . . . Instead you fled
from the court . . . and so failed him in his hour of need. . . ." The bishop
replied: "Hugh, say what you will; I won't answer you today: . . ." Hugh
de Beaumont said: "If I cannot judge you today . . . then you and the
other clergy shall never again judge me." Lanfranc, archbishop of Canterbury, who was something of a legal expert, suggested that the bishop
leave the room, while the court decided whether he must answer. When
the bishop returned, Thomas archbishop of York said: "Lord bishop, our
lord the archbishop and the king's court have judged that you must satisfy the king before you can regain your fief. . . . The bishop made an-

other long argument against being judged by laymen and against being deprived of his bishopric. He asked to be allowed to take counsel with the other bishops. Lanfranc made the obvious reply: "The bishops are judges and so you cannot have them as your counsel." The bishop of Durham again complained that he was being deprived of his bishopric contrary to Church law. Lanfranc answered: "We are not passing judgment on your bishopric but on your fief, and in this fashion we judged the bishop of Bayeux before the father of the present king concerning the fief which he held. . . . The bishop said: "Lord archbishop, I have never mentioned a fief today . . . but I have complained about losing my bishopric. . . ." The archbishop replied: "If I haven't heard you speak of a fief, I still know that you hold a great one, and we will judge you on that." The bishop gave notice that he would appeal to Rome, and was sent out again while the court formulated its decision. When the bishop returned . . . Hugh de Beaumont said: "Lord bishop, the king's court and these barons judge thus—since you will not answer the king on the charges which he made against you . . . you have forfeited your fief."

Source: Simeon of Durham. *Symeonis monachi Opera omnia*, I, ed. T. Arnold. Rolls Series 75. London: Longman, 1882.

DOCUMENT 28
The Bishop of Hamburg Gives a Charter to His Dutch Merchants (1106)

1. In the name of the holy and undivided Trinity. Frederick, by the grace of God bishop of Hamburg, to all the faithful in Christ, gives a perpetual benediction. We wish to make known to all the agreement which certain people living this side of the Rhine, who are called Hollanders, have made with us.

2. These men came to us and earnestly begged us to grant them certain lands in our bishopric, which are uncultivated, swampy, and useless to our people. We have consulted our subjects about this and, considering that this would be profitable to us and to our successors, have granted their request.

3. The agreement was made that they should pay us every year one *denarius* for every hide of land. We have thought it necessary to deter-

mine the dimensions of the hide, in order that no quarrel may hereafter arise about it. The hide shall be 720 royal rods long and thirty royal rods wide. We also grant them the streams which flow through this land.

4. They agreed to give the tithe according to our decree, that is, every eleventh sheaf of grain, every tenth lamb, every tenth pig, every tenth goat, every tenth goose, and a tenth of the honey and of the flax. For every colt they shall pay a *denarius* on St. Martin's day, and for every calf an obol.

5. They promised to obey me in all ecclesiastical matters according to the decrees of the holy fathers, the canonical law, and the practice in the diocese of Utrecht.

6. They agreed to pay every year two marks for every 100 hides for the privilege of holding their own courts for the settlement of all their differences about secular matters. They did this because they feared they would suffer from the injustice of foreign judges. If they cannot settle the more important cases they shall refer them to the bishop. And if they take the bishop with them [that is, from Hamburg to the colony] for the purpose of deciding one of their trials, they shall provide for his support as long as he remains there by granting him one-third of all the fees arising from the trial; and they shall keep the other two-thirds.

7. We have given them permission to found churches wherever they may wish on these lands. For the support of the priests who shall serve God in these churches we grant a tithe of our tithes from these parish churches.

Source: Oliver Thatcher and Edgar H. McNeal. *A Sourcebook for Medieval History.* New York: Scribner's, 1905. No. 298.

DOCUMENT 29
Guibert de Nogent Recounts the Misdeeds of the Bishops of Laon (1115)

CHAPTER I

As I am now going to tell the story of the people of Laon, or rather to put on the stage the tragedy of Laon, I must first trace the source in my opinion of all the trouble to the wrongdoing of the prelates. To their work, which went on far too long, we must add, they say, what was done by Ascelin, also called Adalbero. He, we find, was a native of Lotharingia, having much wealth in goods and lands, who sold up everything and taking huge sums of money to the see over which he presided, adorned his church with exceedingly fine furniture and much increased the prosperity of the church and the diocese, but marred all those benefits by his surpassing wickedness. For what could be more wicked or a greater disgrace to himself than the betrayal of his lord the king, an innocent boy, to whom he had taken an oath of fealty, and his diversion of the current of royal descent to the foreign line of Charles the Great? This crime, like Judas, he committed on the day of our Lord's Supper. In the overthrow of the reigning monarch and his descendants, he certainly did not foresee at the time the usefulness of the change, but only the fulfilment of his wicked will on the innocent.

Chapter II

Now Helinandus, a man of quite a poor family and humble origin, no scholar and of mean person, through his acquaintance with Walter, the old Count of Pontoise, from whose district he came, won the favour of Edward, the King of England, whose wife had some sort of connection with that count, and he became the king's chaplain, partly because he had some French culture. The English King often made him his envoy to Henry, the French king. From that king, who was very avaricious and given to selling bishoprics, by lavish bribes in the form of presents, he obtained a promise that on the death of any French bishop he should succeed to the pontifical insignia. For in his position as chaplain to the king and queen, abounding in wealth as England did at that time, he accumulated huge mountains of money, and therefore when the said opportunity of bribery favoured him, he gained the ear of King Henry. And so it fell out: and being installed at Laon, as he knew he would have no influence through respect for his birth or his learning, he placed his hopes on his wealth, of which he had a great sufficiency and which he had learnt to distribute with much tact, and on his agreeable manners.

And so he gave himself up to the embellishment and building of churches, and whilst seeming to do much for God's glory, he gave indisputable proof that he was only seeking men's esteem and the spread of his own fame by those good works. By such artfulness did he get possession of the Archbishopric of Reims, which he obtained after its great revenues had been squandered for two years under King Philip, a man most mercenary in what belonged to God, and he then received word from the Lord Pope that anyone having one wife could by no means take another. To some one asking plainly the meaning of that, he said that if he could also become Pope he would certainly not be secret about it.

CHAPTER III

After him Enguerrand succeeded, who surpassed the aforesaid bishop both in birth and learning, but in guarding the rights of the Church he was very poor, in comparison with the other. For certain revenues of the bishop, of which royal violence had at one time robbed that See, had been extracted from King Philip by Helinandus himself with entreaties and gifts and their restoration had been confirmed by the king's letters and seal; but this man on his entry, to his own ruin, gave back everything to the king, and during the rule of the three succeeding bishops they have been lost to the church and perhaps will be for ever. Hence in my opinion he has made parties to this simony all succeeding bishops, who shall take up the office with such fear of the king as to shrink from demanding restitution of that which he to his damnation gave for being made bishop.

CHAPTER IV

After his death in this manner, when the bishopric had been vacant for two years, at last we met together to choose a successor. Amongst those present was the same Enguerrand, who, when the former bishop was rejected by the king because of his frivolity, had by his appeal to the king obtained his election. It was plain that he was using every effort of his influence to obtain the election of one who would be under his hand. One who had the favor of the king and the clergy as a candidate, would not for that reason dare to oppose his marriage. To the ruin, therefore, of the city and of the whole province they chose a certain Gaudry, recommended by the King of England, who by report was rich in silver and gold.

The aforesaid person being chosen by the clergy in a vain hope of profit, by the efforts of Enguerrand in the first place with the aid of the rest to their own harm, request for his election is made by the King of

England at the court contrary to canon law. He, although by no means doubtful of the man's election, because he had no title from any church and had been admitted to no holy orders except those of a clerk, used his influence to have him made a sub-deacon and to procure him a canonry in the church of Rouen although up to this time he had lived the life of a soldier only. When all, therefore, had given their assent to his election, Master Anselm, the light of all France, ay, of the whole Latin world in learning and serenity of character, alone opposed it. He, on certain information, was aware of his character, whereas we were unwillingly supporting a stranger. There were some of us, it is true, who did not approve of him, but amongst the others cowards who followed the lead of our powerful rulers.

CHAPTER V

About three years after his appointment he gave the following sign, as it were, to his time. One of the nobles of the city was the castellan of a nun's convent, named Gerard, a man of great energy. He, although of small stature and of lean frame, had so lively a mind and tongue, such energy in the pursuit of war, that he compelled the provinces of Soissons, Laon, and Noyon, to fear him and won the respect of most men. Although he was known far and wide as one of sterling character, sometimes he made biting jests in coarse language against those about him, but never against people of good character.

Dressed in this tunic then, and a purple cloak over it, he went on horseback with some knights to the church. Entering he had stopped before the image of the crucified Lord, his followers dispersing here and there among the various altars to the Saints, and the servants of the conspirators being on the look-out, when word is sent to the Bishop in his palace that Gerard of Crecy (for he took his surname from the Castle of which he was lord) had come down to the church to pray. Taking, therefore, swords under their cloaks, Rorigo, brother of the Bishop (and others) go through the crypt which runs round the apse to the place where he was praying. Now he was stationed at the foot of a column, called a pillar, there being several columns between in a line from the screen to about the middle of the church. And whilst the morning was still dark and there were few people to be seen in the great church, they seized the man from behind as he prayed. He was praying with the fastening of his

cloak thrown behind and his hands clasped on his breast. Seizing the
cloak, therefore, behind, one of them so fastened him in it that he could
not easily move his hands. Whilst he was thus held by the Bishop's stew-
ard, the latter said, "You are taken." And he with his usual boldness,
turned his eye round on him (for he had one only) and looking at him
said, "Go away, you foul letcher!" But the other said to Rorigo, "Strike!"
Who drawing his sword with his left hand wounded him between the
nose and brow. And he, feeling himself wounded, said, "Take me where
you will." Then as they stabbed at him repeatedly and pressed him hard,
he, in desperate case, cried out, "Holy Mary, aid me!" Saying this, he fell
in extreme suffering.

Now there were in that conspiracy with the Bishop himself two
archdeacons of the church, Walter and Guy. Guy was also the Treasurer,
having a house on the other side of the church. From this house there
soon rushed out two servants, who, coming hastily there, took part in the
murder. For by that sacrilegious compact it had been resolved that should
those of the bishop's palace dare to help, they should quickly come forth
from that house. When therefore they had slashed his throat and his legs,
besides giving him other wounds, and he was groaning in the middle of
the church in extreme anguish, a few of the clergy who were then in the
choir, and some women who were going round to pray, murmuring against
them and half dead with fear, yet did not dare to make the least sound.
When the murder had been done, the two picked soldiers returned to
the Bishop's palace and with them were gathered the nobles of the city,
thus betraying their own betrayal; likewise also the archdeacons assembled there. Then the king's Governor, Ivo by name, a very prudent man,
having summoned the royal troops and those of the Abbey of St. John,
whose guardian Gerard had been, attacked the houses of the citizens
who had been in the conspiracy, plundering and burning them and driving the men out of the city. Now the archdeacons and the nobles followed the murderers of Gerard everywhere, making a display of their
fealty to the absent bishop.

CHAPTER VI

But the Bishop, remaining at Rome and pretending delight in the presence of the Apostolic Lord, was listening with eager expectation for some
pleasing news to reach him from French parts. At last the fulfilment of

his wishes was announced and the Lord Pope became aware that a great crime had been done in a great church. The Bishop had an interview with the Pope and by flattering presents shielded himself against suspicion of complicity. And so, more pleased than ever, Gaudry returned home from the City. But since the church, which had been outraged by a wicked act, needed purification, having sent a message to Hubert, the Bishop of Senlis, who was recently dismissed from his office for simony, he summoned him to do that work.

CHAPTER VI BIS

Armed with seals and the Apostolic rescripts the Lord Prelate returned from Rome. But the king, after the murder of Gerard, believing the Bishop to be a party to the crime, which under color of absence he sought to conceal, gave order that all the Bishop's palace should be stripped of corn, wine and meat, and he at Rome was aware of the plundering and the cause of it. And so letters were sent to the King, who had determined that he should be kept out of his See and had deprived him of his property, and other letters were despatched by him to his fellow-bishops and to the abbots of his own and their dioceses; but since between Laon and Soissons we have said before the bridge of the Ailette was the boundary, when he set foot on the first soil of his district, those archdeacons and nobles whom we had excommunicated, hastened to meet him. As therefore he was shut out of the city by the King's orders, with exceedingly rash boldness he threatened to enter it and what was hardly possible for a Caesar or for an Augustus, he declared he would do by force of arms. At length after gaining nothing but ridicule with so many auxiliaries, with the help of intermediaries he made terms for himself and his accomplices in the murder of Gerard, that is, the nobles of the city and both the archdeacons, with Lewis, the King's son (since then king) by means of a huge bribe.

Having entered the city therefore and held a meeting at St. Nicholas of the Wood, during mass, which he was celebrating there, he gave out that he would excommunicate those who had confiscated the property of those men, and had, when Gerard was killed, left the city. When I heard him say this, whispering in the ear of a certain abbot sitting next to me, I said, "Listen, further, to this absurdity. He ought to have excommunicated those who polluted his church with such a horrible crime, whereas he revenges himself on those who inflicted a just vengeance on the murderers."

CHAPTER VII

Now after some time when he had set out for England to extract money from the English king, whom he had served, and who had formerly been his friend, the Archdeacons Walter and Guy, with the nobles of the city, devised the following plan: Of old time such ill-fate had settled on that city that neither God nor any lord was feared therein, but according to each man's power and lust the state was involved in rapine and murder. For to begin with the source of the plague, whenever it happened that the king came there, he who ought to have exacted respect for himself with royal severity, was himself first shamefully fined on his own property. When his horses were led to the water morning and evening, his grooms were beaten and the horses carried off. It was known that the very clergy were held in such contempt, that neither their persons nor their goods were spared, as it is written, "Like as the people, so the priest." . . . Such and like things were done in the city. No one was safe going out at night. There remained for him nothing but plunder, capture and murder.

The clergy with the archdeacons considering this, and the nobles catching at pretexts for exacting money from the people, offer there through agents the choice of making composition by paying a sum to cover them. Now Commune is a new and a bad name of an arrangement for all the poorest classes to pay their usual due of servitude to their lords once only in the year, and to make good any breach of the laws they have committed by the payment fixed by law, and to be entirely free from all other exactions usually imposed on serfs. The people seizing on this opportunity for freeing themselves gathered huge sums of money to fill the gaping mouths of so many greedy men. And they, pleased with the shower poured upon them, took oaths binding themselves in the matter.

A pledge of mutual aid had been thus exchanged by the clergy and nobles with the people, when the Bishop returned with much wealth from England and being moved to anger against those responsible for this innovation, for a long time kept away from the city.

Saying therefore that he was moved with relentless wrath against those who had taken that oath and the principals in the transaction, in the end his loud-sounding words were suddenly quieted by the offer of a great heap of silver and gold. Therefore he swore that he would maintain the rights of the Commune according to the terms duly drawn up at Noyon and Saint-Quentin. The King too was induced by a bribe from the people to confirm the same by oath. O my God, who could say how many disputes arose when the gifts of the people were accepted, how many after oath had been sworn to reverse what they had agreed to, whilst they sought to bring back the serfs who had been freed from the oppression of their yoke, to their former state. At least there was implacable hatred by the Bishop and nobles against the citizens, and whereas he has not the power to crush the freedom of the French, after the fashion of Normandy and England, the pastor is weak and forgetful of his sacred calling through his insatiable greed.

Having therefore summoned the nobles and certain of the clergy on the last day of Lent in the holy days of the Passion of our Lord, he determined to urge the annulment of the Commune, to which he had sworn, and had by bribes induced the King to swear, and the day before the Passover, that is to say, on the day of the Lord's Supper, he summoned the King to this pious duty and instructed the King and all his people to break their oaths, in which snare he had first placed his own neck, on the day, that is, on which his predecessor, Ascelin, had betrayed his King as aforesaid. For on that day, when he should have performed that most glorious of all a prelate's duties, the consecration of the oil and the absolution of the people from their sins, he was not even seen to enter the church. He was intriguing with the King's courtiers for the annulment of the Commune and for the restoration by the King of the laws of the city to their former state. But the citizens fearing their overthrow, promised four hundred (perhaps more) pounds to the King and his courtiers. In reply the Bishop begged the nobles to go with him to interview the King. They promised on their part seven hundred pounds, and King Louis, son of Philip, of conspicuous person and a mighty warrior, hating sloth in business, of dauntless courage in adversity, and in other respects a good man, in this was not very just that he gave ear and attention too much to worthless persons debased by greed.

The King's craving for money being turned therefore, as I said, to feed upon the larger promise, through his consent the oaths of the Bishop and the nobles became void without any regard for honour or the sacred season. That night because of the outbreak of disorder caused by his most unjust blow, although the King had a lodging elsewhere, he was afraid to sleep outside the Bishop's palace. Very early in the morning the King departed and the Bishop assured the nobles they need have no fear about the agreement to pay so much money, knowing that he himself would pay whatever they had promised.

The compact of the Commune being broken, such rage, such amazement seized the citizens that all the officials abandoned their duties and the stalls of the craftsmen and cobblers were closed and nothing was exposed for sale by the innkeepers and hucksters, who expected to have nothing left when the lords began plundering. For at once the property of all was calculated by the Bishop and nobles, and whatever any man was known to have given to arrange the Commune, so much was demanded of him to procure its annulment. These events took place on the day of the Passover, which is called the preparation, and on the holy Sabbath when their minds were being prepared to receive the body and blood of the Lord, they were made ready for murders only here, for perjury there. Why say more? All the efforts of the prelate and the nobles in these days were reserved for fleecing their inferiors. But those inferiors were no longer moved by mere anger, but goaded into a murderous lust for the death of the Bishop and his accomplices and bound themselves by oath to effect their purpose. Now they say that four hundred took the oath.

CHAPTER VIII

The next day, that is, the fifth in Easter week, after midday, as he was engaged in business with Archdeacon Walter about the getting of money, behold there arose a disorderly noise throughout the city, men shouting "Commune!" and again through the middle of the chapel of the Blessed Mary through that door by which the murderers of Gerard had come and gone, there citizens now entered the Bishop's court with swords, battle-axes, bows and hatchets, and, carrying clubs and spears, a very great company. As soon as this sudden attack was discovered, the nobles rallied from all sides to the Bishop, having sworn to give him aid against such an onset, if it should occur.

Next the outrageous mob attacking the Bishop and howling before the walls of his palace, he with some who were succouring him fought them off by hurling of stones and shooting of arrows. For he now, as at all times, showed great spirit as a fighter; but because he had wrongly and in vain taken up another sword, by the sword he perished. Therefore being unable to stand against the reckless assaults of the people, he put on the clothes of one of his servants and flying to the vaults of the church hid himself in a cask, shut up in which with the head fastened on by a faithful follower he thought himself safely hidden. And as they ran hither and thither demanding where, not the Bishop, but the hangdog, was, they seized one of his pages, but through his faithfulness could not get what they wanted. Laying hands on another, they learn from the traitor's nod where to look for him. Entering the vaults, therefore, and searching everywhere, at last they found him in the following manner.

Teudeguld, having incurred the displeasure of Enguerrand, went over wholly to the party of the Commune in Laon. He who had spared neither monk nor clerk nor stranger, in fact no sex, was last of all to be the slayer of a bishop. He, the leader and instigator of this attack, searched most diligently for the Bishop, whom he hated more bitterly than the rest.

And so, as they sought for him in every vessel, this fellow halted in front of that cask, where the man was hiding, and having broken in the head, asked again and again who was there. And he, hardly able to move his frozen lips under his blows, said "A prisoner." Now the Bishop was wont in mockery to call him Isengrin, I suppose, because, of his wolfish look, for so some people call wolves. The wretch, therefore, says to the Bishop, "Is this my Lord Isengrin stored away?" Renulf therefore, sinner though he was, yet the Lord's anointed, was dragged forth from the cask by the hair, beaten with many blows and brought out into the open air in the narrow lane of the clergy's cloister before the house of the chaplain Godfrey. And as he piteously implored them, ready to take oath that he would henceforth cease to be their Bishop, that he would give them unlimited riches, that he would leave the country, and as they with hardened hearts jeered at him, one named Bernard and surnamed de Brueys, lifting his battle-axe brutally dashed out the brains of that sacred, though sinner's, head, and he slipping between the hands of those who held him, was dead before he reached the ground stricken by another thwart blow under the eye-sockets and across the middle of the nose. There brought to his end, his legs were cut off and many another wound inflicted. But Thibaut seeing the ring on the finger of the erstwhile prelate and not being able to draw it off, cut off the dead man's finger and took it. And so stripped to his skin he was thrown into a corner in front of his chaplain's house. My God, who shall recount the mocking words that were thrown at him by passersby, as he lay there, and with what clods and stones and dirt his corpse was covered?

Chapter X

Now on the morrow, as there was hardly any one who passed the bishop's corpse without casting at him some insult or curse, but no one thought of burying him, Master Anselm, who the day before, on the outbreak of the rebellion, had entirely hidden himself, poured out entreaties to the authors of the tragedy to allow the man to be buried, if only because he had the name and rank of a bishop; and they reluctantly consented. Because, therefore, he had lain naked on the ground as though he had been a vile dog, from the evening of the fifth day of Easter to the third hour of the following day, at last the Master ordered him to be taken up and with a salban thrown over him to be carried away to St. Vincent's. One cannot describe the threats and abuse that were showered upon those who cared for his burial or with how many curses the dead man was pelted. Being carried to the church, he had at his funeral none at all of the offices that are paid to any Christian, much less a bishop. The earth being only half scraped out to receive hire, the body was so tightly packed in the tiny coffin, that the breast and belly were crushed even to bursting. With such evil men to lay him out in the manner shown, the worse handling by them of his wretched body, so far as they might, was proved by those who were present, their testimony remaining to this day. That day there was no divine service by the monks in the church.

Chapter XII

After the storm had died away into a calm for a little while and the church began to be restored by the zeal of the clergy, as the wall, where Gerard was killed, seemed to be more weakened by the violence of the fire than the rest, they built at great cost some arches between the middle wall that had been most damaged and the outer structure. And one night with the sound of a great crash it was so shattered by a thunderbolt, that the arches joining the wall were torn asunder and the wall partly inclined out of the perpendicular had now to be pulled down from the foundations. O wondrous judgment of God! Why does Thy stern wrath, O Lord, pass sentence on such things, when Thou didst allow a man standing in prayer to Thee of some sort to be punished, if an unfeeling wall under which that act was done, was not suffered to go unpunished? Nor was Thy displeasure at such a wrong itself a wrong, O Lord.

CHAPTER XIV

And so the Bishop, having died in this manner, they began to approach the King for the election of another. Without any previous election they were given the Dean of Orléans, because a certain Stephen who had influence with the King and was unable to get a bishopric himself, wanted the deanery, and so obtained the Bishopric for the Dean and got the deanery himself. And when he was brought to be consecrated, and they took divination about him, they came on a blank page; as though it had been prophesied about him, "I will prophesy nothing about him, since his acts will be almost nothing." For a few months after, he died. Yet he restored some of the bishop's house. When he died, one was elected lawfully against his will. Lawfully, I say, in this respect, that he took office without paying for it, nor had he any wish to have dealings in simony.

Source: © C. Swinton Bland. *The Autobiography of Guibert, Abbot of Nogent-sous-Coucy*. Broadway Translations. London: George Routledge and Sons, 1925.

DOCUMENT 30
The Concordat of Worms:
The End of the Investiture Conflict (1122)

1. Calixtus, bishop, servant of the servants of God, to his beloved son, Henry, by the grace of God emperor of the Romans, Augustus.

We hereby grant that in Germany the elections of the bishops and abbots who hold directly from the crown shall be held in your presence, such elections to be conducted canonically and without simony or other illegality. In the case of disputed elections you shall have the right to decide between the parties, after consulting with the archbishop of the province and his fellow-bishops. You shall confer the regalia of the office upon the bishop or abbot elect by giving him the sceptre, and this shall be done freely without exacting any payment from him; the bishop or abbot elect on his part shall perform all the duties that go with the holding of the regalia.

In other parts of the empire the bishops shall receive the regalia from you in the same manner within six months of their consecration, and shall in like manner perform all the duties that go with them. The undoubted rights of the Roman church, however, are not to be regarded as prejudiced by this concession. If at any time you shall have occasion to complain of the carrying out of these provisions, I will undertake to satisfy your grievances as far as shall be consistent with my office. Finally, I hereby make a true and lasting peace with you and with all of your followers, including those who supported you in the recent controversy.

2. In the name of the holy and undivided Trinity.

For the love of God and his holy church and of pope Calixtus, and for the salvation of my soul, I, Henry, by the grace of God, emperor of the Romans, Augustus, hereby surrender to God and his apostles, Sts. Peter and Paul, and to the holy Catholic church, all investiture by ring and staff. I agree that elections and consecrations shall be conducted canonically and shall be free from all interference. I surrender also the possessions and regalia of St. Peter which have been seized by me during this quarrel, or by my father in his lifetime, and which are now in my possession, and I promise to aid the church to recover such as are held by any other persons. I restore also the possessions of all other churches and princes, clerical or secular, which have been taken away during the course of this quarrel which I have, and promise to aid them to recover such as are held by any other persons.

Finally, I make true and lasting peace with pope Calixtus and with the holy Roman church and with all who are or have ever been of his party. I will aid the Roman church whenever my help is asked, and will do justice in all matters in regard to which the church may have occasion to make complaint.

All these things have been done with the consent and advice of the princes whose names are written below: Adelbert, archbishop of Mainz; Frederick, archbishop of Cologne, etc.

Source: Oliver Thatcher and Edgar H. McNeal. *A Sourcebook for Medieval History*. New York: Scribner's, 1905. Nos. 85 and 86.

DOCUMENT 31
The Call for the Election of an Emperor (1125)

Adelbert, archbishop of Mainz; Frederick, archhbishop of Cologne; Udalric, bishop of Constance; Buco, bishop of Worms; Arnold, bishop of Speier; Udalric, abbot of Fulda; Henry, duke of Bavaria; Frederick, duke of Suabia; Godfrey, count palatine; Berengar, count of Sulzbach, along with the other princes, ecclesiastical and secular, who were present at the funeral of the late emperor, send their greeting and most faithful services to their venerable brother, Otto, bishop of Bamberg.

After the burial of our late lord and emperor, we who were there present thought it expedient to counsel together in regard to the condition of the state. We were unwilling to make any definite plans, however, without your presence and advice, and so we determined to call a diet to meet at Mainz on St. Bartholomew's Day [August 25], hoping that this decision would meet your approval. It is our thought that the princes should meet then and take the necessary action in regard to the serious problems that confront us, the general state of the kingdom, the question of a successor, and other matters. In thus calling a diet without first gaining your approval, we have not meant to infringe in any way upon your rights or to arrogate to ourselves any peculiar authority in this matter. We ask you to bear in mind the oppression of the church in these days and to pray earnestly that in the providence of God this election may result in the freeing of the church from its yoke of servitude and in the establishing of peace for us and for our people. You are instructed to declare a special peace for your lands, to be kept during the time of the diet and four weeks thereafter, so that all may come and return in perfect security; and to come to the diet yourself in the customary manner, that is, at your own expense and without inflicting any burden upon the poor of the realm.

Source: Oliver Thatcher and Edgar H. McNeal. *A Sourcebook for Medieval History*. New York: Scribner's, 1905. No. 87.

DOCUMENT 32
Henry I of England and the Bishops' Peace (1135)

Henry, king of the English to . . . all faithful sons of Holy Church in Normandy, greeting. Know that in the presence of Hugh, archbishop of Rouen, and the bishops John of Lisieux, Audin of Evreux, John of Séez and Algar of Coutances, and by the common advice and consent of all my barons listed below, it has been decided and determined concerning manslayers who kill men contrary to the rules of the Truce and Peace of the Church. namely: If anyone wishes to accuse such a manslayer and challenge him to a judicial duel, the duel shall be held in my court. If the accused loses, the bishop in whose diocese this takes place shall have his fine of nine pounds from the goods of the convicted man by the hands of my judge. . . . If no one wishes to challenge the manslayer to a duel, the accused shall clear himself in the church of God by the agency and through the judgment of the Church. If he is convicted there . . . the same thing shall be done about a fine to the bishop. . . . And if any manslayer . . . makes peace with me, the fine to the bishop shall not be included in the arrangements, but he must pay the bishop or make a separate peace with him. Witnesses: [9 barons]. Done at Rouen in the year of grace, 1135.

Source: E. J. Tardif. *Le tres ancien coutumier de Normandie.* Rouen, 1881.

DOCUMENT 33
Description of Santiago de Compostela (mid-12th c.)

THE DIMENSIONS OF THE CHURCH

Now the basilica of S. James is in length fifty-three times a man's stature, measuring from the western doorway to the altar of the Saviour, in width, thirty-nine times, measuring from the Door of the Franks to the south portal. The interior height is fourteen times a man's stature.

It is not worth anyone's while to know what the external length and height are.

The church has nine aisles on the lower level, and six on the upper, also a principal apsidal chapel, namely that containing the altar of the Saviour, and a sanctuary with ambulatory; a nave and two transepts; and it has eight small apsidal chapels, each with an altar.

Six of the nine aisles we speak of as small, and three as great. The first principal aisle stretches from the west portal to the four middle piers which dominate the church, and it has a lesser aisle to the right and to the left. There are two other naves in the two transepts, of which the first extends from the Door of the Franks to the four piers of the crossing, and the second from these same piers to the south portal; both have two lesser lateral aisles. These three principal naves reach to the vault of the church, and the six lesser aisles only to the middle of the piers. Each of the great arms measures eleven and a half times a man's stature in breadth. We call a man's stature just eight palms.

There are twenty-nine piers in the great nave, fourteen to the right hand, and as many to the left, and one comes between the two inner portals, . . . standing between the arches. In the naves of the transept of the church, from the Door of the Franks to the south portal, there are twenty-six piers, twelve at the right hand and as many at the left; two of them, placed within before the doors, stand between the arches and portals.

In the apse of the church, besides, there are eight single columns about the altar of the Blessed James.

The six aisles which are above in the upper story of the church are the same in length and width as the corresponding aisles below. On one side the walls bound them, and on the other, the piers rising from the lower part of the great naves and pairs of shafts of the kind called semicylindrical by the masons. There are as many piers in the lower part of the church as in the naves above; and as many as are the arches below, so many are they in the galleries above. But in the gallery passages there are, between successive piers, in each case, two of the shafts called by the masons cylindrical columns.

In the church there is indeed not a single crack, nor any damage to be found; it is wonderfully built, large, spacious, well-lighted; of fitting size, harmonious in width, length, and height; held to be admirable and beautiful in execution. And furthermore it is built with two stories like a regal palace. For he who visits the galleries, if sad when he ascends, once he has seen the preeminent beauty of this temple, is rejoiced and filled with gladness.

The Windows

The glazed windows in the basilica proper number sixty-three, and in each and every chapel surrounding the choir there are three. In the vault of the basilica about the altar of the Blessed James which is in the apse there are five windows from which the altar of the Apostle receives a good light. In the galleries above are windows to the number of forty-three.

The Lesser Portals

The church has, in addition to seven small entrances, three principal portals: one which faces the west, the main portal; another to the south, and still another to the north. In each portal there are two doorways, and in each doorway, two doors. The first of the minor portals is called that of S. Mary; the second, of the Via Sacra; the third, of S. Pelagius; the fourth, that of the Chapter; the fifth, the Stoneyard Portal; the sixth likewise, Stoneyard Portal; the seventh, the Grammar School Portal, which also communicates with the dwelling of the archbishop.

The North Portal

And beyond this Paradise is the north portal, the Door of the Franks, of the basilica of St. James, with two entrances, which have the following beautiful sculptured decoration. Outside at each opening there are six columns, some of marble, others of stone: three to the right and three to the left: six, that is to say, at one entrance, and six at the other; and so there are twelve columns. Above the shaft between the two portals, on the outer side, there is let into the wall the seated figure of Our Lord in Majesty; with His right hand He gives benediction, and in His left He holds a book. And round about His throne are the Four Evangelists, as if supporting the throne. At His right is carved Paradise, with another figure of the Lord reproving Adam and Eve for their sin; He appears also to the left, driving them forth from Paradise. And round about are sculptured a multitude of images of saints, animals, men, angels, women, flowers, and other created things whose nature and quality we cannot relate because of their great number. But over the doorway to the left as we enter the basilica—within the arch, that is—is carved the Annunciation of the Blessed Virgin Mary; there, too, the Angel Gabriel addresses her. To the left above the doors of the entrance at the side, the months of the year and many other beautiful works are represented in sculpture. Here are, also, two great fierce lions extending out from the wall, one to the right and one to the left, who continually look down as if keeping their eyes upon the doors.

On the upper part of the jambs are four apostles, each holding a book in his left hand, and with his raised right hand giving a benediction to those entering the basilica. On the left-hand portal are Peter at the right and Paul at the left; on the right-hand portal are the Apostle St. John at the right and the Blessed James at the left. Above the head of each Saint is carved the head of a bull, corbeled out from this jamb.

THE SOUTH PORTAL

The South Portal has two entrances, as we have said, with four door-valves. At the right door on the exterior, that is, in the first band above the doors, the Betrayal of Our Lord is wonderfully carved. There He is bound to the pillar by the hands of the Jews; here He is flagellated, there Pilate sits enthroned, as if judging Him. And above, on the other band, is sculptured the Blessed Mary, Mother of Our Lord, with her Child, in Bethlehem, and the three Kings who are come to visit the Boy and the Mother, offering Him three gifts; and the star also is carved there, and the angel warning the Kings not to return to Herod. On the jambs of this doorway are two apostles like warders of the doors, one to the right and one to the left.

Similarly there are two other apostles placed at the other doorway, to the left; on the jambs, that is to say. And in the first band of this doorway, above the doors, that is, is carved the Temptation of Our Lord. There are before the Lord hideous angels like spectres setting Him upon the pinnacle of the Temple; others offer Him stones, urging Him to make bread of them; others spread out before Him the kingdoms of the world, pretending that they will give them to Him if He will fall down and worship them—thus may it not be! But there are also others, white or good angels, behind His back, and still other angels above with censers, ministering unto Him.

On this same portal, there are four lions, one to the right of one doorway, and another by the other doorway. Above the middle shaft between the two doorways are two ferocious lions, one of which holds his hind-quarters against the hind-quarters of the other. There are eleven columns on this same portal, at the right-hand door, five, and at the left-hand door, five, and an eleventh which comes between the two doorways, separating the arches. And these columns, some of marble, others of stone, are marvelously carved with images of flowers, men, birds, and animals. The marble columns here are of white marble.

Nor ought we to forget the female figure set near the Temptation of Our Lord: she holds in her hands the rotting head of her lover, cut off by her husband, who forces her to kiss it twice each day. What a great and admirable judgment upon an adulterous woman, which should be recounted to everyone!

Above the four doors the upper zone, near the triforium level of the church, is beautifully resplendent with an admirable band of figures sculptured on slabs of white marble. There is a standing figure of the Lord, and St. Peter holding the keys in his hands is at His left, while the Blessed James is at his right between two cypress trees; next to him stands St. John his brother, while at the right and left are apostles and others. The wall above and below, on the right side and on the left, is most excellently sculptured with flowers, men and saints, beasts, birds, fish, and other works, which are beyond the possible limits of our recital. But it might be said that there are four angels above the archivolts, each with a trumpet, announcing the Day of Judgment.

THE WEST PORTAL

The West Portal, with two doorways, in beauty, size, and in the works upon it, excels the other portals. It is greater and handsomer, and more wonderfully carved than the others; it is provided with a great number of steps of approach; it is adorned by various marble columns and decorated with many kinds of creatures and in various ways; it is sculptured with images of men, women, beasts, birds, saints, angels, flowers, and works of divers kinds, so many that they cannot be included in our description. In the upper part, however, is a wonderful carving of the Lord's Transfiguration as it occurred on Mount Tabor. Our Lord is represented there in a white cloud, His face shining like the sun, His garments refulgent like snow, the Father above speaking to Him; and Moses and Elias who appeared with Him, telling Our Lord of His decease which was to be accomplished in Jerusalem. The Blessed James is there, as are Peter and John, to whom, before any others, the Lord revealed His transfiguration.

THE TOWERS OF THE CHURCH

There are to be nine towers on the church—two over the portal by the fountain, two over the South Portal, two over the West Portal, one over each of the winding stairways, and a larger one over the crossing in the middle of the basilica.

The splendid basilica of the Blessed James is gorgeous with these and other very beautiful works. It is all built of very strong, living stone, brown, and very hard. Within it has various paintings, and without it is roofed in the best manner with lead and tiles. But of these things we have mentioned, some are already entirely finished and others are yet to be completed.

THE ALTARS OF THE BASILICA

The basilica has its altars arranged in the following order. First, adjoining the Door of the Franks, which is on the left side, comes the altar of St. Nicolas; next, the altar of the holy Cross; then in the ambulatory, that is, the altar of St. Fides, the virgin, then the altar of the Apostle and Evangelist St. John, the brother of St. James; next comes the altar of the Saviour in the principal absidiole; then the altar of the Apostle St. Peter, then the altar of St. Andrew, then the altar of the Bishop St. Martin; then comes the altar of the Baptist St. John.

Between the altar of St. James and that of the Saviour stands the altar of St. Mary Magdalene, where the pilgrims' morning masses are sung.

Above in the galleries there are customarily three altars, of which the principal one is that of the Archangel St. Michael; there is another altar, to the right, dedicated to St. Benedict, and still another dedicated to the Apostle St. Paul and the Bishop St. Nicholas to the left, where also the archbishop's chapel customarily is.

THE BODY AND THE ALTAR OF ST. JAMES

But as we have thus far described the church, now we must consider the venerable apostolic altar. Within the said venerable basilica, the revered body of the Blessed James lies under the high altar raised in his honor, enclosed by a marble sarcophagus, in state, as the tradition has it, in a very fine arched sepulchre of wonderful workmanship and fitting size. That the body is immovable is well known from the testimony of Theodomir, Bishop of this city, who found it in time past, and was unable to stir it from its place. So let the folk beyond the mountains blush when they claim to have any part of it, or relics of him. For the entire body of the Apostle is there; it is brightened by heavenly jewels; it is graced with unfailing odors, fragrant and divine; it is embellished by the splendor of celestial lights, and unceasingly honored by angelic adoration.

Above the sepulchre of St. James is a small altar which his disciples made, tradition has it, and which, for love of the Apostle and his disciples, no one has since wished to destroy. And above this is a large and admirable altar five palms high, twelve long, and seven wide. I have with my own hands thus measured it. There is also a small altar made of three pieces of stone under this great altar, which is closed at the back and on the right and left sides, but open in front so that the old altar can clearly be seen when the silver altar frontal is removed.

And if anyone should wish to send a covering or altar-cloth for the apostolic altar, he should make it nine palms in width and twenty-one in length. And if any one for love of God and the Apostle should send an antependium to cover the altar in front, let him see that it is made seven palms wide and thirteen long.

The Silver Frontal

The frontal before the altar is gloriously wrought of gold and silver. In the centre of it is sculptured the Lord's Throne; there the Four and Twenty Elders are, placed as the Blessed John, brother of St. James, saw them in his Apocalypse—twelve to the right and as many to the left, round about, holding zithers and golden phials of sweet spices in their hands. In the midst of the Throne sits the Lord in Majesty, holding the Book of Life in His left hand, and, giving blessing with His right. Around His Throne are the Four Evangelists, as if holding up the Throne. The Twelve Apostles are placed at His right and His left, three at the right in the first, and three in the upper register; similarly there are at the left, three in the first, the lower register, and three in the upper. There are very finely wrought flowers in the border round about and very lovely columns between the apostles. This fitting and beautiful frontal has this inscription in verse on the upper part:

DIEGO II BISHOP OF THE SEE OF SANTIAGO MADE THIS FRONTAL IN THE FIFTH YEAR OF HIS EPISCOPATE. EIGHTY-FIVE MARKS OF THE SILVER CAME FROM THE TREASURY OF SANTIAGO; AND BELOW, THIS INSCRIPTION: AL- FONSO WAS KING, AND RAIMUNDO HIS SON-IN-LAW WAS DUKE WHEN THE BEFORE MENTIONED BISHOP FINISHED THE WORK.

THE CIBORIUM OF THE APOSTOLIC ALTAR

The canopy which covers this venerable altar is marvellously wrought inside and out with paintings and representations of various kinds. It is square, well proportioned in height and width, and carried on four columns. On the inside, in the lowest register, are certain special Virtues which St. Paul mentions, represented as women, eight, in number. There are two at each corner. And above their heads are standing angels, hold- ing in their raised hands a throne, which is at the crown of the vault. On the throne is the Lamb of God holding a cross with His foot. There are as many angels as Virtues.

Outside, in the first register, are four angels, who announce the Res- urrection of Judgment Day with blaring trumpets. Two are in the front, and two behind in the other face at the rear. Similarly placed there are four prophets, Moses and Abraham on the left-hand side, and Isaac and Jacob on the right, each one holding in his hand a scroll with his prophecy.

The Twelve Apostles are seated round about in a row above, with the Blessed James in the middle of the facade or front face, his left hand hold- ing a book, his right hand making the sign of benediction. At his right is another apostle, and at his left, still another, in the same register. Sim- ilarly, there are three other apostles. on the right side of the ciborium, three on the left, and likewise three at the back.

On the covering above are seated four angels, as if guarding the altar, while at the four angles where this roofing begins are carved the Four Evangelists in their own likeness.

The ciborium is painted on the inner parts; its exterior is sculptured as well as painted.

At its summit is built a kind of three-arched top stage, in which is carved the Divine Trinity. In the first arch, which faces the west, stands the Person of the Father; in the second, which faces between south and east, the Person of the Son; and in the third, which faces north, the Person of the Holy Spirit. Again, above this upper stage there is a shining silver ball, on which a precious cross is set.

THE MASONS OF THE CHURCH AND THE FINE QUALITY OF ITS CONSTRUCTION

The master-masons who first labored at the building of the basilica of the Blessed James were named Bernard the elder, a builder of genius, and Robert, who, with about fifty other masons, worked assiduously at it under the very faithful administration of Lord Wicartus, the Canon Lord Seferedus, and the Abbot Lord Gundesindus in the reign of Alfonso, King of Spain, and under the Bishop Lord Diego I, a strenuous militant churchman and noble man. The church was begun in the Era 1116. . . . From the year in which the first stone was laid in its foundations until that in which the last stone was put into place, forty-four years elapsed. And this church, from the time it was begun until the present day, has flourished in the glory of the miracles of the Blessed James. In it health is bestowed on the sick, sight returned to the blind; the tongue of the mute is unloosed; hearing is restored to the deaf, normal carriage afforded the lame, relief conceded the possessed; and what is better, the prayers of faithful people are heard, vows are fulfilled, the bonds of sin are broken; to the stricken the skies are opened; to the grieving, consolation is given; and all foreign nations from all the earth's climes troop thither, bearing with them gifts of praise to the Lord.

THE DIGNITY OF THE CHURCH OF SANTIAGO

Nor is it to be forgotten that for love and honor of the Apostle, the blessed Pope Calixtus (worthy of good memory) translated and gave to the Basilica and City of Santiago the archepiscopal dignity of the City of Mérida, which has been a metropolis in the land of the Saracens. And for this he ordained and confirmed Diego, a most noble man, to be the first archbishop of the Apostolic See of Compostela. This same Diego was previously bishop of Santiago.

Source: Kenneth J. Conant. *The Early Architectural History of the Cathedral of Santiago de Compostela*. Cambridge: Harvard University Press, 1926.

DOCUMENT 34
Hugh d'Amiens, Archbishop of Rouen, on the Cult of the Carts (1145)

Hugh, priest of Rouen to the Reverend Father Thierry, Bishop of Amiens; may you ever prosper in Christ. The great works of the Lord are shown in all His designs. At Chartres they commenced in humility to draw carts and beams for the construction of the church, and this humility brought forth miracles. The fame of these spread abroad and excited our Normandy. Therefore our diocesans, having accepted our blessing, went to Chartres and fulfilled their vows. After this, in a similar manner, they commenced to come from throughout our diocese to their own cathedral church of Rouen, having made this condition, that no one should come in their company unless he should first confess and repent, and unless he should lay aside wrath and envy. Thus those who were formerly enemies came into abiding concord and peace. These requisites filled, one among them is made chief, at whose command they drag with their own arms the carts, advancing in humility and silence, and bringing thus their offering not without discipline and tears. These three conditions which we have related, confession with penitence, the laying aside of all malevolence, humility and obedience in following their leader, we required from them when they came to us, and we received them piously, and absolved and blessed them if these three conditions were fulfilled. While in this spirit they were accomplishing their journey, very many miracles took place in our churches, and the sick who had come with them were made whole. And we permitted our diocesans to go out of our see, but we forbade them to go to those excommunicated or under the interdict. These things were done in the year of the incarnation of the word 1145. Farewell.

Source: Arthur Kingsley Porter. *Medieval Architecture*, I. Cambridge: Harvard University Press, 1904.

DOCUMENT 35
John of Salisbury on the Duties of Knights to
the Church (1159)

Knights rightfully have many privileges. . . . They are freer [than other men] and they enjoy many privileges. . . . There is no knight who is not bound to the church by a tacit or express oath. . . . And now a solemn custom has grown up, that on the day when a man is girt with the belt of knighthood, he goes solemnly to a church, places his sword on the altar like an offering . . . and, as it were dedicates himself to the altar and promises to God the service of his sword. . . . Thus when knights offer their sword, and . . . redeem the first token of their rank from the altar, they bind themselves to the perpetual service of the Church. They can do much for the church, but must not do anything against it. . . . For the military arm falls easily into violence and is accustomed to plunder other men's property.

Source: John of Salisbury. *Policratius*, ed. C.C.I. Webb. Oxford: Oxford University Press, 1909.

DOCUMENT 36
The Constitutions of Clarendon I (1164)

Moreover, a certain part of the recognized customs and authority of the kingdom is contained in this draft, of which part these are the chapters.

Ch. I. If a controversy comes up between laymen, or between laymen and clerics, or between clerics, concerning advowson and presentation of churches; it shall be treated or closed in the court of the lord king.

Ch. II. Churches in the fee of the lord king cannot be given in perpetuity without his assent and permission.

Ch. III. Clerics charged and accused of anything, being summoned by a justice of the king, shall come to his court, to answer there for what it seems to the king's court he should respond to there; and in the ecclesiastical court for what it appears he should respond to there; in such a way that the king's justice shall send to the court of the holy church to see in what manner the matter will be treated there. And if the cleric shall be convicted or shall confess, the church ought not to examine him as for the remainder.

Ch. IV. It is not lawful for archbishops, bishops, and persons of the kingdom to leave the kingdom without the permission of the lord king. And if they go out, if it pleases the lord king, they shall give assurance that neither in going, nor in staying, nor in returning will they seek the hurt or harm of king or kingdom.

Ch. V. The excommunicated should not give a pledge to continue, nor take an oath, but only a pledge and surety of remaining in the judgment of the church so that they may be absolved.

Ch. VI. Laymen shall not be accused unless by true and lawful accusers and witnesses in the presence of the bishop, in such a way that the archdeacon does not lose his right, nor any thing which he ought to have from it. And if those who are complained of are such that no one wishes or dares to accuse them, the sheriff, being requested by the bishop, shall cause twelve lawful men of the neighborhood or town to swear in the presence of the bishop that they will discover the truth in the matter, according to their knowledge.

Ch. VII. No man who is a tenant-in-chief of the king, nor any of the ministers on his demesne, shall be excommunicated, nor shall the lands of any one of them be placed under an interdict, unless first the lord king, if he is in the country, or his justiciar if he is outside the kingdom, agrees that justice shall be done to that man: and in such a way that what pertains to the king's court shall be terminated there; and with regard to that which belongs to the ecclesiastical court, it shall be sent thither in order that it may be handled there.

Ch. VIII. Concerning appeals, if they should arise, they should go from the archdeacon to the bishop, from the bishop to the archbishop. And if the archbishop fails to deliver justice, they must come finally to the lord king, in order that by his command the argument may be ended in the court of the archbishop, thus it must not proceed further without the assent of the lord king.

Ch. IX. If a quarrel arises between a cleric and a layman or between a layman and a cleric concerning any tenement which the cleric wants to take as free alms, but the layman as a lay fee: let it be decided by an investigation of twelve lawful men through the judgment of the chief justiciar of the king, in the presence of the justiciar himself, whether the tenement belongs to free alms or to lay fee. And if it is recognized as belonging to free alms the pleading will be in the ecclesiastical court, but if to the lay fee, unless both call to the same bishop or baron, the pleading will be in the king's court. But if, for that fee, both call to the same bishop or baron, the pleading shall be in his court; in such a way that, because of the recognition that was made, he who first was seized shall not lose his seisin, until the case has been proven for the plea.

Ch. X. Anyone in a city or castle or borough or demesne manor of the lord king, if he be summoned by the archdeacon or bishop for some crime for which he ought to answer to them, and he is unwilling to give satisfaction to their summons, may quite permissibly be put under the interdict; but he ought not to be excommunicated until the chief minister of the lord king of that town is summoned in order to compel him by law to come to give satisfaction. And if the minister of the king fails in this matter, he himself shall be at the mercy of the lord king, and the bishop can thereafter restrain the accused by ecclesiastical justice.

Ch. XI. Archbishops, bishops, and all persons of the kingdom who hold from the king in chief have their property of the lord king as a barony, and answer for them to the justices and ministers of the king, and comply with and perform all the royal customs and duties; and, like other barons, they ought to be present with the barons at the judgments of the court of the lord king, until it comes to a judgment leading to loss of life or limb.

Ch. XII. When an archbishopric, bishopric, abbey, or priory in the gift of the king is vacant, it ought to be in his hands; and he will thence receive all the revenue and income from it, just as demesne ones. And when it has come to providing for the church, the lord king should summon the more powerful persons of the church, and the election ought to take place in the lord king's own chapel with the assent of the lord king and the counsel of the persons of the kingdom whom he has summoned for this purpose. And there, before he is consecrated, the person elected shall do homage and fealty to the lord king as to his liege lord, for his life and limbs and his earthly honor, saving his order.

Ch. XIII. If any of the magnates of the kingdom have prevented an archbishop or bishop or archdeacon from doing justice to himself or his men, the lord king should do justice to them. And if by chance anyone has prevented the lord king his justice, the archbishops, bishops, and archdeacons ought to bring him to justice in order that he may make amends to the lord king.

Ch. XIV. Chattels of those in forfeiture of the king may not be detained in a church or churchyard, contrary to the king's justice, because they belong to the king, whether they are found in the churches or outside them.

Ch. XV. Pleas concerning debts, which are owed either with or without security being placed are in the king's justice.

Ch. XVI. The sons of peasants may not be ordained without the consent of the lord on whose land they are known to have been born.

Source: William Stubbs, ed. *Select Charters.* Oxford: Oxford University Press, 1921.

DOCUMENT 37
The Service of Knights Owed by the Archbishop of York to Henry II (1166)

To his dearest lord, Henry, by the grace of God, king of the English, and duke of the Normans and of the men of Aquitaine, count of the Angevins, his man Roger, by the same grace, archbishop of York, legate of the apostolic see, gives greeting. Your dignity has ordered all your liegemen, cleric and lay, who hold from you in chief in Yorkshire to send to you, by their letters carrying seals outside: how many knights each one has by the old enfeoffment of the time of the king [Henry] your grandfather, that is to say, from the year and the day in which he was alive and dead; and how many knights he has enfeoffed from the new enfeoffment, after the death of your grandfather of good memory. And in this short report there are how many knights' fees there are on the demesne of each, and the names of all these, both of the new and the old enfeoffments, since you want to know if there are any who have not yet done allegiance to you and whose names are not written in your roll, so that they may do allegiance to you before the first Sunday of Lent. I, one of those subject in all things to your orders, have searched with all diligence in my tenement, as the brief time allowed, and in this return declare these things to you, my lord.

In the first place know my lord that there is no knight's fee on the demesne of the archbishopric of York, since we have a sufficient number of enfeoffed knights to perform all the service which we owe you, just as our predecessors did it, and we have even more knights than we owe you as you may learn from the present list. For our predecessors enfeoffed more knights than they owed to the king, not for the necessary service which they owed, but because they wanted to provide for their relatives and servants.

These are the names of those enfeoffed in the time of King Henry [I]: [There follows a list of thirty-nine knights and the service owed. They range from Hugh of Verly, who holds a fee of four knights, to Leofred, who holds a thirteenth part of a knight's fee.]

After the death of King Henry there were enfeoffed: Peter the butler, half a knight's fee; Peter the chamberlain, the twentieth part of a knight's fee; Geoffrey of Burton, a twelfth of a knight's fee and Gervase of Bretton a third of a knight's fee.

And since, my lord, I exact from certain of these men more service than they are now doing, and in truth others are withholding services which are said to pertain not to themselves, but to the table and the demesne of the archbishop, I humbly beg that this my return is not able to harm me or my successors, and that we can recover or retain the rights of the church. Farewell, my lord. [Added are seven names, each holding, with one exception, only fractions of a knights' fee.]

Source: *Liber rubeus de scaccario*, I. Rolls Series. London: Longman, 1896.

DOCUMENT 38
The Canonization of Thomas à Becket
(12 March 1173)

Bishop Alexander, servant of the servants of God, to his beloved sons the prior and monks of the church of Canterbury greeting and apostolic benediction.

The whole body of the faithful must rejoice at the marvels of that saintly and revered man, Thomas, your archbishop. But then you should be filled with still greater joy and exultation, you who have very often gazed with faith at his miracles, and whose church especially deserves to be honored by his most sacred body. We, moreover, having contemplated the fame of the merits by which his life was so wondrously enlightened, not just the universal and celebrated fame of his miracles, but even the testimony in which I have complete confidence of our dear sons, Albert of St. Lawrence in Lucina and Theodwin of St. Vitalis, cardinal priests and legates of the apostolic see, and of many other people; and having consulted in council with our brethren and a multitude of clergy and laity present in the church, we have solemnly canonized him on Ash Wednesday and decreed that he should be enrolled in the fellowship of holy martyrs. We command, by apostolic authority, that you and the whole body of the faithful in England celebrate his feast each year on the day on which he ended his life by his glorious passion with suitable reverence. Since, therefore, it is right and very fitting for you that his holy body should be buried with the reverence and honor suitable to it, we command you by apostolic rescript to form a solemn procession on some especial day when the clergy and people are assembled, to lay his body devoutly and reverently with respect in the altar, or to place it in some appropriate coffin, as may be convenient, raised above the altar; and to obtain his protection by your devout prayers to God for the salvation of the faithful and the peace of the universal church. Given at Segni, 12 March.

Source: *Materials for the History of Thomas Becket*, VII, ed. James Craigie Robertson. Rolls Series 119. London: Longman, 1885.

DOCUMENT 39
Gervase on the Rebuilding of Canterbury Cathedral (1174–84)

In the year of grace one thousand one hundred and seventy-four, by the just but occult judgment of God, Christchurch at Canterbury, in the forty-fourth year from its dedication, that glorious choir which had been so magnificently completed by the care and industry of Prior Conrad was consumed by fire.

Now the manner of the burning and repair was as follows. In the aforesaid year, on the nones of September at about the ninth hour [5 September 1174, between 3 and 4 PM], during an extraordinarily violent south wind, a fire broke out before the gate of the church. Outside the walls of the monastery three cottages were half destroyed. From there, while the citizens were assembling and subduing the fire, cinders and sparks carried aloft by the high wind, were deposited upon the church.

Being driven by the fury of the wind between the joints of the lead, they remained there among the half rotten planks. Shortly glowing with increasing heat, they set fire to the rotten rafters. From there the fire spread to the larger beams and their braces. No one could see the damage because the well-painted ceiling below and the sheet lead roof covering above concealed the fire between them.

Meantime the three cottages, where the mischief had started, were destroyed. The excitement subsided and everybody went home, while the neglected church was being consumed by the internal fire unknown to all. Beams and braces burning, the flames rose to the slope of the roof. The sheets of lead yielded to the increasing heat and began to melt. Thus the raging wind, finding a freer entrance, increased the fury of the fire; and the flames began to show themselves. A cry arose in the church yard: "See! see! the church is on fire."

The people and the monks assembled in haste and drew water. Brandishing their hatchets, they ran up the stairs full of eagerness to save the church, already, alas! beyond their help. When they reached the roof and saw the black smoke and scorching flames that filled it, they abandoned the attempt in despair. Thinking only of their own safety, they hastily descended.

And now that the fire had loosened the beams from the pegs that bound them together, the half-burned timbers fell on the seats of the monks in the choir below; the seats, consisting of a great mass of woodwork, caught fire, and thus the mischief grew worse and worse. It was marvelous, though sad, to see how that glorious choir itself fed the fire that was destroying it. The flames, multiplied by the mass of timber, extended upwards fifteen cubits [about 25 feet], scorched and burned the walls, and most especially, injured the columns of the church.

Now the people ran to the ornaments of the church and began to tear down the pallia and curtains, some to save them, but some to steal them. The reliquary chests were thrown down from the high beam and, thus, broken, and their contents scattered. But the monks collected the relics and carefully preserved them from the fire. There were some, who, inflamed with a wicked and diabolical greed, did not fear to steal the things of the church, which they had saved from the fire.

In this manner the house of God, hitherto delightful as a paradise of pleasures, was now made a despicable heap of ashes, reduced to a dreary wilderness, and laid open to all the injuries of the weather.

Imagine now what mighty grief oppressed the hearts of the sons of the Church under this great tribulation; I truly believe the afflictions of Canterbury were no less than those of Jerusalem of old. The wailings of the monks were like the lamentations of Jeremiah. The mind cannot conceive, nor words express, their grief and anguish. Truly that they might alleviate their miseries with a little consolation, they put together as well as they could, an altar and station in the nave of the church, where they might wail and howl, rather than sing, the daily and evening services. Meanwhile the patron saints of the church, St. Dunstan and St. Elfege, had their resting place in that wilderness. Lest the saints suffer even the slightest injury from the rains and storms, the monks, weeping and lamenting with incredible grief and anguish, opened their tombs and extricated them in their coffins from the [damaged] choir, but only with the greatest difficulty and labor, as if the saints themselves resisted the change.

They arranged them as decently as they could at the altar of the Holy Cross in the nave. Just as the children of Israel were ejected from the land of promise, even from a paradise of delight, that it might be like people, like priest, and that the stones of the sanctuary might be poured out at the corners of the streets; so the monks remained in grief and sorrow for five years in the nave of the church, separated from the people only by a low wall.

Meantime the brotherhood sought counsel as to how and in what manner the burned church might be repaired, but without success; for the columns of the church, commonly termed the pillars, were exceedingly weakened by the heat of the fire, and were scaling in pieces and hardly able to stand, so that they frightened even the wisest out of their wits.

French and English builders were therefore summoned, but even these differed in opinion. On the one hand, some undertook to repair the aforesaid columns without disturbing the walls above. On the other hand, there were some who asserted that the whole church must be pulled down if the monks wished to exist in safety. This opinion, true as it was, excruciated the monks with grief, and no wonder, for how could they hope that so great a work should, by human ingenuity, be completed in their lifetimes.

However, among the other workmen there had come a certain William of Sens, a man active and ready, and a workman most skillful both in wood and stone. Him, therefore, they retained, on account of his lively genius and good reputation, and dismissed the others. And to him, and to the providence of God, was the execution of the work committed.

And he, residing many days with the monks and carefully surveying the burned walls in their upper and lower parts, within and without, concealed for some time what he found necessary to be done, lest the truth should kill them in their present state of grief.

But he went on preparing all things that were needed for the work, either by himself or by the agency of others. And when he found that the monks began to be somewhat comforted, he ventured to confess that the pillars damaged by the fire, and all that they supported, must be destroyed if the monks wished to have a safe and excellent building. At length they agreed, being convinced by reason and wishing to have the work as good as he promised, and above all things to live in security. Thus they consented patiently, if not willingly, to the destruction of the choir.

And now he addressed himself to the procuring of stone from beyond sea. He constructed ingenious machines for loading and unloading ships, and for drawing cement and stones. He delivered molds for shaping the stones to the sculptors who were assembled, and diligently prepared other things of the same kind. The choir, condemned to destruction, was pulled down, and nothing else was done in this year.

The Master began, as I stated long ago, to prepare all things necessary for the new work, and to destroy the old. In this way the first year was taken up. In the following year, after the feast of St. Bertin [5 September 1175], but before the winter, he erected four pillars, that is, two on each side, and after the winter two more were put up, so that on each side were three in order, upon which and upon the exterior wall of the aisles he framed seemly arches and vaults, that is, three keystones on each side. I put keystone for the whole vault because the keystone placed in the middle locks up and binds together the parts which converge to it from every side. With these works the second year was occupied.

In the third year he placed two pillars on each side, the two extreme ones of which he decorated with marble columns placed around them. He decorated these principal pillars because at that place the choir and transept arms were to meet. Having added the keystones and vaults [of the aisles], he built the lower triforium [the false gallery] with many marble columns from the great tower to the decorated pillars, that is, as far as the crossing. On top of this he built another triforium [the clerestory wall passage] of other materials and also the clerestory windows. And next he built three keystones of the main vaults, namely, from the tower as far as the crossing. All of which things appeared to us, and to all who saw them, incomparable and most worthy of praise. At so glorious a beginning we rejoiced and conceived good hopes of the end, and provided for the acceleration of the work with diligence and spirit. Thus was the third year occupied and the beginning of the fourth.

In the summer of the fourth year, commencing from the crossing, he erected ten pillars, that is, five on each side. The first two were ornamented with marble columns to correspond to the other two principal ones. On these ten he placed the arches and vaults. And having, in the next place, completed the triforia [false gallery and clerestory wall passage] and the upper windows on both sides, at the beginning of the fifth year, he was preparing with machines for the turning of the great [crossing] vault, when suddenly the beams broke under his feet, and he fell to the ground, stones and timbers accompanying his fall, from the height of the capitals of the upper vault, that is to say, from the height of fifty feet. Thus sorely bruised by the blows from the beams and stones, he was rendered helpless to himself and to the work. But no other person than himself was injured in the least. Only against the master was this vengeance of God, or spite of the devil, directed.

The master, thus hurt, remained in his bed for some time under medical care in expectation of recovering. But he was deceived in this hope, for his health mended not. Nevertheless, as the winter approached, and it was necessary to finish the crossing vault, he gave charge of the work to a certain ingenious and industrious monk, who was the overseer of the masons; an appointment that caused much envy and malice, because it made this young man appear more skillful than richer and more powerful monks. But the master, reclining in bed, commanded all things that should be done in order. And thus was completed the vault between the four principal pillars. In the keystone of this vault the choir and transept arms seem, as it were, to meet. Two vaults, one on each side of the crossing were put up before the winter; when heavy rains stopped the work. In these operations the fourth year was occupied and the beginning of the fifth. But on the eighth day from the said fourth year, on the idus of September [13 September 1178], before the master's accident, an eclipse of the sun occurred at about the sixth hour.

And the master, perceiving that he derived no benefit from the physicians, gave up the work, and crossing the sea, returned to his home in France. Another succeeded him in the charge of the works; William by name, English by nation, small in body, but in workmanship of many kinds acute and honest. In the summer of the fifth year he finished the transept arms on each side, that is, the south and the north, and turned the vault over the high altar, the completion of which the rains of the previous year had hindered, although everything was prepared. Moreover, he laid the foundation for the enlargement of the church at the eastern part, because a chapel of St. Thomas was to be built there.

For this was the place assigned to him; namely, the chapel of the Holy Trinity, where he celebrated his first mass, where he was wont to prostrate himself with tears and prayers, under whose crypt he was buried for so many years. This was the place where, for his merits, God had performed so many miracles, where poor and rich, kings and princes, had worshiped him; and from which the sound of his praises had gone forth to all lands.

Master William, on account of these foundations, began to dig in the cemetery of the monks, from whence he was compelled to remove the bones of many holy monks. These were carefully collected and deposited in a large trench, in that corner which is between the chapel and the south side of the infirmary house. Having, therefore, laid a most substantial foundation for the exterior wall with stone and cement, he erected the wall of the crypt as high as the bases of the windows.

Thus was the fifth year employed and the beginning of the sixth.

It has been above stated, that after the fire nearly all the old portions of the choir were destroyed and changed into something new in a more noble fashion. The differences between the two works may now be enumerated. The pillars of the old and new work are alike in form and thickness but different in length. For the new pillars were elongated by almost twelve feet. In the old capitals the work was plain, in the new ones exquisite in sculpture. There the circuit of the choir had twenty-two pillars, here are twenty-eight. There the arches and everything else was plain, or sculptured with an axe and not with a chisel. But here almost throughout is appropriate sculpture. There were no marble columns, but here are innumerable ones. There, in the circuit around the choir, the [groin] vaults were plain, but here the vaults are arch-ribbed and have carved keystones. There a wall set upon pillars divided the transept arms from the choir, but here there is no such partition, and the spaces converge together in one keystone, which is placed in the middle of the great vault which rests on the four principal pillars. There, there was a ceiling of wood decorated with excellent painting, but here is a vault beautifully constructed of stone and light tufa. There, was a single triforium [passage in the wall], but here are two in the main elevation of the choir and a third in the side aisles. All of this will be better understood from inspection than by any description.

This must be made known, however, that the new work is higher than the old by so much as the clerestory windows of the choir, as well as of its aisles, are raised above the marble tabling.

Because in future ages it may be doubtful why the breadth which was given to the choir next the tower should be so much contracted at the head of the church, it may not be useless to explain the causes thereof. One reason is that the two towers of St. Anselm and of St. Andrew, placed in the circuit on each side of the old church, would not allow the width of the choir to proceed in the direct line. Another reason is, that it was agreed [and necessary] that the chapel of St. Thomas should be erected at the head of the church, where the chapel of the Holy Trinity stood, and this was much narrower than the choir.

The master, therefore, not choosing to pull down the said towers, and being unable to move them, set out the width of the choir in a straight line, as far as the beginning of the towers. Then, receding slightly on either side from the towers, and preserving as much as he could the width of the aisle outside the choir, on account of the frequent processions, he gradually and obliquely narrowed his work, so that from opposite the altar, it might begin to contract, and from there, at the third pillar, it might be so narrowed as to coincide with the breadth of the chapel, which was named of the Holy Trinity. Beyond these, four pillars were set on the sides at the same distance as the last, but of a different form; and beyond these other four were arranged in a half circle, and upon these the upper stories on each side were brought together and terminated.

The outer wall, which extends from the aforesaid towers, first proceeds in a straight line, is then bent into a curve, and thus in the round tower [the Corona] the wall on each side comes together. All which may be more clearly and pleasantly seen by the eyes than taught in writing. But this much was said so that the differences between the old and new work might be made manifest.

Now let us carefully examine what were the works of our mason in the seventh year from the fire, which, in short, included the completion of the new and handsome crypt, and above the crypt the exterior walls of the aisles up to their marble capitals. The windows, however, the master was neither willing nor able to turn, on account of the approaching rains. Neither did he erect the interior pillars. Thus was the seventh year finished, and the eighth begun.

In the eighth year the master erected eight interior pillars, and turned the arches and the vaults, including the clerestory windows, in the circuit. He also raised the tower [the Corona] up to the bases of the highest windows under the vault.

In the ninth year no work was done for want of funds.

In the tenth year the upper windows of the tower, together with the vault, were finished. Upon the pillars was placed a lower and an upper triforium, with windows and the great vault. Also the upper roof where the cross stands aloft was finished, and the roof of the aisles as far as the laying of the lead. The tower was covered in, and many other things done this year.

In this year Baldwin, bishop of Worcester, was elected to the rule of the church of Canterbury on the eighteenth kalend of January [15 January 1184], and was enthroned there on the feast of St. Dunstan.

Source: Robert W. Willis. *The Architectural History of Canterbury Cathedral.* London: Longmans and Company, 1843.

DOCUMENT 40
The Bishop of the Artois and the Count of Flanders Agree on Rights (1177)

Given the disagreements which are wont to arise over contracts and agreements because of the uncertain memory of man. . . . I Fumaldus, by God's grace Bishop of Artois, and I Philip, Count of Flanders and Vermandois, compose this agreement with regard to the dispute we have over our rights, especially those relating to secular jurisdiction; and we certify this agreement with our seals. In the past there have been many disputes between our predecessors; in our time, with the consent and by the express wish of the chapter of Artois and of the men of the count, we declare the disputes terminated by this solution.

All litigation involving 60 *solidi* or less which may arise in the area bounded by the Strate gate and the Tenard bridge, and within the walls throughout the entire quarter, shall be subject to the justice of the bishop.

This applies to all cases. Understood also are the breaking of all prohibitions, no matter by whom; the falsifying of all measures, and cheating in the measurement of cloth and all other things with the exception of counterfeiting: perjury or corrupting judges and cases of dueling also shall be the bishops. . . .

Done in the year of our Lord, 1177.

Source: Georges Espinas and Henri Pirenne. *Recueil des documents rélatifs à l'histoire de l'industrie drapière en Flandres*, I. Brussels, 1906.

DOCUMENT 41
Pope Innocent III to the Archbishop of Rouen on Absent Canons (1198)

Since it is written that whoever does not work shall not eat [2 Thess. 3:10], we believe it wrong that clergymen do not serve those churches from which they have their livings. You have informed us that certain canons of the church of Rouen receive incomes and livings from the church, but do not live there, as they should, and that the church of Rouen is thereby unjustly deprived of the services of the clergy whom she supports. Therefore we grant your petition, venerable brother in Christ, and by our apostolic authority give you full power to use ecclesiastical discipline to compel them to live in their churches, as the law and custom of the church require.

Source: Oliver Thatcher and Edgar H. McNeal. *A Sourcebook for Medieval History*. New York: Scribner's, 1905. No. 121.

DOCUMENT 42
Innocent III Pronounces a Papal Interdict on France (1200)

Let all the churches be closed; let no one be admitted to them except to baptize infants; let them not be otherwise opened except for the purpose of lighting the lamps, or when the priest shall come for the Eucharist and holy water for the use of the sick. We permit mass to be celebrated once a week on Friday early in the morning to consecrate the Host for the use of the sick, but only one clerk is to be admitted to assist the priest. Let the clergy preach on Sunday in the vestibules of the churches, and in place of the mass let them disseminate the word of God. Let them recite the canonical hours outside the churches, where the people do not hear them; if they recite an epistle or a gospel let them beware lest the laity hear them; and let them not permit the dead to be interred, or their bodies to be placed unburied in the cemeteries. Let them, moreover, say to the laity that they sin and transgress grievously by burying bodies in the earth, even in unconsecrated ground, for in so doing they arrogate to themselves an office pertaining to others. Let them forbid their parishioners to enter churches that may be open in the king's territory, and let them not bless the wallets of pilgrims except outside the churches. Let them not celebrate the offices in Passion week, but refrain even till Easter day, and then let them celebrate in private, no one being admitted except the assisting priest, as above directed; let no one communicate even at Easter, except he be sick and in danger of death. During the same week, or on Palm Sunday, let them announce to their parishioners that they may assemble on Easter morning before the church and there have permission to eat flesh and consecrated bread. Women are expressly forbidden to be admitted into the churches for purification, but are to be warned to gather their neighbors together on the day of purification and pray outside the church, nor may the women who are to be purified enter even to raise their children to the sacred font for baptism until they are admitted by the priest after the expiration of the interdict. Let the priest confess all who desire it in the portico of the church; if the church have no portico we direct that in bad or rainy weather, and not otherwise, the nearest door of the church may be opened and confessions heard on its threshold (all being excluded except the one who is to confess) so that the priest and the penitent can be heard by those who are outside the church. If, however, the weather be fair, let the confession be heard in front of the closed doors. Let no vessels of holy water be placed outside of the church, nor shall the priests carry them anywhere, for all the sacraments of the church beyond these two which were reserved are absolutely prohibited. Extreme unction, which is a holy sacrament, may not be given.

Source: *Documents Illustrative of Feudalism*, ed. Edward P. Cheney. Translations and Reprints from Original Sources of European History, v. IV, no. 3. Philadelphia: Department of History, University of Pennsylvania, 1897.

DOCUMENT 43
The Rebuilding of Auxerre Cathedral and
the Collapse of the Old Towers (1215–17)

1215. How the bishop had the old building of the church of Auxerre demolished in order to construct the new. At the same time the construction of new churches everywhere heightened people's zeal. And so the bishop, seeing his own church at Auxerre, which was of ancient and crude construction, suffering from neglect and old age, while others all around were lifting their heads in marvelous beauty, determined to provide it with [a] new building so that it might not be inferior to these others in form and treatment. He had the east end completely torn down so that, as the squalor of the old was removed, it might become rejuvenated in the elegant shape of its reconstruction. The building of the first years, as the church lifted its head aloft beyond what had been hoped for, proclaimed the great generosity with which he poured large sums of money into it; indeed he disbursed for the work's expenses about seven hundred livres of his own in the first year, apart from the offerings of the faithful and the income from the land under his jurisdiction which he had assigned to it at the beginning; and at times in the remaining years, ten livres a week, at times approximately a hundred sols [sous], apart from the sums aforementioned and the taxes from his own and neighboring dioceses.

1217. Concerning the fall and miracle of the towers. Incidentally it is urgent that . . . that miracle be told . . . which is known to have occurred in the demolition of the old structure. Now in the year 1217 on the Sunday before Advent, we were celebrating the day in honor of the Holy Trinity. In the old church there were on either side two towers of no small height and of vast solidity, one south, one north, containing beneath them the whole width of the choir and the choir stalls. Since the buttresses [antae] of the old structure, which used to support them firmly, had been removed for the new building, these towers began to crack, at first only by, a small fissure, thanks to their cohesion over so many years. No one anticipated that they could collapse so speedily. During this service . . . [not only the smaller but the larger bells were being rung] . . . the southern tower spread with a more than ordinary gap; some, observing this, began to talk, and this reached the clergy. The architect was summoned as the third hour approached. He was asked whether there were any immediate danger of collapse of the towers and whether the clergy could safely celebrate the divine service below. Upon his steadfast assurance that there was nothing to fear, one of his disciples who was present said it was not safe to remain under them through the hour. The architect started to upbraid him for bringing unnecessary fear upon the clergy, pointing to certain beams stretched from tower to tower which were keeping the whole structure from falling. When he was more pressingly asked to give no assurance except of what was certain, he said, as if overcome by the persistence of his questions, "I can say nothing certain at all, being ignorant of what the future is preparing." At these words, as by some sort of presentiment, there was a consensus of opinion shared by all that, after the procession, which was now impending, was over (for it was the third hour), Mass should be celebrated in the church of the Blessed Mary, which adjoined the cathedral. This was done. Nonetheless, in customary fashion, as if there were no fear, all the bells were formally and solemnly rung. Only a strong frame would have withstood their striking, according to human reckoning; but the collapse was postponed so that both the divine power which could restrain their sudden collapse and the mercy which wanted to spare might be more evident when all the striking had ceased. Further, even as the place of holding the divine services was moved, so also were the books which were in daily use, and likewise all those that were kept in the closet under the south tower, as if everyone expected the tower to fall immediately. After Mass had been celebrated and the canons were sitting together at their meal, the southern tower, shaken violently, fell onto the opposite tower with a sudden crash, its foundations having been impaired deep within. . . . The people, aroused by the crash, came running. The northern tower still stood and seemed to rest on a solid base: all of a sudden, after scarcely half an hour, it fell to earth and cast the whole mass of its weight on the one that had fallen earlier. . . .

The devotion of the people, evoked by the proclamation of the priests, made them eager to remove the rubble. The outer walls of both towers had survived the collapse. What remained of the south tower had a fissure and cavity that constantly threatened immediate collapse; nevertheless, the dedicated people and others hired for wages exerted themselves to remove the rubble, and the danger of imminent collapse did not deter them in their zeal.

Source: Victor Mortet and Paul Deschamps. *Recueil de textes rélatifs à l'histoire de l'architecture et à la condition des architectes en France au moyen âge*, II. Paris: Picard, 1929.

DOCUMENT 44
Frederick II Forbids Municipal Freedoms and Communes (1218)

In the name of the holy and undivided Trinity. Frederick, etc. . . . (2) In various parts of Germany, through the failure to enforce the law and through neglect, certain detestable customs have become established which hide their bad character under a good appearance. By them the rights and honor of the princes of the empire are diminished and the imperial authority is weakened. It is our duty to see that these bad customs, or rather these corrupt practices, shall no longer be in force. (3) Wishing, therefore, that all the grants and concessions of liberties and privileges which we have made to the princes of the empire shall have the broadest interpretation and that the said princes may have full and undisturbed possession of them, we hereby remove and depose in every town and city of Germany all the city councils, burgomasters, mayors, aldermen, and all other officials, by whatever name they may be called, who have been established by the people of the said cities without the permission of their archbishop or bishop. (4) We also dissolve all fraternities or societies, by whatever name they may be called. (5) We also decree that, in every city or town where there is a mint, no kind of money except that which is coined in that place shall be used in the sale and purchase of all kinds of goods and provisions. (6) In times past the archbishops and bishops governed the cities and all the lands which were given them by the emperor, and we wish them to continue to do so forever, either in person or through the officials whom they may appoint for this purpose, in spite of the fact that certain abuses have crept in, and in some cities there are those who resist them. But this resistance to their lord is illegal. (7) In order that these wicked abuses may be stopped and may not have even a pretense of authority, we revoke and declare invalid and worthless all the privileges, open letters, and sealed letters, which we or our predecessors or the archbishops or bishops have given to any person, either public or private, or to any city, in favor of these societies, communes, or councils, to the disadvantage of the princes and of the empire. This document has the form of a judicial decision, being published by a decree of the princes with our full knowledge.

Source: Oliver Thatcher and Edgar H. McNeal. *A Sourcebook for Medieval History*. New York: Scribner's, 1905. No. 315.

DOCUMENT 45
The Annals of St. Nicaise on the Civic Uprisings in Reims (1233–36, 1241)

1233. This year Reims was at peace, but certain citizens under the archepiscopal ban and under the chapter ban, fearing that an inquisition into usury would be made against them, conspired against the chapter, hurling threats and curses. The canons, fearing for their lives, fled the city on November 9, 1235. And for two years and two months the canons were forced to live in exile at Cormicy and Courville. During this period, the citizens, while royal power favored and incited them, besieged the archbishop's fortress with siege engines, mangonels [catapults] and stones taken from the parish churches in which they had been hidden. They killed the archbishop's marshall in the square; others were wounded by arrows and by stones. They took over some houses that faced the fortress and immediately enclosed the city with earthen walls, which they were later forced to take down. A legal case against the citizens was begun by the chapter in the papal court at Rome. The archbishop was in agreement with this step and provided half the funds to bring the case.

1237. And a suit was brought before his lordship, Pope Gregory VII. The facts of this case are preserved under seal in the archives of the church in Reims and are kept in written form in the registers of Pope Gregory.

1238. In this year Henry of Braine, Archbishop of Reims, came to the city of Reims with weapons and seized certain officials and burghers under his jurisdiction. Some of them the archbishop held in prison for a long time and a certain number of others who were under his ban were banished and they were not allowed back for as long as the archbishop lived. On the same day he ordered torn down several houses in his ban and he also ordered the demolition of the fortifications [crenellations] which the citizens had built on their houses. All of these thing were done because the burghers and other citizens had caused the baliff and servants of the archbishop to flee the city and they had done other misdeeds against the archbishop and were not willing to make remedy. In the same year the archbishop issued a general interdiction on the whole city of Reims and excommunicated all of the citizens in his jurisdiction.

1240. In this year Henry of Braine, of blessed memory, archbishop of Reims died in Courville on July 6 and was brought to Reims Cathedral and buried in front of the high altar. After his death the citizens under the jurisdiction of the archbishop who had all been excommunicated by this same archbishop and who had remained for a long time in excommunication sought absolution from the chapter at Reims, according to the rules of the church. When there had been discussion about the rules for a long time, they obtained absolution from the chapter through the intercession of good men according to this formula: the burghers and thirty other citizens from among those prominent citizens who were under the jurisdiction of the archbishop made remedy to the chapter on behalf of themselves and all of the others who had been excommunicated in the aforesaid ban for all the misdeeds and all of the breaches of justice and complaints because of which they had been excommunicated by the archbishop, and they swore that, in addition, they would adhere to the orders and regulations of the chapter and they gave as a sign of good faith (restitution) 1,000 marks of silver that they would themselves adhere to the orders of the chapter at Reims and that they would faithfully follow them.

1241. This year on September 7, the vigil of the birth of the blessed Virgin Mary the chapter at Reims entered the new chevet [the architectural choir east of the transept].

Source: *Annales S. Nicasii Remenses*, ed. G. Waitz. MGH, Scriptores XIII. Hannover: MGH, 1881. Translation by Edward Dolin and William Clark.

DOCUMENT 46
The Limit of the Authority of
the Archbishop of Cologne (1237)

Frederick II, etc. The archbishop of Cologne asked whether his jurisdiction extended beyond the city walls or not. The decision was that his jurisdiction extends beyond the city walls to the distance which is generally called a "ban-mile," and within that he may legally sit in judgment on all the men who are under his jurisdiction.

Source: Oliver Thatcher and Edgar H. McNeal. *A Sourcebook for Medieval History*. New York: Scribner's, 1905. No. 309.

DOCUMENT 47
Occupational Statutes of Paris (1258)

CHAPTER 48. OF MASONS, STONE CUTTERS, PLASTERERS AND MORTARERS

In the city of Paris anyone who wishes to be a mason may be one, provided he knows his trade, and works according to the practices and customs of his profession, which are defined thus:

No one may have more than one apprentice in his business, and if he has one he must keep him for six years of service. He may well keep him beyond this time if the man is available, but for pay. If he keeps him less than six years he will be fined twenty Paris sous, payable to the chapel of Saint Blaise, unless the apprentices are his own sons born to him in wedlock.

The mason may lawfully take a second apprentice on the same terms as he took the first one after the first one has completed five years.

The king who now rules, to whom may God grant long life, has entrusted, for as long as he may see fit, authority over all masons to Master William de Saint-Patu. The said Master William swore in Paris in the palace lodge that he would protect the guild of masons as best he could, with honesty and justice to the poor as well as to the rich, to the weak as well as to the powerful, as long as the king wished him to serve that guild. Master William then gave his oath in the presence of the provost of Paris in the Châtelet.

Mortarers and plasterers come under the same conditions and organization as the masons.

The master who in the name of the king heads the guild of masons, mortarers and plasterers of Paris can have two apprentices only under the same conditions, as above stipulated. Should he have more apprentices he shall be fined as above stated.

Masons, mortarers and plasterers may have as many helpers and servants in their business as they please as long as they do not show any of them the fine points of their craft.

All masons, mortarers and plasterers must swear to protect their craft by committing themselves to work loyally and well and to report to the master of the guild any case of infringement on the usage and customs of the craft which may come to their attention.

Masters with apprentices whose term of apprenticeship is fulfilled must come before the guild master and testify to the fact that their apprentice has accomplished his term faithfully and well, whereupon the guild master shall ask the apprentice to promise under oath to observe the practices and customs of the craft loyally and well.

No one may practice his craft after nones [3 P.M.] have been rung at Notre-Dame on Saturdays at any time during the year or after vespers [6 P.M.] are sung at Notre-Dame unless he is about to close an arch or a stairwell, or is about to lay the last stones of a doorway leading to the street. Should anyone work beyond these hours, with the exception of the above-indicated or similar work that cannot be postponed, he must pay a fine of four deniers [a denier was a medieval Parisian penny] to the guild master, and the guild master may take away the tools of him who repeats the offense.

Mortarers and plasterers are under the jurisdiction of the master who, in the name of the king, heads the above-mentioned guild.

If a plasterer delivers plaster for use by anyone, the mason who is employed by him to whom the plaster is sent is under oath to watch that the measure be right and honest. If he is in doubt, he must remeasure it or have it measured before his eyes. If he finds the measure to be wrong, the plasterer has to pay a fine of five sous: two sous to the above-mentioned chapel of Saint Blaise, two sous to the guild master, and twelve deniers to him who will have measured the plaster. It must, however, be proved that the same amount of plaster was missing from every donkey-load delivered for the specific job as was missing from the sack which has been measured; one sack-load by itself cannot be measured.

Nobody may be a plasterer in Paris unless he pays five Paris sous to the appointed guild master. After having paid he must promise under oath not to mix any other material with the plaster and to give good and honest measure.

If a plasterer mixes material with his plaster which should not be used, he must pay a fine of five sous to the guild master every time he repeats the offense. If the plasterer makes a habit of cheating and does not improve or repent, the guild master may suspend him from the craft; and if the plasterer will not obey the guild master, the latter must inform the provost of Paris, who must in turn force the plasterer to abandon the craft.

Mortarers must promise under oath and in the presence of the guild master and other masters of the craft that they will not make mortar of other than good binding material and, should they make it of other material so that the mortar does not set while the stones are being placed, the structure must be undone and a fine of four deniers must be paid to the master of the guild.

Mortarers may not take on an apprentice for less than six years of service and one hundred Paris sous to teach him.

With the king's authorization the guild master has jurisdiction over minor infringements and fines of masons, plasterers and mortarers and of their helpers and their apprentices. Furthermore, he has jurisdiction over the enterprises of their trade, over unauthorized (*sanz sanc?*) builders and over claims; with the exception of property claims.

Should anyone from the above-mentioned crafts, when summoned before the guild master, fail to obey, the fine to be paid to the said master is set at four deniers; if he appears on the designated day and is guilty, he makes a pledge, and if he does not pay within the designated time he has to pay [an additional] fine of four deniers to the guild master. If he denies any wrongdoing but is at fault he also pays four deniers to the guild master.

The guild master may levy only one fine per quarrel. If the one who has to pay the fine is so furious and so beside himself that he refuses to obey the order of the master or to pay his fine, the master may bar him from the craft.

If anyone belonging to any of the above-mentioned crafts who has been excluded by order of the guild master continues to work beyond the date of exclusion, the master may take away his tools until he has paid the fine; and if he resists with force, the guild master should inform the provost of Paris, who should put down his violence.

Masons and plasterers must do guard duty and pay the taxes and other dues that all other citizens of Paris owe the king.

Mortarers have been exempt from guard duty since the time of Charles Martel, as wise men have heard it said from father to son.

The appointed guild master is exempt from guard duty as reward for the services he renders as master of the guild.

Exempt from guard duty are those who are over sixty years of age, and he whose wife is in bed for as long as she is there, provided they inform the overseer of the guard appointed by the king.

Source: G. B. Depping. *Reglements sur les arts et métiers de Paris*. Translated by W. Clark. Paris: Imprimerie de Crapelet, 1837.

DOCUMENT 48
Building in the French Gothic Style (1280)

Richard of Ditensheim, deacon . . . tore down the monastery constructed by the Reverend Father . . . Peter Crudolfus, for it was in ruins because of its great age and was in danger of damaging the structures next to it. Having summoned the master mason most skilled in architecture, who had then recently come from the city of Paris in the land of France, he ordered the church to be built of ashlar stone in the French style. Truly, then, this master built a church of marvelous workmanship, elaborately adorned within and without with images of the saints, with molded window frames and piers, a work that caused much toil and large expenditure, and even now today it so appears to human gaze; thus as people come from all directions, they marvel at so noble a work, praise the master, revere Richard as the servant of God, rejoice that they have seen him, and his name is spread abroad far and wide . . . and he is very often mentioned by those to whom he is not known.

Source: Victor Mortet and Paul Deschamps. *Recueil de textes rélatifs à l'histoire de l'architecture et à la condition des architectes en France au moyen âge*, II. Paris: Picard, 1929.

DOCUMENT 49
Durandus on the Symbolism and Meaning of Churches (1286)

OF A CHURCH AND ITS PARTS.

1. First of all, let us consider a church and its parts. The word church hath two meanings: the one, a material building, wherein the Divine Of-

fices are celebrated: the other, a spiritual fabric, which is the Collection of the Faithful. The church, that is the people forming it, is assembled by its ministers, and collected together into one place by "Him who maketh men to be of one mind in a house" (Psalm 68:7). For as the material church is constructed from the joining together of various stones, so is the Spiritual Church by that of various men.

2. The Greek ecclesia is in Latin translated by convocatio, because it calls men to itself: the which title does better befit the spiritual than the material church.

The material typifies the spiritual Church: as shall be explained when we treat its consecration. Again, the Church is called Catholic, that is universal, because it has been set up in, or spread over, all the world, because the whole multitude of the faithful ought to be in one congregation, or because in the Church is laid up the doctrine necessary for the instruction of all.

3. It is also called in Greek synagoga, in Latin congregatio, which was the name chosen by the Jews for their place of worship: for to them the term synagogue more appropriately belongs though it be also applied to a church. But the Apostles never call a church by this title, perhaps for the sake of distinction.

4. The Church Militant is also called Zion: because, amidst its wanderings, it expects the promise of a heavenly rest: for Zion signifies expectation. But the Church Triumphant, our future home, the land of peace, is called Jerusalem: for Jerusalem signifies the vision of peace. Also, the church is called the House of God: also sometimes Kyriake, that is, the Lord's House. At others Basilica, (in Latin, a royal palace), for the abodes of earthly kings are thus termed: and how much more fittingly our Houses of Prayer, the dwelling-places of the King of Kings! Again, it is called temple, from tectum amplum, where sacrifices are offered to God: and sometimes the tabernacle of God, because this present life is a journey, and a progress to a lasting Country: and a tabernacle is an hostelrie: as will be explained when we speak of the Dedication of a church. And why it is called the Ark of the Testimony, we shall say in the ensuing chapter, under the title Altars. Sometimes it is called Martyrium, when raised in honour of any Martyr; sometimes capella, (chapel,) . . . sometimes caenobium, at others sacrificium; sometimes sacellum; sometimes the House of Prayer: sometimes monastery: sometimes oratory. Generally, however, any place set apart for prayers is called an oratory.

Again, the Church is called the Body of Christ: sometimes a Virgin, as the Apostle said, "That I may present you as a chaste virgin to Christ" (II Cor. 11:2): sometimes a Bride, because Christ has betrothed Her to Himself, as in the Gospel: "He that has the Bride is the Bridegroonm" (John 3:29): sometimes a Mother, for daily in Baptism She beareth sons to God: sometimes a Daughter, according to that saying of the Prophet, "Instead of your fathers you shall have children" (Psalm 45:16): sometimes a widow, because "She sits solitary through her afflictions, and, like Rachel, will not be comforted." . . .

7. Now a church is to be built on this fashion. The foundation being prepared, according to that saying, "It fell not, for it was founded upon a rock" (Matt. 7:25). . . .

8. The foundation must be so contrived, as that the Head of the Church may point due East . . . that is, to that point of the heavens, where the sun arises at the equinoxes; to signify, that the Church Militant must behave Herself with moderation, both in prosperity and adversity: and not towards that point where the sun rises at the solstices, which is the practice of some. . . .

10. The cement, without which there can be no stability of the walls, is made of lime, sand, and water. The lime is fervent charity, which joins to itself the sand, that is, undertakings for the temporal welfare of our brethren: because true charity taketh care of the widow and the aged, and the infant, and the infirm, and they who have it study to work with their hands, that they may possess wherewith to benefit them. Now the lime and the sand are bound together in the wall by a mixture of water. But water is an emblem of the Spirit. And as without cement the stones cannot cohere, so neither can men be built up in the heavenly Jerusalem without charity, which the Holy Ghost works in them. All the stones are polished and squared,—that is, holy and pure, and are built by the hands of the Great Workman into an abiding place in the Church. . . .

14. The arrangement of a material church resembles that of the human body: the Chancel, or place where the Altar is, represents the head: the Transepts, the hands and arms, and the remainder,—towards the west,— the rest of the body. The sacrifice of the Altar denotes the vows of the heart. . . .

15. Furthermore, the church consists of four walls, that is, is built on the doctrine of the Four Evangelists; and has length, breadth, and height: the height represents courage,—the length fortitude, which patiently en-

dures till it attaines its heavenly Home; the breadth is charity, which, with long suffering, loves its friends in God, and its foes for God; and again, its height is the hope of future retribution, which despises prosperity and adversity, hoping "to see the goodness of the Lord in the land of the living" (Psalm 27:13).

16. Again, in the Temple of God, the foundation is Faith, which is conversant with unseen things: the roof, Charity, "which covers a multitude of sins" (I Peter 4:8). The door, Obedience, of which the Lord says, "if you will enter into life, keep the commandments" (Matt. 19:17). The pavement, humility, of which the Psalmist says, "my soul cleaves to the pavement" (Psalm 119:25).

17. The four side walls, the four cardinal virtues, justice, fortitude, temperance, prudence. . . . But some churches are built in the shape of a Cross, to signify, that we are crucified to the world, and should tread in the steps of The Crucified. . . . Some also are built in the form of a circle: to signify that the Church hath been extended throughout the circle of the world. . . .

18. The Choir is so called from the harmony of the clergy in their chanting, or from the multitude collected at the divine offices. . . .

19. The Exedra is an apse, separated a little from a temple or palace; so called because it projects a little from the wall. . . .

21. The towers are the preachers and Prelates of the Church, which are Her bulwark and defense. . . .

22. The cock at the summit of the church is a type of preachers. For the cock, ever watchful even in the depth of night, gives notice how the hours pass, wakens the sleepers, predicts the approach of day, but first excites himself to crow by striking his sides with his wings. There is a mystery conveyed in each of these particulars. The night is this world: the sleepers are the children of this world who are asleep in their sins. The cock is the preacher, who preachs boldly, and excites the sleepers to cast away the works of darkness, exclaiming, "woe to them that sleep, awake you that sleep!" (Eph. 5:14). . . .

24. The glass windows in a church are Holy Scriptures, which expel the wind and the rain, that is all things hurtful, but transmit the light of the True Sun, that is, God, into the hearts of the Faithful. These are wider within than without, because the mystical sense is the more ample, and precedes the literal meaning. Also, by the windows the senses of the

body are signified: which ought to be shut to the vanities of this world, and open to receive with all freedom spiritual gifts. . . .

26. The door of the church is Christ: according to that saying in the Gospel, "I am the door" (John 10:9). The Apostles are also called doors. . . .

27. The Piers of the church are Bishops and Doctors: who specially sustain the Church of God by their doctrine. . . . The bases of the columns are the Apostolic Bishops, who support the frame of the whole Church. The capitals of the Piers are the opinions of the Bishops and Doctors. For as the members are directed and moved by the head, so are our words and works governed by their mind. The ornaments of the capitals are the words of Sacred Scripture, to the meditation and observance of which we are bound.

28. The pavement of the church is the foundation of our faith. But in the spiritual Church the pavement is the poor of Christ: the poor in spirit, who humble themselves in all things. . . .

29. The beams which join together the church are the princes of this world, or the preachers who defend the unity of the Church, the one by deed, the other by argument.

Source: John Mason Neale and Benjamin Webb. *The Symbolism of Churches and Church Ornaments*. Leeds, 1843.

DOCUMENT 50
Etienne de Bonneuil Is Sent to Work at Uppsala (1287)

To all who see this writ, Renaut le Cras, Provost of Paris, gives greeting. Be it known to all that we, in the year of grace 1287, on the Friday before the feast of Our Lady [September 8], examined and confirmed the following contract.

To all who will see this letter, Renaut le Cras, Provost of Paris, gives greeting. We make known that before us appeared Etienne de Bonneuil, to be master mason and master of the church of Uppsala in Sweden, proposing to go to said country as he had agreed upon. And he acknowledged having rightfully received and obtained advance payment of forty Paris livres from the hands of Messrs. Olivier and Charles, scholars and clercs at Paris, for the purpose of taking with him at the expense of said church four mates and four yeomen (*bachelers*), seeing that this would be to the advantage of said church for the cutting and carving of stone there. For this sum he promised to take said workmen to said land and to pay all their expenses.

The said . . . Etienne declared himself in our presence well paid and promised to deliver the said workmen as soon as he and the men who accompany him arrive in that country, and to compensate them sufficiently in such a manner that they consider themselves well paid for everything.

And should it happen that said Etienne de Bonneuil or the mates whom he has consented to take with him to the land of Sweden should perish on the sea on their way, owing to storms or in some other manner, he and his companions and their heirs shall be clear and absolved of the entire above-mentioned sum of money. And should they go from life to death no one may claim that part of the contract in which said Etienne commits himself under oath to be held bound in person and with all his goods movable and immovable, present and future, wherever he may be found, to stand trial before us or our successors or in whatever court of justice he may find himself. Furthermore, that in that case none of the said sum of money may be claimed either by the two clercs or by those whose agents they are in said church of Sweden, either from said Etienne or from those whom he will take with him, nor from their heirs.

In witness whereof we have put on this contract the seal of the provost's office at Paris in the year of grace 1287, on the Saturday before the feast of Saints Gile and Leu [August 30], and now have sealed the transcript of these papers with the seal of the provost's office in Paris on the day indicated above.

Source: Victor Mortet and Paul Deschamps. *Recueil de textes rélatifs à l'histoire de l'architecture et à la condition des architectes en France au moyen âge*, II. Paris: Picard, 1929.

DOCUMENT 51
The Expertise of Chartres Cathedral (1316)

In the year 1316, on the Thursday after the feast of the Nativity of the Holy Virgin Mary, the report on the defects of the church made by the masters delegated by the chapter to investigate these defects, was recorded as follows.

Gentlemen, we report to you that the four arches which help to carry the vaults are good and strong, the piers which carry the ribs are good, and the center of the vault which carries the keystone is good and strong. It will not be necessary to take down more than half the vault to the point where one can see what needs to be done. We have also advised that the scaffolding be moved above the molding (enmerllement) of the stained glass window. This scaffolding will also help to protect your choir screen and the people who walk under it, and it will also be useful when making whatever other scaffoldings may turn out to be convenient and necessary in the vault.

Here are the defects which exist in the church of Notre Dame of Chartres as seen by Master Pierre de Chelles, master of the fabric of the cathedral of Paris, Master Nicolas de Chaumes, master of the works of his majesty our king, and by Master Jacques de Longjumeau, master carpenter and juror in Paris, in the presence of Monsignor Jean de Reate, canon of Chartres, originally from Italy, Master Simon Daguon, master of the fabric [at Chartres], Master Simon the carpenter, and Master Berthaust, jurors of this cathedral fabric and responsible to the dean of the chapter.

First, we have seen the vault over the crossing; here repair work is indeed necessary, and if it is not done within a short time there might be great danger.

Furthermore, we have seen the flying buttresses which shoulder the vaults; the joints must be reset in mortar and tightened, and if this is not done very soon great damage may well occur.

Also, there are two piers shouldering the towers which require repair work.

Furthermore, repair work is necessary on the piers connected with the galleries above the portals [porches], and it is recommended that at each bay a further support be added to help carry what is above. One part of the support must rise from above the foundation on the ground to strengthen the corner pier, and the other part must move above to where the body of the church is again free and must have full dimensions in order to reduce the pressure; this should be done in all places where it is judged to be necessary.

In addition we have seen and explained to Master Berthaust how he can work on the statue of the Magdalene right where it is, without moving it.

Furthermore, we have looked into the large tower and observed that it needs repair work very badly, that one of the panels of its sides has large fissures and is in ruins, and that one of the finials is broken and in pieces.

Moreover, the porches are defective in front. The roofing is rotten and thin, for which reason it would be good to put an iron rod into each bay to help support it, which would be wise in order to remove all danger.

We have also seen to it, for the good of the church, that the first scaffolding be moved above the window molding for work on the vault of the crossing.

Furthermore, for the good of the church, we have examined the roof shaft which carries the angel aloft and which is completely rotten and unable to connect with the shaft of the nave of the church because the latter is broken where it connects with the joints of the woodwork from above. If this is to be well repaired, two boards should be laid together with those on the chevet; the angel should be placed on top of the second one of these. The greater part of the wood at this end should be replaced and used elsewhere.

Furthermore, the wooden bell carriage for the small bells is inadequate, for it has been old for a long time. The bell carriage for the large bells is also inadequate and must be improved soon.

Furthermore, four of the splices at the ridge of the roof must either be replaced, for the present ones are rotten at one end, or be thoroughly repaired if the chapter does not wish to replace them as we proposed to your masters.

Victor Mortet. "L'expertise de la cathédrale de Chartres en 1316." *Congrès archéologique de France. (Chartres, 1900)* Pp. 308–29.

DOCUMENT 52
Jean de Jandun's Description of Notre-Dame in Paris (1323)

In Paris, the privileged sanctuary of the Christian religion, beautiful buildings consecrated to God have been founded in such great numbers that there are probably not many cities, even among the most powerful cities of Christianity that can count so many houses of God. Among these houses, the imposing church of the most glorious Virgin Mary, Mother of God, shines brilliantly at the first rank, like the sun among the stars. And if certain people, by the freedom of their appreciation can only see a few things easily, testify to the beauty of other churches before her, I think, if they examine the whole [church] and the details, will quickly abandon that opinion. Where can you find, I ask you, two towers of such magnificence, so perfect, so high, so large, so strong, enriched with such a variety and multiplicity of decoration. Where can you encounter, I beg you, so complex a series of lateral vaults both below and above. When do you find, I repeat, the splendid light from such a ring of chapels. That's not all: tell me in what other church will I see a transept of comparable grandeur where this arm separates the choir from the nave. Finally, it gives me pleasure to say, where could I see two similar rose windows opposite one another in a straight line, roses the resemblance to which gives them the name of the fourth vowel [o]. Below, smaller roses, rosettes arranged with marvelous art, some in circles, others in lozenges, surrounding the glittering windows embellished in precious colors and with figures painted with the most exquisite delicacy. In truth, I think that this church offers to those who look attentively such a subject for admiration that the soul never tires of contemplating it.

Source: Le Roux de Lincy and L. M. Tisserand. *Paris et ses historiens aux XIVe et Xve siècles*. Histoire générale de Paris, Collection des documents. Translated by Clark. Paris: Imprimerie impériale, 1867.

DOCUMENT 53
Henry Knighton, Bishop of Lincoln, on the Effects of the Black Death (1348)

In this [1348] and the following year there was a general death of people throughout the world. It began first in India, then it passed to Tharsis, thence to the Saracens, Christians and Jews in the course of one year; from one Easter to the next. . . .

In one day there died 812 people in Avignon according to the reckoning made to the pope. . . . 358 Dominicans died in Provence in Lent; in Montpellier only seven friars were left from 149. . . . At Marseilles only one Franciscan remained of 150. . . .

Then the grievous plague came to the seacoasts from Southampton, and came to Bristol, and it was there as if all the strength of the town had died, as if they had been hit with sudden death, for there were few who stayed in their beds more than three days; or two days or even one half a day. Then the death broke out everywhere the sun goes. And more than 380 died at Leicester in the small parish of St. Leonard. More than 400 died in the parish of the Holy Cross; 700 died in the parish of St. Margaret of Leicester. And so it was in greater number in each parish. Then the bishop of Lincoln sent throughout his diocese and gave general power to each and every priest, regular as well as secular, to hear confessions and absolve with full and complete episcopal authority, except only in the instance of debt. In which case, if he was able by himself while he lived he should pay it, or others surely would do this for him from his possessions after his death. Likewise the pope granted full remission of all sins to whoever was absolved while in peril of death, and he granted this power to last from Easter to the next following. And everyone could elect his confessor as it pleased him. In this year there was a great pestilence among the sheep everywhere in the kingdom; so that in one place more than 500 sheep died in one pasture, and they became so putrid that neither beasts nor birds would touch them. And because of the fear of death there were low prices for everything. . . . For a man could have one horse which before was worth 40s. for one half a mark. . . . And sheep and cattle wandered through fields and among crops and there was no one who was concerned to drive and collect them, but an unknown number died in ditches and hedges throughout every region for lack of herders. For there was such a lack of servants and helpers that there was no one who knew what he ought to do. . . .

The workers, nevertheless, were so elated and contrary that they did not heed the mandate of the king [prohibiting higher wages] but if anyone wanted to hire them, he had to give them as they desired; either lose their crops and fruit or grant the selfish and lofty wishes of the workers. . . .

After the aforesaid pestilence, many large and small buildings in all the cities, boroughs and villages collapsed and were levelled with the earth for lack of inhabitants; likewise many villages and hamlets were deserted. No house was left in them for everyone who had lived in them had died, and it was probable that many such villages were never to be inhabited again.

Source: Joseph Rawson Lumby, ed. *Chronicon Henrici Knighton*. Rolls Series 92. London: Longman, 1895.

GLOSSARY

Abbey: A monastery; a community of men or women living under religious vows; the buildings, especially the church, used by the community.

Aisle: Corridor in a church; the aisles flank and run parallel to the central space of the nave and are separated from it by arcades (Figure 1).

Altar: The structure at which the liturgical rites are performed, especially the Eucharist, or Mass of the faithful. The form and the symbolism were borrowed from the table used at the Last Supper, when the Eucharist is thought to have been created.

Ambulatory: A processional passage way around a shrine or the central apse in a church (Figure 1).

Apse: A vaulted semicircular structure that, in a church, faces the nave and frames or houses the altar. A large church may have additional, small apses opening off the ambulatory or the transept.

Arcade: A series of arches resting on columns or piers and usually carrying a wall or other superstructure, as in the main arcade of a church.

Archbishop: A higher-level bishop, also known as a metropolitan or primate, having jurisdiction over an ecclesiastical province, or archdiocese, which includes several dioceses headed by bishops. The archbishop had the ultimate authority in naming bishops, a right much disputed in the Middle Ages by secular rulers.

Archivolt: The molding following the contour of an arch and framing the opening or the sculpted tympanum.

Ashlar masonry: Masonry of squared, even-faced blocks of stone laid in horizontal courses.

Baptistery: A building, a room, or a space set aside for baptismal rites.

Base: The carved architectural element on which a column or pier stands.

Basilica: From the Greek word *basilikos* meaning royal. In Early Christian architecture, a church of longitudinal plan consisting of a high central nave lit by clerestory windows, flanked by lower side aisles, followed by a transept and an apse, which either framed or contained the altar. In ancient architecture it was a longitudinal meeting hall, often with aisles around all four sides.

Bay: A regularly repeated compartment, or unit of space, bound by architectural members that define its limits and articulate its volume. It can also be a lateral slice through an entire building that contains all the repeating spatial units (Figure 2).

Bishop: The highest order of ministers in the Christian church; the word comes from an Anglo-Saxon corruption of the Greek *episcopus* (overseer). A bishop presides over a diocese and is responsible for all the churches within that area. Bishops must have taken priest's orders and must be consecrated to a particular cathedral see by the archbishop in whose archdiocese the cathedral is located.

Blind arcade: An arcade placed against a wall as decoration.

Buttress: A mass of masonry built to strengthen a wall and to counter the outward thrust of an interior vault. *See also* **flying buttress**.

Canon: A nonmonastic clergyman belonging to a cathedral or collegiate church chapter. Canons were organized into chapters with their own officers and responsibilities beginning in the eighth century. This is the group that actually owns a cathedral church and has the responsibility of running and maintaining it.

Capital: The decorative upper part of a column, or pier that creates a transition from the vertical support to the horizontal lintel or arcade.

Cathedra: The bishop's official chair or throne.

Cathedral: The church containing the bishop's **cathedra**, thus his principal church.

Centering: The timber frame or scaffolding built to support an arch or vault during its construction.

Choir: The architectural choir is the entire east end of the church. The liturgical choir is that part of the church reserved for the clergy and singers. The liturgical choir is not always situated in the architectural choir, as at Reims Cathedral (Figure 1).

Choir screen: A screen between the choir and the nave separating the clergy and the congregation; in England called a rood screen when it supports the "rood," or cross; in France called a jubé.

Clerestory: The top zone of windows in a church that stands "clear" of the lower stories and, thus, can have windows to admit light.

Column: A cylindrical, vertical supporting element that consists of three parts: base, shaft, and capital. Shafts are occasionally monolithic but usually composed of stacked drums.

Crossing: In church architecture, the intersection of nave and transept arms (Figure 1).

Crypt: A vaulted chamber usually beneath the apse and choir, housing tombs or a chapel.

Deacon: From the Greek word meaning servant, minister. A cleric whose rank in the ministry is just below that of the priest (presbyter) and bishop. The deacon assists a priest, acts as reader, leads prayers, distributes communion, receives offerings, and distributes alms. An archdeacon is the principal administrative officer in a diocese.

Diocese: The district and churches under the jurisdiction of a bishop.

Elevation: The side view of a building, either interior or exterior (Figure 2).

Facade: The front of a building containing the major public entrance or entrances; usually to the west but also applied to the transepts of a church if they are treated as entrances.

Flying buttress: The device in Gothic architecture that transfers the outward thrust of the nave vault over the side aisles through masonry arches to massive upright piers along the outer walls. Its most important function, however, is to act as a wind brace against the enormous wind pressure on the high roof of the church (Figure 2).

Fresco: Mural painting in which pigments in water are applied to wet plaster that absorbs the colors. Fresco was commonly used to decorate the interiors of churches beginning in the Early Christian period. It was widely used in southern Europe, but seldom used in northern Europe after c. 1100.

Gallery: The vaulted and windowed second story of a Romanesque or Early Gothic church, especially in England and Normandy. Early examples are unvaulted spaces as tall as the side aisles below them. The term *tribune* is commonly used for a gallery, but it more accurately refers to a royal box from which to observe church services.

Gargoyle: A waterspout often carved as a monster or animal during Late Gothic times.

Grisaille: Monochromatic painting on stained glass. The result is a pearly, translucent glass that allows more light in the interior.

Hall church: A church with nave and aisles of equal height.

Historiated: Decorated with a narrative subject, as historiated capitals.

Horseshoe arch: An arch of more than a semicircle that can be pointed as well as rounded.

Iconography: The symbolism of a work of art.

Iconology: The study of the meaning of images.

Jamb: The side of a door or window; often splayed and decorated with statue-columns, figures attached to the architectural columns mounted on the jambs of a doorway.

Keystone: The wedge-shaped central stone of an arch or vault.

Lancet window: A tall, narrow, pointed window with no interior tracery.

Lantern tower: A tall tower erected over the crossing of a church. The tower is given windows to light the crossing.

Lintel: The horizontal element spanning an opening.

Liturgy: The public services or rites of worship in the church, the principal one of which is the Mass or Eucharist; also written texts giving the order of service.

Martyr: One who suffered death for the faith. The anniversary of a martyr's death was celebrated by the church (saint's day). Until 1969, a relic of a martyr or a saint had to be placed in every consecrated altar.

Martyrium: A church built over the tomb of a martyr in Early Christian times. Old St. Peter's in Rome was a martyrium.

Monastery: A community of religious men or women (monks or nuns), living according to a rule. It can also refer to the buildings housing the completely self-sufficient community. The word is synonymous with abbey.

Mosaic: A surface decoration composed of small colored stones or glass cubes (tesserae) laid in cement or plaster forming figurative or abstract designs. Mosaics were most common in the Mediterranean world, less in northern Europe where they were often "replaced" by painting.

Narthex: The vestibule of a church; a transverse hall in front of the nave.

Nave: From the Latin for ship. Central vessel of a church, extending from the entrance to the crossing or choir (Figure 1).

Oculus: A round window.

Ogee: An S-shaped curve; in an ogee arch the two S-shaped curves are reversed to meet in a central point.

Pier: A solid masonry support with a shape other than cylindrical.

Pilaster: A flat vertical element projecting from a wall or pier; often divided into base, shaft, and capital.

Pinnacle: A small turret, usually ornamental, but also used to load a buttress as a wind brace.

Plinth: The projecting base of a column or of a wall.

Pointed arch: An arch composed of two segments of a circle. Tests have proved that a pointed arch is stronger than a round or semicircular arch, as well as being useful for adjusting to a uniform height.

Presbyter: A priest who is the chief assistant to the bishop and ranks higher than a deacon. Presbyters became overseers and administrators of the church. They were in the service of the bishop rather than the chapter, although they were usually members of the chapter.

Relics: The venerated remains of saints or objects associated with saints.

Respond: A shaft or pilaster attached to a wall to support an arch.

Sacristy: A room in a church near the altar where liturgical vessels and vestments are kept.

Tracery: Ornamental stone work that turns a window opening into a design surface. Tracery can also be applied to both interior and exterior wall surfaces as ornament. There are two kinds of tracery: plate tracery is created by cutting through a thin wall of stone to create the divisions and framing of the windows; bar tracery consists of carved elements, often imitating architectural forms, that are set in the window openings to create the patterns into which the iron framework and stained glass are set. The conceptual difference between the two is important in the history of the window.

Transept: The cross-volume of a church, usually as high and as wide as the nave and the choir of a Gothic church. In Early Christian and Carolingian times the transept might be lower than the nave and choir (Figure 1).

Triforium: In the elevation of the church, the space at the height of the aisle roofs between the nave arcade and the clerestory. This second story can take many forms, ranging from simple holes in the wall to fully articulated wall passages, so a more precisely descriptive term is preferable.

Trumeau: The central doorpost of a portal supporting a lintel and tympanum.

Tympanum: The area between the lintel and the arch of a portal. In Romanesque and Gothic churches the tympanum will be filled with sculpture.

Vault: A masonry ceiling or covering built on the principle of the arch. The oldest and simplest form is the barrel vault, a tunnel-like extension of the arch. The barrel vault usually requires continuous support along the two sides, which made opening windows below it difficult. Almost as old, but more complex is the groin vault in which two barrel vaults of equal size intersect at right angles, which allows the vault to be supported at the four corners. Barrel vaults and groin vaults were exploited by ancient Roman builders, although both forms were known much earlier. The rib vault and the later fan vault are the only forms "invented" during the Middle Ages. The rib vault was constructed in two stages, as discussed in Chapter 4. When pointed arches were used, it became easier to cover irregularly shaped spaces because the ribs were the means to regularize the height before the web was laid over the surface. The fan vault was a late Gothic invention of the Perpendicular style in which semi-cones appear to be rotated from the outside walls. They touch in the center or apex of the vault and are connected by flat panels. The panels that make up the vault are decorated with patterns of ribs and tracery paneling to give the appearance of an ornamental rib vault.

Vestry: A room adjacent to the east end of a church used for the storage of vestments and liturgical implements.

Voussoir: A wedge-shaped block used in the construction of an arch. The central voussoir is known as the keystone.

Westwork: A complex structure at the west end of a church consisting of superimposed entrance, a chapel, and often a throne room flanked by towers or stair turrets.

ANNOTATED BIBLIOGRAPHY

Armi, C. Edson. *Design and Construction in Romanesque Architecture*. Cambridge: Cambridge University Press, 2004. An excellent new analysis of the achievements of early Romanesque architecture in Burgundy and northern Italy.

Barral i Altet, Xavier. *The Early Middle Ages*. Cologne: Taschen, 1997. One of Taschen's Encyclopedia of World Architecture volumes; well-illustrated, readable text with lots of well-chosen examples in color.

Barral i Altet, Xavier. *The Romanesque*. Cologne: Taschen, 1998. This Taschen volume has an informative, readable text that attempts to consider the topic anew and has lots of good color illustrations.

Binding, Gunther. *High Gothic*. Cologne: Taschen, 1999. Despite an inaccurate title and a very idiosyncratic text, the color illustrations are usually of high quality.

Binding, Gunther. *Medieval Building Techniques*. Translated by Alex Cameron. Stroud: Tempus, 2004. Authoritative collection of some 900 illustrations of medieval building techniques and tools illustrated in drawings of examples from the twelfth to the fifteenth centuries.

Binski, Paul. *Becket's Crown*. New Haven: Yale University Press, 2004. A new analysis of Gothic buildings in England from Canterbury to 1300.

Binski, Paul. *Painters*. Medieval Craftsmen. London: British Museum, 1991. Most of the discussion is focused on European panel paintings, but there are useful analyses and comments on wall paintings with good illustrations.

Bony, Jean. *French Gothic Architecture of the 12th and 13th Centuries*. Berkeley: University of California Press, 1983. A terse and tight text that re-

flects its origins as a lecture series of 1961, this classic volume still bris-
tles with ideas that have inspired a generation to rethink older theories
and ideas. Its richness and freshness are revealed by careful, considered
reading.

Branner, Robert. *Gothic Architecture*. New York: George Braziller, 1961. A well-
illustrated introductory survey that still has useful ideas and a good approach to the topic.

Brown, Sarah, and David O'Connor. *Glass-Painters*. Medieval Craftsmen. London: British Museum, 1991. A good account of how stained glass is made,
together with a brief survey from the earliest examples to the fifteenth century.

Calkins, Robert G. *Medieval Architecture in Western Europe*. Oxford: Oxford University Press, 1998. A good, well-illustrated, introductory survey that is
stronger in the later chapters.

Camille, Michael. *Gothic Art, Glorious Visions*. New York: Harry N. Abrams,
1996. Although the text is short on architecture, the intelligence of the
author and the significance of the questions he proposes far outweigh this
problem.

Cherry, John. *Goldsmiths*. Medieval Craftsmen. London: British Museum, 1991.
A good introduction to the uses of gold and silver in the Middle Ages,
well illustrated with examples and scenes of goldsmiths at work.

Coldstream, Nicola. *Masons and Sculptors*. Medieval Craftsmen. London: British
Museum, 1991. An excellent introduction to the topic with an international perspective.

Coldstream, Nicola. *Medieval Architecture*. Oxford: Oxford University Press,
2002. A broad survey in a brief text full of insights and ideas.

Erlande-Brandenburg, Alain. *Gothic Art*. New York: Harry N. Abrams, 1989.
The text is old-fashioned and very dated in its ideas, but the breadth of
coverage and the hundreds of illustrations make up for it. Look, but don't
read!

Fernie, Eric. *The Architecture of Norman England*. Oxford: Oxford University
Press, 2000. The new standard, this excellent book is full of insights and
new ideas.

Frankl, Paul. *Gothic Architecture*. Pelican History of Art, revised edition by Paul
Crossley. New Haven and London: Yale University Press, 2000. Originally
written in the 1920s, the text was already old-fashioned when first pub-

lished in 1962. Its value now lies in Crossley's introduction and updates to the notes and bibliography; the text itself is a relic.

Geary, Patrick J. *Furta Sacra: Thefts of Relics in the Central Middle Ages.* Rev. ed. Princeton: Princeton University Press, 1990. The standard treatment of relic theft; a well-researched study that makes fascinating reading.

Gimpel, Jean. *The Cathedral Builders.* Translated by Teresa Waugh. New York: Harper and Row, 1984. An enjoyable, readable text written with verve and the excitement of discovery.

Grant, Lindy. *Architecture and Society in Normandy, 1120–1270.* New Haven: Yale University Press, 2005. A new analysis of the beginnings of Gothic in Normandy through the creation of the Norman Gothic style and the impact of the French conquest in 1204.

Hiscock, Nigel, ed. *The White Mantle of Churches: Architecture, Literacy, and Art Around the Millennium.* International Medieval Research 10: Art History Subseries 2. Turnhout: Brepols, 2003. An important collection of articles incorporating new research on the topics noted in the title.

Holloway, R. Ross. *Constantine and Rome.* New Haven: Yale University Press, 2004. An important, new assessment of the early sites in Rome.

Horn, Walter. "On the Origins of the Mediaval Bay System." *Journal of the Society of Architectural Historians* 17 (1958), pp. 2–23. Horn sees the origins of the thinking that produced the idea of the bay in medieval architecture in the long-standing tradition of building with timber.

Horn, Walter, and Ernest Born. *The Plan of St.-Gall.* 3 vols. Berkeley: University of California Press, 1979. A monumental study on the only surviving drawing of the plan of a self-sufficient Carolingian monastery, which Horn believed was followed at St.-Gall. Other scholars see the plan as an intellectual document rather than as a guide to construction.

Kimpel, Dieter, and Robert Suckale. *L'architecture gothique en France 1130–1270.* Translated by Françoise Neu. Paris: Flammarion, 1990. An important text, originally published in German in 1985, that takes a socio-political approach, incorporating considerable archeological and documentary research, with wonderful photographs by the Hirmers.

Kostof, Spiro. "The Architect in the Middle Ages, East and West." In *The Architect: Chapters in the History of the Profession,* ed. Spiro Kostof, pp. 59–95. New York: Oxford University Press, 1977. Written from the standpoint of the architect, this chapter provides innumerable insights. The bibliography is dated, but it cites important older sources.

Kraus, Henry. *Gold Was the Mortar.* London: Routledge & Kegan Paul, 1979. An excellent introduction to the financing of cathedral construction through the in-depth analysis of seven examples, six in France and one in England.

Krautheimer, Richard. *Early Christian and Byzantine Architecture.* Pelican History of Art, 4th ed. Harmonsworth and New York: Viking Penguin, 1986. The classic treatment of the subject, dramatically updated for each new edition and still fundamental.

Laule, Ulrike, et al. *Architecture of the Middle Ages.* Berlin: Feierabend, 2004. A richly illustrated new introduction and survey. The superb architectural photography by Achim Bednorz makes it especially useful.

Laule, Ulrike, et al. *Churches, Cathedrals, Monasteries: Sacred German Architecture.* Berlin: Feierabend, 2005. The title should be "Germanic," since it includes Prague, Strasbourg, and Vienna, as well as an excellent survey of German examples in Achim Bednorz's superb photographs.

Le Goff, Jacques. *The Birth of Purgatory.* Translated by Arthur Goldhammer. Chicago: University of Chicago Press, 1984. A thorough analysis of the scholarly background and the arguments of the scholars in the formulation of the doctrine of Purgatory.

Lillich, Meredith Parsons. "King Solomon in Bed, Archbishop Hincmar, the *Ordo* of 1250, and the Stained-Glass Program of Reims Cathedral," *Speculum* 80 (2005), pp. 764–801. A superb new study of the evidence that results in the identification of the nave program for the first time. Not only is this a model study, but it includes a full listing of Lillich's other important articles on the stained glass of Reims.

Mark, Robert. *Light, Wind, and Structure.* Cambridge: MIT Press, 1990. An excellent, readable introduction to the technical aspects of construction and engineering.

Mark, Robert, ed. *Architectural Technology up to the Scientific Revolution.* Cambridge: MIT Press, 1993. A collective study that investigates a wide range of topics in medieval architecture that are not covered elsewhere.

McClendon, Charles. *The Origins of Medieval Architecture.* New Haven: Yale University Press, 2005. An important new analysis of architecture from 600–900 AD by one of the best scholars of the period.

Nussbaum, Norbert. *German Gothic Church Architecture.* New Haven: Yale University Press, 2000. The best treatment of the topic in any language, one that will be the standard for many years. This English translation is the latest edition.

Pearsall, Derek. *Gothic Europe, 1200–1450*. Harlow: Pearson, 2001. A historian's view of the age of cathedrals, with an intelligent, readable text. Over all, the majority of examples are in England, while the rest of Europe gets short shift.

Prache, Anne. *Great Cathedrals of Europe*. Ithaca/London: Cornell University Press, 1999. A lavishly illustrated volume with a good general text. Detailed bibliography for every building mentioned.

Price, Lorna. *The Plan of St Gall in Brief*. Berkeley: University of California Press, 1982. A good introduction to the plan that amounts to an abridgement of the monumental three-volume work by Walter Horn with the reconstruction drawings of Ernst Born.

Radding, Charles M., and William W. Clark. *Medieval Architecture, Medieval Learning*. New Haven/London: Yale University Press, 1992; paper, 1994. An intellectual historian and an architectural historian analyze parallels in conceptual thinking in the Romanesque and Gothic periods. Extensive, specialized bibliography.

Raguin, Virginia Chieffo, Kathryn Brush, and Peter Draper, eds. *Artistic Integration in Gothic Buildings*. Toronto: University of Toronto Press, 1995. Seventeen international scholars explore the ways in which Gothic buildings are analyzed and studied in this important collection.

Sadler-Davis, Donna. *The Sculputral Program of the Verso of the West Façade of Reims Cathedral*. Bloomington: Indiana University, unpublished Ph.D. Dissertation, 1984. This is one of the most important iconographic studies of Reims and is available from University Microfilms, Ann Arbor, Michigan.

Schütz, Bernhard. *Great Cathedrals*. New York: Harry N. Abrams, 2002. Another lavishly illustrated volume, but discussing only selected examples. The text is marred by a number of silly errors in terminology that should have been caught. Another case of enjoying the illustrations and ignoring the text.

Scott, Robert A. *The Gothic Experience*. Berkeley/London: University of California Press, 2003. An interesting, underillustrated text in which an enthusiastic sociologist looks at Gothic cathedrals, mostly in England. There is too much dependence on interpretations taken from dated and questionable secondary sources. Parts IV and V are the best.

Stalley, Roger. *Early Medieval Architecture*. Oxford: Oxford University Press, 1999. A good synthesis in a short, smart text.

Stokstad, Marilyn. *Medieval Art*, 2nd ed. Boulder: Westview, 2004. The best survey of medieval art and architecture with a smart, sensitive, and well-written text by a scholar who conveys her love and understanding of the material. There is a good bibliography and an extensive glossary.

Strafford, Peter. *Romanesque Churches of France: A Traveller's Guide*. London: Giles de la Mare Publishers, 2005. An excellent introductory book for the traveler arranged by modern geographic regions, with convenient maps. The author knows and loves the material and presents it well. No bibliography.

Toman, Rolf, ed. *The Art of the Gothic*. Cologne: Konemann, 1999. A group of important European scholars contributed mostly good texts that are only overshadowed by the amazing range of photographs by Achim Bednorz.

Toman, Rolf, ed. *Romanesque*. Berlin: Feierabend, 2002. A reduced version in size and text of the preceeding volume, saved by the quality of the reproductions of Bednorz's photographs.

Toman, Rolf, ed. *Romanesque: Architecture, Sculpture, Painting*. Cologne: Konemann, 1997. A collective effort by a team of specialists unified by the wealth of illustrations, most by Achim Bednorz.

Turner, Jane, ed. *The Dictionary of Art*, 34 vols. London: Macmillan, 1996. A major reference that is now updated on line, this dictionary has articles by major scholars in a wide variety of categories. Look up cathedrals by their cities, but also by their style (e.g., Romanesque). The range of articles on the technical side (masonry, arch, etc.) is also very useful. The bibliographies with each entry are excellent. Together with the Bony text cited earlier, this is the starting point for all serious research.

Vroom, Wilhelms Hermanus. *De financiering van de kathedraalbouw in de middeleeuwen, in het bijzonder van de dom van Utrecht*. Maarssen: Gary Schwartz, 1981. Despite the narrow focus on Utrecht, this is an excellent analysis of the surviving late medieval financial records; use the English summary, pp. 628–36.

Wu, Nancy, ed. *Ad Quadratum: The practical application of geometry in medieval architecture*. Aldershot and Burlington: Ashgate Publishing, 2002. A good introduction to the wide variety of scholarship devoted to the study and analysis of geometry.

Internet Research

All research on medieval cathedrals on the Web should be through "approved" sites, such as the Web page of the International Center of Medieval Art, http://www.medievalart.org. Most museums with major collections of medieval art also have their own Web pages, most of them well illustrated. In addition, usually reliable information can be found by searching through the names of the cities or the names of the cathedrals through such major search engines as Google and Yahoo. In many cases, however, these sites will not reflect the most recent scholarly research about the buildings and will more often present older ideas about chronology. In addition, almost all will attempt to convert you, reflecting their continuing roles as religious centers. Many will have useful images that can be downloaded. Avoid nonapproved sites, most of which are notable only for the absolutely stunning stupidities they attempt to pass off as knowledge.

INDEX

About the Author

WILLIAM W. CLARK is Professor of Art History at Queens College. He is the author of *Medieval Architecture, Medieval Learning: Builders and Masters in the Age of Romanesque and Gothic*, among other titles.